Gowing of
The Royal Fusiliers

T. Gowing
sergeant-major Royal Fusiliers

Gowing of
The Royal Fusiliers

The Experiences of a Fusilier on Campaign
During the Crimean War, the Indian Mutiny
and the Umballah Campaign-1853-72

T. Gowing

Gowing of
The Royal Fusiliers
The Experiences of a Fusilier on Campaign
During the Crimean War, the Indian Mutiny
and the Umballah Campaign-1853-72
by T. Gowing

FIRST EDITION

Leonaur is an imprint
of Oakpast Ltd

Copyright in this form © 2010 Oakpast Ltd

ISBN: 978-0-85706-337-3 (hardcover)
ISBN: 978-0-85706-338-0 (softcover)

http://www.leonaur.com

Publisher's Notes

The opinions of the authors represent a view of events in which he was a participant related from his own perspective, as such the text is relevant as an historical document.

The views expressed in this book are not necessarily those of the publisher.

Contents

Introduction by the Leonaur Editors	7
Preface	11
Enlistment	13
Disembarkation in the Crimea	20
The Battle of the Alma	26
Sebastopol & Balaclava	35
The Inkermann Battles	46
Malta & Back to the Front	66
Night Attack	76
Sebastopol	84
The Battle of Tchernaya	104
The Final Bombardment of Sebastopol	112
The Storming of the Town	118
After the Siege	135
Sergeant Walsh's Crimea Experience	139
Lieut. Hope and the 7th Fusiliers	153
Embarked For Home	160
The Commencement of the Mutiny in 1857	170
Lucknow & Beyond	195
With the Royal Fusiliers in the Punjaub and Elsewhere	203
The Afghan Campaign of 1863	245

The Royal Fusiliers	270
Military Commanders in the Army	280

Introduction by the Leonaur Editors

The author of this book, Timothy Gowing was once one of the most well known soldiers of the Royal Fusiliers. He was born in Halesworth, Suffolk in 1834, the son of a Baptist minister. As he approached his twentieth birthday he came to the conclusion that a military life was his ambition and he decided to join the army, enlisting as a private soldier in H.M. 7th Regiment of Foot—The Royal Fusiliers.

This was a period of long spells of peace time soldiering for many, but the Crimean War had broken out and after a short period of training Gowing was marched aboard ship and sent on his way to the battle front. His experiences at war against the Russians form a substantial and interesting part of the book you are now holding. The violent conflagration that was the Indian Mutiny flared up hard on the heels of the Crimean War and many regiments and men who had but recently been in action before Sebastopol now found themselves on the sub-continent fighting a very different war and enemy. Gowing was, after a period on Malta recovering from wounds, one of their number and he takes his reader on campaign in India with him.

By now he had gained his sergeants stripes—first as a Regimental Drill Sergeant and later as Colour Sergeant and Sergeant-Major. He turned down a commission on two occasions principally on financial grounds, though on the second occasion he would have become on officer of his own regiment—The Royal Fusiliers. In 1864 he completed his ten years army service and could have once become a civilian, but instead he re-enlisted for yet another ten years to ensure he qualified for an army pension with which to support himself and his family in later life. Much of second ten years of military service was spent in India.

Gowing's personal life in India was tragic. He married and became father to twelve children. Cholera struck in 1869 and six of the eight children the couple still had within their care died on the same day. His wife was also pronounced dead—but miraculously recovered.

Aged only 42 years old, Gowing and his wife with just two surviving children sailed home to England in 1876. He took up residence in Southport, and fathered another seven children. The Gowing's lived in a number of Lancashire and Yorkshire towns and it was during this period that he wrote his recollections of his military service. He decided to publish the book himself and sell it to the factory, mill and office workers of the northern towns and cities to augment his army pension of 2/6d per day. The proceeds from the sale of his book were—apart from his pension—his only income. However, by the standards of the time he was quite successful and he sold thousands of copies.

Until quite recently copies of Gowing's book could be found regularly in the secondhand book shops of English towns, to the degree that, irrespective of their age, individual books could be purchased comparatively inexpensively. Gowing added substantially to his text on several occasions and a number of versions of it were in circulation at the same time. Unfortunately, much of this additional material had little to do with his personal experiences of military life.

Under most circumstances the Leonaur editors do not edit the work of the authors of the books that carry the Leonaur imprint. There are, however, exceptions and Timothy Gowing's book is one of them. Authors from this period often digressed from their principal theme—invariably into the realms of religious diatribe and travelogue. Whist Gowing was not particularly guilty of the latter, given his background readers might not be surprised to discover he was given to a measure of the former. Additionally, Gowing thought himself something of a poet and since he was his own editor and publisher his efforts as a bard became, without impediment, part of his book.

For reasons that the modern reader might only guess at Gowing also decided to become a biographer of several of the 'great and good,' of whom he had no personal experience, and take it upon himself to pen 'histories' of military campaigns which occurred many decades before he was born. In addition he included anecdotes about people and events that also had nothing to do with his own experiences and saw fit to put before his readers polemics under titles such as, 'Great Britain—A Military Power?' As a result subsequent editions of his book became incrementally more bloated and much less successfully focused on events that he had not witnessed.

We try not to be judgemental about the approach the authors of the books we publish take to their subject matter. However, we do feel that a book is simply better for concentrating on its core subject particularly when that is the reason modern readers will purchase the book. In the case of this book that central subject matter is, of course, the personal experiences of a Fusilier in the Age of Victoria. In the hope and conviction that you will agree with us, all such extraneous material has been removed from the edition you are now holding.

The result is, of course, a much shorter book than Gowing himself will have known or may have preferred, but it is one which is considerably more focused, more accessible and more enjoyable to read.

The Leonaur Editors

Preface

Having been much encouraged by the rapid sale of 18,500 copies of the first editions of my book, and being urged by a number of friends to go more deeply into the subject, I have revised and considerably enlarged it, (see Leonaur Introduction), and hope that the following pages will prove of interest, not only to the rising generation, but to all thinking people. I have confined myself strictly to a narrative of facts, whether the incidents related came under my own observation or otherwise. A number of gentlemen have kindly given me valuable assistance.

I took part in some of the most desperate scenes in those arduous campaigns of the Crimea, the Indian Mutiny, and Afghanistan. At the Alma I was one of those who led the way up the fatal heights; at Inkermann I was in the thick of the fight, and was wounded. I was beside that Christian hero, when he fell in his country's cause, with the words on his lips—"For England's home and glory—follow me."

It would be well if thousands of the fast young men of the present day (*at the time of first publication*), took a lesson from the life of that exemplary soldier. I was also engaged in those memorable struggles that were carried on, night after night and day after day, before Sebastopol; and was wounded a second time in that bloody attack on the Redan, in which a Norfolk man—the late General (then Colonel) Windham—gained an immortal name. In giving my experiences during that campaign I may in some respects seem to be repeating an "oft-told tale," yet, as a personal narrative, it will, I think, be new to many, and will afford information not elsewhere to be found.

The letters to my parents from the seat of war in the Crimea and India, from 1857 to 1876, I have ventured to publish, trusting they will prove of more than passing interest, and set more than one thinking, "Where is my boy tonight?"

Many of them were written under great difficulty in a bleak tent or hut, with the thermometer far below freezing point, with my wet rags frozen on my back; often my overcoat stiff with frost. Others from some of the hottest stations in India, with the sweat rolling off one like rain; the only covering would be a mosquito shirt and drawers, made of the finest muslin, with the thermometer indicating 125 or 130 degrees of heat in your room.

The descriptions of the different fights, both by day and night, particularly the storming of Sebastopol, and the aspect of the interior of those bloodstained walls after the siege, will help to depict in their true colours the horrors of war.

In the chapters on the Indian Mutiny I have narrated some of the most atrocious deeds that were perpetrated, and shown how vengeance was most surely meted out to the miscreants who were guilty of them.

The description of the Afghan campaign of 1863 will, I hope, clearly prove that we had some rough work before the sons of the Himalayas were subdued; while the manners and customs of the people of India, which I have briefly dwelt on, will, I feel certain, afford

With confidence I now submit my work to my fellow-countrymen, trusting that none will criticise too harshly the humble literary efforts of one who has tried to do his duty upon many a hard-fought field, and who is ready to do it again rather than see that flag we love so well trampled in the dust.

T. Gowing,
Late Sergeant-Major, R. F.,
and Allahabad Garrison.

Chapter 1

Enlistment

I was now fast approaching my twentieth year—a dangerous age to many unsettled in mind; and the thrilling accounts that were constantly coming home from the East, worked me up to try my luck as others had done before me, so, in the early part of January 1854, I enlisted into one of the smartest regiments of our army, the Royal Fusiliers. I selected this regiment for its noble deeds of valour under Lord Wellington, in the Peninsular. They, the old Fusiliers, had made our enemies, the French, shake on many a hard-fought field. Let the reader just look over the record of the *Battles of the British Army*, or *Napier's Peninsula*, and he will remember the Royal Fusiliers, as a Briton, with pride, as long as he lives. View them at *Albuera*, 16th May, 1811. I would borrow Napier's pithy language about them—

> Nothing could stop the astonishing Infantry: how, inch by inch and foot by foot, they gained the heights of Albuera with a horrid carnage; swept the entire host of France from before them; gave them a parting volley, and then stood triumphant, fifteen hundred unconquerable British soldiers left out of the proud army of England, which that morning had succeeded six thousand combatants.

"They had not died for nothing," for the French military historians acknowledged that ever after that they approached the British Infantry with a scared feeling of distrust, for these never knew when they were beaten. A corps like that might be destroyed, but not easily defeated. Thus, my lot was cast with a regiment that had in days of yore planted the Standard of Old England in many a "hot corner," and was destined to do it again. The deeds of the good loyal old corps had been handed down from father to son; and I found some of the right sort of stuff in it, men that would do or die, and dare everything that lay in their power to keep up the reputation of the regiment, whose motto was *Death or Victory*.

On joining I was about 6ft. high, very active and steady, was soon brought to the notice of my officers, and went up the ladder of promotion pretty quickly. A month or two after I had joined, had got over the goose step, and had been taught how to "catch flies," war was declared by our Government, in conjunction with France, against Russia. All regiments were at once put upon a war footing, and thousands who had an appetite for a little excitement or hard knocks, rushed to the Standard; while those who only liked pipe- claying and playing at soldiers, soon got out of the way by retiring upon "urgent private affairs."

Those of my readers who are old enough will remember the pitch of excitement to which the blood of Old England was worked up: the eyes of the whole world were turned upon us; the deeds of our forefathers had not been forgotten—their exploits had astonished the civilised world; both by land and sea they had been the admiration of all, whether friend or foe, when led by such commanders as the immortal Nelson and the Iron Duke. We, their descendants, were about to face in deadly conflict the strongest and most subtle nation of the civilized world, that could bring into the field one million of bayonets, swayed by despotic power.

But numbers were not taken into consideration, our only cry was "Let's get at them." The Fusiliers were quickly made up to about one thousand strong; and embarked at Southampton on the 5th of April, 1854, for the East, under command of an officer who afterwards proved himself one of the bravest of the brave. Colonel Lacy Walter Yea, a soldier in every sense of the word, both in the field and out of it; just the right man in the right place to command such a corps as the Royal Fusiliers.

In marching out of the Barracks at Manchester to the railway station, one could have walked over the heads of the people, who were wrought up to such a pitch of excitement as almost amounted to madness. Our inspiring band in front struck up "The British Grenadiers," "The Girl I left behind me," "We are going far away." Fathers shook hands with their sons, and bade them farewell, while mothers embraced them; and then the bands struck up "Cheer! boys, cheer!" which seemed to have a thrilling effect upon the multitude, and to give fresh animation to the men.

The expressions from the vast crowd as our men marched along were, "Pur them. Bill," "Remember Old England depends upon you," "Give them plenty of cold steel and then pur them," "Keep up your pecker, old boy—never say die," "Leave your mark upon them if you get a chance." At last the noble old corps reached the railway station, and then there were deafening shouts. Some cried, "We'll meet again, and give you a warm reception when you come back ;" then, after one hearty "God bless you" from a vast multitude, away they went behind the iron horse. We had a number of Manchester men in our ranks, and, although that town is noted for its peace principles, they let the enemy know at the Alma, Inkermann, and throughout the campaign, that they knew how to fight.

Well, reader, the old Fusiliers have gone to help to carry out the orders of our Government and Her Most Gracious Majesty—"God bless her." But your humble servant is left behind to have a little more knocked into his head in the way of marching and counter-marching, and the young idea had to be taught how to shoot. It did not matter much where one went—all the talk was about the gallant old corps, wishing them God-speed and a safe return to their native isle. The depôt was soon removed from Manchester to Winchester, where I completed my drill, and with steadiness went up to the rank of corporal; and, about the 15th of June, a strong draft was selected to join the service companies then in Turkey.

After having passed a close medical inspection, Corporal T. G. was told off for the draft; and it is not an easy thing to describe my feelings. I deemed myself, I must acknowledge, a proud man; and felt that the honour of our dear old isle hung upon my shoulders; I pictured myself coming home much higher in rank, and with my breast covered with honours, the gifts of a grateful country; but I little dreamed of the hardships that were before me. My comrade, a good honest Christian, quoted the following lines with a sparkling eye, at the same time brandishing a stick over his head:—

Not once or twice in our proud island's story,
The path of duty was the way to glory.

He fell at the Alma, The Searcher of all hearts knew well that he was more fit to face Him than I was; his whole life was that of a Christian from the day I first knew him, and he was never ashamed of his colours.

We marched out of Winchester about twelve hundred strong, detachments of various regiments, with a light heart, nearly the whole of the good people of that city marching with us. The same scenes were enacted as at Manchester, when the regiment went off; we had hard work to get through the people; there was many a fond farewell from broken-hearted mothers, and many a tear was shed, for all that was near and dear to many were just off to a foreign land, to back up the comrades who had gone before.

With a ringing cheer from some thousands of people wishing us God-speed and a safe return to our native homes, away we went, and were conveyed to Portsmouth in safety, duly arriving at the port which had in days of yore witnessed the departure of thousands of the bravest sons of England to return no more. We found the people of Portsmouth a warm-hearted set, and they gave us a genuine reception in sailor-like fashion. In marching through the streets, which were thronged with pretty girls, the bands in front struck up "The Girl I left behind me." We had various greetings as we passed on to the Dockyard, such as, "Stick to them, my boys," "Give it them if you get a chance, "Remember old England depends upon you," "We'll not forget you."

With one tremendous cheer we passed on into the Dockyard, and thousands of voices joined in shouting "Farewell, God bless you." We soon found ourselves on board a noble ship—about twelve hundred fine young fellows determined to "do or die," little dreaming of the hardships we should have to encounter, hardships that no pen or tongue can adequately describe. We cheered heartily for Old England and England's Queen. An old General Officer told us to cheer when we came back, and we replied that we would, for we were just in the right frame of mind to carry the Standard of Old England through thick and thin, prepared to dare all the legions that the "*Czar* of all the Russias" could bring against us, and to stand shoulder to shoulder with our allies the French, in a foreign land. Napoleon's words were now to be verified.

The strongest nation in the world had thrown down the gauntlet at the feet of France and England, and Waterloo was now to be avenged by our uniting against the disturber of the peace of Europe. The following pages will prove that, with all their boasted strength, and that although fighting behind one of the strongest fortifications in the whole world, the Russians came off second best, and had to submit to the dictates of the flag that for near one thousand years has proved itself, under good guidance, second to none.

Peter the Great, though he mentioned the gold of England, forgot her steel and her "dumplings" that were so hard to digest, and the haughty legions of Russia soon had to endure such a pounding at the hands of the sons of Albion and Gaul, that they were glad to relinquish the prey which they had almost within their grasp.

Well, off we went, steaming and sailing, out of Portsmouth, with any amount of cheering and shouting. Next morning some of our fellows appeared as if one good man could beat a dozen of them; they looked in a most pitiable plight. They had not brought their sea legs with them and it was blowing rather fresh—what the sailors call a nice breeze—and those who could work and eat might do so for about forty-eight hours; but the greater portion of those who had, only a few hours previous, been making all the row they could, were lying all over the decks, huddled up like so many dying ducks.

I never was seasick, but I have every reason to believe, from what I have seen of it, that it is not at all desirable; my comrade, a strong young man of some twenty-four years, was quite knocked up for some days, so I suppose I must not be too hard upon the poor victims of *mal-de-mer*. In a few days, most of the men were all right again; we passed two or three of our ocean bull-dogs and plenty of other ships homeward-bound; had nothing particular to note, but that we were going out to defend a rotten cause, a race that almost every Christian despises. However, as soldiers we had nothing to do with politics,— we had simply to carry out the orders of Her Most Gracious Majesty and her Government.

We called at the Rock and took in coal, staying there one day, so that we had a good look at that wonderful place, which is the eyesore of Spain, and likely to remain so, for she will never get it again. It is immensely strong, nature and art having combined to render it well-nigh impregnable, and our people are not likely to be starved into a capitulation, as we constantly keep there some seven years' food for about ten thousand troops. I do not believe an enemy's ship could float near it, while on the land side the approach is very narrow and most securely defended. At any rate, the Spaniards will scarcely be foolhardy enough to make the attempt; if they do, they will find it a very hard nut to crack.

Off we went again, up the Mediterranean and on to Malta. We found it unpleasantly hot, but there was plenty of life—the place seemed full of Maltese, English, French, Germans, Swiss, Italians, in fact representatives of all nations of the earth, except Russians, and these we were on the way to look up. Malta appears to be admirably defended; we had a good look around it and at some of its huge forts. The Maltese boys, or I should rather say children, much amused us by their smartness in diving right under the ship and coming up with a piece of the coin of the realm in their mouths, immediately going down again after another. I never witnessed any one staying under water so long as these boys did, they seemed to be quite at home paddling on their side around the ship, in fact they appeared to have quite an amphibious nature.

As soon as we got coal, off we went again—on to Varna. They quickly put us on shore, and right glad were we to get there, for it is not very comfortable in a troopship—shut up, with scarcely standing room, constantly being pitched and tossed about, especially if you should happen to lose your balance and come down "soft upon the hard," with your face in contact with some of the blocks, and have a lot of sailors grinning at you—for they do not seem to have any pity for a poor fellow staggering about like a drunken man.

Well, we parted with our sailors on the best of terms; we had found them a fine jolly lot. At Varna we found ourselves mixed up with Turks, Egyptians, French, English, Maltese, Jews, Greeks, &;c., it was a regular Babel. Our new allies, the French, were remarkably civil, and their artillery were fine-looking men. We were at once marched off. to join our regiments. The old 7th formed a part of the Light Division under Sir G. Brown, at Monistier, about twenty miles from Varna. Sir G. Brown was a veteran who had won his spurs on many a hard fought field against our old enemies the French; but we were now allies, and all old sores must be forgotten and buried six feet deep; we had now one common foe—the Russians—to face; and shoulder to shoulder we were about to fight.

Monistier appeared a very pleasant place. There were all sorts of sports got up in the camp to keep up the men's spirits, which was much needed; we had an unseen enemy in the midst of us—cholera—that was daily finding and carrying off its victims. We were soon away, cholera-dodging, from camp to camp, or place to place; it was sweeping off our poor fellows so very fast. Our colonel looked well after his regiment, particularly the draft. We, were equally divided amongst the companies; they found us plenty of work to do, making trenches, batteries, gabions, marching and counter-marching.

The French and ourselves got on capitally, particularly the *Zouaves*, whom we found a very jolly set, though they afterwards proved themselves a troublesome lot to the enemy. It did not matter much where we went, we everywhere found Turkey a most unhealthy place; while the Turks and Bashi-Bazouks were a cut-throat looking crew, particularly the latter. We marched back to Varna, and it began to be rumoured that we should soon be off somewhere else. In the early part of August, the harbour of Varna was partly full of transports, ready to ship us off again, and we were heartily glad to get out of that; for we had lost a very great number of men through cholera and fever.

We lost the first English officer in Turkey, Captain A. Wallace, who died from an injury received in a fall from his horse while out hunting. The Turks struck me as a queer lot, particularly the women, who did not seem to put themselves out in the least, but were dirty and lazy-looking.

CHAPTER 2

Disembarkation in the Crimea

The time was now fast approaching for us to depart, and towards the latter end of August we began to get ready for a move. On the 7th of September, 1854, we sailed under sealed orders, and left Turkey behind us. We were now off, and it was a grand sight. Each steamer towed two transports; a part of the fleet was in front, a part on either side, and part behind us. We had some eight hundred ships of various sizes, and it seemed as if no power on earth were capable of stopping us. The Russian fleet might well keep out of our way. This voyage was truly a source of delight to the proud and war-like feelings of a Briton. As each ship with her consort steamed majestically out of the harbour of Varna, the hills on either side echoed for the first time with the loyal strains of England and France. The bands in a number of ships played "Rule Britannia," "God Save the Queen," and the French and Turkish National Anthems.

We dashed past the huge forts on either side of us, with the Turkish, English, and French flags floating proudly to the wind, and the guns at each fort saluting us. I had a good look at them with a capital glass; they appeared of an enormous size, and the guns large enough to creep into. I have heard that no fewer than six midshipmen crawled into one of them to get out of the wet; but I will not vouch for the truth of the story. The guns are about thirty inches in diameter, and some of them unscrew in the centre; they are shotted with a granite ball, which is raised by a crane and weighs about 800lbs.; while the charge consists of about 110lbs., of powder. Sir John Duckworth had some of his squadron sunk or destroyed by these nice "little pills," when he forced the Dardanelles, in 1807, and was compelled to beat a retreat.

We were only too glad to get away from Turkey; their towns look very well at a distance, but none of them will stand a close inspection, for they are filthy beyond description. We steamed up the Black Sea, bidding defiance to the Russian Fleet. It was the first time that a British Fleet had ever entered these waters. We spent a few days very pleasantly—our bands every evening playing a selection of lively airs; but at length we cast anchor and got ready for landing. Two days' rations were served out to each man, the meat being cooked on board.

The composition of the Russian Fleet, which fled at our approach, and took shelter under the guns of Sebastopol, was as follows:—

7 120-gun Ships	4 16-gun Brigs
13 84 ,, ,,	4 12 ,, ,,
3 60 ,, Frigates	6 16 ,, Schooners
1 54 ,, ,,	2 8 ,, ,,
1 52 ,, ,,	4 12 ,, Cutters
2 44 ,, ,,	3 10 ,, ,,
2 20 ,, Corvettes	28 With one or two Guns
3 18 ,, ,,	30 Transport Vessels.
4 18 ,, Brigs	

Nearly all these ships were built in British waters, and all on the capture of Sebastopol were sent to the bottom, cither by our guns or by the Russians to prevent them falling into our hands. A few that took shelter at Nicolaieff only escaped.

We were now approaching the enemy's shore for soldiering in reality, and about to find out whether the sons of Albion had degenerated since the days of their forefathers, who had earned our proud flag into all parts of the world, and had proved victorious both by sea and land. The honour of old England was, we realised, now in our hands. One good look at the older men was quite enough, they meant to do or die; while our commander, Lord Raglan, inspired us with confidence that he would lead us on to victory.

The reader may now prepare himself for some rough, hard soldiering and fighting.

On the 14th September, 1854, we landed at Old Fort. At a signal from the Admiral-in-chief we all got ready, and the first consignment of the Light Division were soon off at rapid pace. It was a toss-up between us and a boat-load of the 2nd Batt. Rifle Brigade, as to who should have the honour of landing first on the enemy's shore; but with all due respect I say the Fusiliers had it, though there was not much to boast of, as it was afterwards said the Rifles were a very good second (*see note at the end of chapter.*) We were not opposed in landing; a few *Cossacks* were looking on at a respectful distance, but made no attempt to molest us. It would have been madness on their part to have done so, considering the enormous force we could have brought to bear upon them.

A company of ours, and one or two of the Rifles, were at once sent forward to be on the lookout; Sir G. Brown went with them and nearly got "nabbed;" they could have shot him, but wanted to take him alive, believing that he was "a big bug;" some of our people, however, noticed their little game, crept close up to the general, and when the *Cossacks* thought of making a dash, set to work and emptied some of their saddles, while the remainder scampered off as fast as their horses' legs could carry them. Sir G. Brown had thus a narrow escape—as narrow as any he had previously experienced in the Peninsula and elsewhere.

The greater portion of our army quietly landed—the French disembarking some little distance from us. These had their little tents with them, and so had the small detachment of Turks who were with us, but there was not a single tent for the English Army—so much for management. Thousands of Britain's sons, who had come to fight for Queen and Country, were thrown ashore, as it were, without shelter of any kind.

A portion of the infantry with a few guns were first landed; but I must say that our condition as an army in an enemy's country was pitiable in the extreme. We had no tents, our officers had no horses, except a few ponies; Sir George Brown's sleeping compartment and dining-room were under a gun-carriage: even as bad off as we were our position was to be envied, for, although we were drenched to the skin, we were on *terra firma,* The poor marines and sailors in the men-of-war boats, were towing large rafts, with horses, guns, and detachments of artillerymen, amid a heavy swell from the sea, that was now running high—it was as dark as pitch, the horses almost mad with excitement, kicking and plunging. A number of poor fellows found a watery grave, rafts being upset in the heavy surf whilst attempting to land—the sea dashing with all its majestic force upon the sandy beach, although we could not see it. We made fires the best way we could, with broken boats and rafts; It was a fearful night!

When morning broke, we presented a woeful appearance; but we soon collected ourselves and assembled on the common. Next day we managed to get hold of a few country carts, or waggons, full of forage, that were being drawn by oxen and camels. We were all anxious to get at the enemy, and longed to try our strength against any number of boasting Russians. Our united army stood as follows:—English, or rather Britons, four divisions of infantry, each division then consisting of two brigades, each brigade of three regiments; to each division of infantry was attached a division of artillery, consisting of two field-batteries, four nine-pounder guns and two twenty-four pounder howitzers; we had a small brigade of light cavalry with us, attached to which was a six-pounder troop of horse-artillery; in all we mustered 26,000 men and 54 field guns.

Our gallant allies, the French, had about 24,000 men and 70 field guns. The Turks had about 4,500 men, no guns or cavalry, but they managed to bring tents with them. Thus the grand total now landed, and ready for an advance to meet the foe at all hazards, was 54,000 men, with 124 field guns. And the subsequent pages will tell how that force often met and conquered, amidst the storms of autumn, the snows of winter, and the heats of summer; nothing but death could thwart that dauntless host, whose leaders knew no excuses for weakness in the day of trial. We were all ready to cry shame on the man who would desert his country in the hour of need—

The first night in the Crimea was a night long to be remembered by those who were there. It came on to rain in torrents, while the wind blew a perfect hurricane; and all, from the commanders down to the drummer boys, had to stand and take it as it came. And the rain did fall, only as it does in the tropics. We looked next morning like a lot of drowned rats. What our people were thinking about I do not know. Had the enemy come on in strength nothing could have saved us. We were now in an enemy's country—that enemy most powerful and subtle; it was known that they were in force not far from us, though their strength was unknown—yet we were absolutely unprovided with camp equipment or stores.

They say fortune favours the brave, and, happily, the Russians let the opportunity slip. Next day we were as busy as bees landing all sorts of warlike implements—artillery, horses, shot, shell, and all that goes to equip an army, except shelter. The "unseen enemy" was still with us, daily finding its victims. Our men worked like bricks, were determined to make the best of a bad job. We dried our clothing on the beach, and the next night strong lines of picquets were thrown out to prevent surprise, while we lay down, wrapped in our cloaks. On the 16th, we still kept getting all sorts of things on shore in readiness to meet the enemy; but our people seemed to forget that we were made of flesh and blood.

The French were well provided with tents and other comforts; we still had none. On the 17th there was the same work getting ready for a start; but the morning of the 18th saw us on our legs advancing up the country. We then suffered from the want of water; what we did get was quite brackish. On the morning of the 19th we marched fairly off with the French on our right. We continued to suffer very heavily; a number of men fell out for the want of a few drops of water, but it could not be got, and we continued to march all day without sighting the enemy, except only a few *cossacks*, who kept a respectful distance from us. The Light Division was in front, and we found out afterwards that was to be our place whenever there were any hard knocks to be served out.

It began to get a little exciting in the afternoon. In front of us was a handful of cavalry—apart of the 11th Hussars; and presently a battery of Horse Artillery dashed off at a break-neck pace and began pounding away at something we could not see. We saw that day the first wounded man on our side—a corporal of the 11th Hussars; his leg was nearly off. We soon got accustomed to such eights, passed on, and took no notice. As we topped the rising ground we could see the enemy retiring; our cavalry were still in front, feeling the way—as they advanced the *cossacks* kept slowly retiring. We still advanced until it began to get dark, when strong picquets were thrown out—we collected what we could to make our bivouac fires, for we still had no tents.

Some of our poor fellows died that night sitting round the scanty fires, or wrapped in their cloaks. I shall ever remember that night as long as I live. We sat talking for some little time of our homes and friends far away. My comrade had just had about an hour's sleep; when on waking he told me he bad a presentiment that he should fall in the first action. I tried to cheer him up and drive such nonsense out of his head.

I thought he was not well, and he replied that he was very ill, but should be out of all pain before tomorrow's sun set; however, he was determined to do his duty, let the consequence be what it might, adding, "May the dear Lord give me strength to do my duty for my Queen and Country, for I could not, my boy," grasping my hand, "bear the thought of being branded as a coward."

Still retaining a firm manly grip he continued, "for God has washed all my sins away in Jesus' blood. Come," he continued, "let's walk about a little; I am getting cold." Afterwards, getting hold of my arm, he stopped, looked me full in the face, and twice repeated the solemn words, "Eternity, Eternity, know and seek the Lord while he may be found, call upon Him while He is near, for you cannot tell what tomorrow will bring forth, and it may be too late then." Then he repeated parts of hymns, which I had often heard sung when a boy. I can safely say he was one who was ready for anything—life or death. As he had said "his life was hid with Christ in God." We pledged that we would do all that we could for each other in life or in death; I little thought that his end was so near.

Such were some of the men who carried the standard that has braved the battle and the breeze for a thousand years up the heights of Alma, and I can say truly, that it is not the drunkard or the blackguard who makes a thorough soldier, either in the field or out of it. As I proceed with my narrative, I will give other examples—for instance, Sir H. Havelock, Colonel Blackader, Major Malan, Lord Raglan, and also poor Captain Hedley Vicars, of the 97th, one of the bravest of men, who loved the Lord with all his heart and soul, and was not at all backward in telling poor sinners what that Lord had done for him. As he would often say, "Religion is a personal matter; have mercy upon me, oh God, for I am vile."

CHAPTER 3

The Battle of the Alma

Well, to my story; the morning of the 20th found us once more on our legs. Marshal St. Arnaud rode along our line; we cheered him most heartily, and he seemed to appreciate it; in passing the 88th, the Marshal of France called out in English, "I hope you will fight well today;" the fire-eating old Connaught Rangers at once took up the challenge, and a voice loudly exclaimed "Shure, your honour, we will, don't we always fight well?" Away we then went at a steady pace, until about midday—the Light and Second divisions leading, in columns of brigades.

As we approached the village of Burlak, which was on our side of the river, or what was called the right bank, the blackguards set fire to it, but still we pressed on; we by the right, the Second division by the left. We now advanced into the valley beneath, in line, sometimes taking ground to the right, then to the left, and presently we were ordered to lie down to avoid the hurricane of shot and shell that the enemy was pouring into us. A number of our poor fellows lay down to rise no more; the enemy had the range to a nicety. Our men's feelings were now wrought up to such a state that it was not an easy matter to stop them.

Up to the river we rushed, and some,—in fact all I could see,—got ready for a swim, pulling off their knapsacks and camp kettles. Our men were falling now very fast; into the river we dashed, nearly up to our arm pits, with our ammunition and rifles on the top of our heads to keep them dry, scrambled out the best way we could, and commenced to ascend the hill. From east to west the enemy's batteries were served with rapidity, hence we were enveloped in smoke on what may be called the glacis. We were only about 600 yards from the mouths of the guns, the thunderbolts of war were, therefore, not far apart, and death loves a crowd. The havoc among the Fusiliers, both 7th and 23rd, was awful, still nothing but death could stop that renowned Infantry.

There were 14 guns of heavy calibre just in front of us, and others on our flanks, in all some 42 guns were raining death and destruction upon us. A number of our poor fellows on reaching the top of the slippery bank were shot down and fell back dead, or were drowned in the Alma. The two Fusilier Regiments seemed to vie with each other in performing deeds of valour. General Codrington waved his hat, then rode straight at one of the embrasures, and leaped his grey Arab into the breastwork; others, breathless, were soon beside him. Up we went, step by step, but with a horrid carnage.

When one gets into such a "hot corner" as this was, one has not much time to mind his neighbours. I could see that we were leading; the French were on our right, and the 23rd Fusiliers on our left. This was Albuera repeated—the two Fusilier regiments shoulder to shoulder—only the French were on our right as Allies, whereas in the former battle they were in front as bitter foes.

The fighting was now of a desperate kind. My comrade said to me "We shall have to shift those fellows with the bayonet, old boy," pointing to the Russians. We still kept moving on, and at last General Sir G. Brown, Brigadier Codrington, and our noble old Colonel, called upon us for one more grand push, and a cheer and a charge brought us to the top of the hill. Into the battery we jumped, spiked the guns, and bayoneted or shot down the gunners; but, alas, we were not strong enough, and we were in our turn hurled, by an overwhelming force, out of the battery, and down the hill again. The old 7th halted, fronted, and lay down, and kept up a withering fire upon the enemy at point-blank range, which must have told heavily upon their crowded ranks. Help was now close at hand.

Up came the Guards and Highlanders. His Royal Highness the Duke of Cambridge was with them, and he nobly faced the foe. He had a good tutor in that hero of a hundred fights, Sir Colin Campbell. They got a warm reception, but still pressed on up that fatal hill. Some will tell you that the Guards retired, or wanted to retire; but no, up they went manfully, step by step, both Guards and Highlanders, and a number of other regiments of the 2nd Division, and with deafening shouts the heights of Alma were ours. The enemy were sent reeling from them in hot haste, with artillery and a few cavalry in pursuit. If we had only had three or four thousand cavalry with us, they would

VIEW OF THE HEIGHTS OF ALMA.

not have got off quite so cheaply; as it was, they got a nasty mauling, such an one es they did not seem to appreciate.

After gaining the heights—a victory that set the church bells of Old England ringing and gave schoolboys a holiday, we had time to count our loss. Alas, we had paid the penalty for leading the way. We had left more than half our number upon the field, dead or wounded, and one of our colours was gone, but, thank God, the enemy had not got it; it was found upon the field, cut into pieces, and with a heap of dead and wounded all around it. Kinglake, the author of *The Crimean Campaign*, says in the boldest language that "Yea and his Fusiliers won the Alma." As one of them, I can confirm that statement—we had to fight against tremendous odds.

The brunt of the fighting fell upon the first Brigade of the Light Division, as their loss will testify. At one time the 7th Fusiliers confronted a whole Russian Brigade and kept them at bay until assistance came up. Our poor old colonel exclaimed, at the top of the hill, when he sounded the assembly, "A colour gone, and where's my poor old Fusiliers, my God, my God!" and he cried like a child, wringing his hands. After the enemy had been fairly routed, I obtained leave to go down the hill. I had lost my comrade and I was determined to find him if possible. I had no difficulty in tracing the way we had advanced, for the ground was covered with our poor fellows—in some places sixes and sevens, at others tens and twelves, and at other places whole ranks were lying. "For these are deeds which shall not pass away, and names that must not, shall not wither."

The Russian wounded behaved in a most barbarous manner; they made signs for a drink, and then shot the man who gave it them. My attention was drawn to one nasty case. A young officer of the 95th gave a wounded Russian a little brandy out of his flask, and was turning to walk away, when the fellow shot him mortally; I would have settled with him for his brutish conduct, but one of our men, who happened to be close to him, at once gave him his bayonet, and despatched him. I went up to the young officer, and finding he was still alive, placed him in as comfortable a position as I could, and then left him, to look for my comrade.

I found him close to the river, dead; he had been shot in the mouth and left breast, and death must have been instantaneous. He was now in the presence of his glorified captain. He was as brave as a lion, but a faithful disciple. He could not have gone 100 yards from the spot where he told me we should "have to shift those fellows with the bayonet." I sat down beside him, and thought my heart would break as I recalled some of his sayings, particularly his talk to me at midnight of the 19th; this was about six p.m., on the 20th. I have every reason to believe that he was prepared for the change. I buried him, with the assistance of two or three of our men. We laid him in his grave, with nothing but an overcoat wrapped around him, and then left him with a heavy heart.

In passing up the hill I had provided myself with all the water bottles I could, from the dead, in order to help to revive the wounded as much as possible. I visited the young officer whom I saw shot by the wounded Russian, and found he was out of all pain: he had passed into the presence of a just and holy God. The sights all the way were sickening. The sailors were taking off the wounded as fast as possible, but many lay there all night, just as they had fallen. Dear reader, such is war. I rejoined my regiment on the top of the hill, and was made sergeant that night. We remained on the hill until the 23rd, and lost a number of men from cholera.

The 21st and 22nd were spent in collecting the wounded—both friend and foe. Ours were at once put on board ship and sent to Scutari; some hundreds of the enemy were collected in a vineyard on the slopes, the dead were buried in large pits—and a very mournful and ghastly sight it was, for many had been literally cut to pieces. It was a difficult matter really to find out what had killed some of them. Here men were found in positions as if in the act of firing; there, as if they had fallen asleep; and all over the field the dead were lying in every position it was possible for men to assume. Some of those who had met death at the point of the bayonet, presented a picture painful to look upon; others were actually smiling. Such was the field of the Alma.

The first battle was now over, and as I wrote to my parents from the heights, I thanked God I was still in the land of the living, and what's more with a whole skin (except an abrasion on the head caused by a stone), which a few hours before had appeared impossible. The three regiments that led the way suffered fearfully, the 7th Royal Fusiliers on the right, the 23rd Royal Welsh Fusiliers in the centre, and the 33rd on the left. Any one of these three regiment suffered more than the whole brigade of Guards or Highlanders combined; not that I wish to speak disparagingly of the gallant Guards or the noble Highlanders, I only wish to show on whom the brunt of the fighting fell.

Volumes could be written upon the Alma—the battle that opened the guns of France and England in unison, but I must confine my narrative to what actually passed under my own eyes, or in my own regiment. Canrobert, a French marshal, might well in the excitement exclaim, "I should like to command an English Division for a campaign, and it would be the d—— take the hindmost; I feel that I could then attain my highest ambition!"

A Russian wounded general, in giving up his sword, as prisoner of war, stated that they were confident of holding their position for some days no matter what force the Allies could bring against them, adding that they came to fight men and not devils. Prince Menschikoff quitted the field in a hurry, for he left his carriage behind and all his state papers. He, poor man, had to eat a lot of humble pie, and we are told that he was furiously mad. He had been over confident that he could hold us in check for three weeks, and then put us all into the sea; he just held the heights for three hours after the attack commenced. Ladies even came out of Sebastopol to witness the destruction of the Allies; but I fancy their flight must have been most distressing, while their feelings were not to be envied.

The Russian officers were gentlemen, but their men were perfect fiends. The night after the battle and the following morning, this was proved in a number of cases, by their shooting down our men just after they had done all they could for them. Our comrades at once paid them for it either by shooting or bayoneting them on the spot; this was rough justice, but it was justice, nevertheless; none of them lived to boast of what they had done.

Poor Captain Monk of ours was the talk of the whole regiment that evening. It appears that a Russian presented his rifle at him, close to his head. The captain at once parried it and cut the man down. A Russian officer then tackled him in single combat, and he quietly knocked him down with his *fist*, with others right and left of him, until he had a heap all round him, and at last fell dead in the midst of them. Sir G. Brown's horse was shot from under him just in front of us, but that fire-eating old warrior soon collected himself, jumped up waving his sword and shouting, "Fusiliers, I am all right, follow me, and I'll remember you for it!" and then, as Marshal Ney did at Waterloo, led the way up that fatal hill on foot, animating the men to the performance of deeds of valour. Britons, where is the man who would not respond to such a call? The eyes of the civilized world were upon us.

Up the hill we went, for our blood was up, and the strength of all the Russians could not stop us; they might call us red devils if they liked, we were determined to do our duty for Queen and country. We remained on the heights until the 23rd. The 57th joined us there, just too late for the battle; but the old "die-hards" left their marks upon the enemy at Inkermann and throughout the siege of Sebastopol.

The following letter, written immediately after the battle, will, perhaps, prove interesting here:—

Heights of Alma,
September 20-21, 1854.

My Dear Parents,

I wrote you from Turkey that I would most likely tell you a little about the enemy before long. Well, we have met them and given them a good sound drubbing at the above-named place; and thank God, I am still in the land of the living, and, what's more, with a whole skin, which a few hours ago appeared impossible. To describe my feelings in going into action, I could not; and I hope you will excuse my feeble attempt at describing the terrible fight we have just passed through.

As soon as the enemy's round shot came hopping along, we simply did the polite—opened out and allowed them to pass on—there is nothing lost by politeness, even on a battlefield. As we kept advancing, we had to move our pins to get out of their way; and presently they began to pitch their shot and shell right amongst us, and our men began to fall. I know that I felt horribly sick—a cold shivering running through my veins—and I must acknowledge that I felt very uncomfortable; but I am happy to say that feeling passed off as soon as I began to get warm to it. It was very exciting work, and the sights were sickening; I hope I shall never witness such another scene.

We were now fairly under the enemy's fire—our poor fellows began to fall fast all around me. We had deployed into line, and lay down, in order to avoid the hurricane of shot and shell that was being poured into us.

We still kept advancing and then lying down again; then we made a rush up to the river, and in we went. I was nearly up to my armpits; a number of our poor fellows were drowned, or shot down with grape and canister (that came amongst us like hail) while attempting to cross. How I got out I cannot say, as the banks were very steep and slippery. We were now enveloped in smoke, and could not see much.

Up the hill we went, step by step, but with a fearful carnage. The fighting now became very exciting, our artillery playing over our heads, and we firing and advancing all the time. The smoke was now so great that we could hardly see what we were doing, and our poor fellows were falling all around. It was a dirty, rugged hill. We got mixed up with the 95th. Someone called out, "Come on young 95th, the old 7th are in front." The fighting was now desperate.[1] General Sir George Brown, Brigadier Codrington, our noble Colonel Yea, and, in fact, all our mounted officers, were encouraging us to move on; and, at last, with a ringing cheer we topped the heights, and into the enemy's battery we jumped.

Here we lost a great number of our men; and, by overwhelming numbers, we, the 23rd, 33rd, 95th, and Rifles, were mobbed out of the battery, and a part of the way down the hill again; and then we had some more desperate fighting. We lay down and blazed into their huge columns as hard as we could load and fire; and in about twenty minutes, up came the Guards and Highlanders and a number of other regiments; and, with another ringing cheer for Old England, at them we went again and re-topped the heights, routing them from their batteries. Here I got a crack on the head with a piece of stone, which unmanned me for a time. When I came round I found the enemy had all bolted.

Do not let anyone see this, as they would only laugh at my poor description of our first battle. The poor old Fusiliers nave suffered very heavily. My poor comrade was killed just after getting out of the river. He is the one whom I have often spoken about. I am confident that he is gone to a far better home than this. Dear parents, what a sight the whole field presents! I would again thank God with a sincere heart for protecting me, I hope, for some good purpose. I hope that you will be able to make out this scrawl, as the only table I have is a dead Russian. I went down the hill yesterday evening and found my poor comrade dead.

The wounded Russians behaved worse than the brute beasts of the field; they shot some of our officers and men just after they had done all they could for them, but they did not live

---

1. A nice warm reception for a prodigal son. I was not 21, and it set me thinking of the comfortable home in Norwich that I had left.

long to talk of what they had done, for they were at once shot or bayoneted. On some parts of the field the killed of the poor old 7th, 23rd, 33rd, and 95th, lay thick. You will notice that I could not finish this letter yesterday. I hope you will excuse the paper (it's the best I have) and likewise my poor description of our maiden fight. You may tell them in Norwich, or anywhere else, that your poor boy led the way up this fatal hill—for it was the 7th Fusiliers, 23rd Fusiliers, and 33rd Duke of Wellington's, 95th, and Rifles, that led the van.

The Guards and Highlanders, and the entire 2nd Division, backed us up well. We have still that horrible disease—Cholera—amongst us. One of my company died with it last night, after storming the heights. Please send a paper. Direct, Sergeant T. Gowing, Royal Fusiliers.

    Goodbye, dear parents, and God bless you all.

        From your rough, but affectionate son,

            T. Gowing, Royal Fusiliers.

Chapter 4

Sebastopol & Balaclava

The morning of the 23rd saw us early on our feet, and *en route* for the fortress known by the worldwide name of Sebastopol. We marched all day, our men fast dropping out from sickness. Our first halting-place was at Katcha, where we had a splendid view. Our friends the *Cossacks* kept a little in front of us. On the 24th away we went again; nothing particular occurring, except that our Unseen Enemy—cholera—was still in the midst of us, picking off his victims. The commander-in-chief of the French, the gallant and gay Marshal St. Arnaud, succumbed to it. But we pressed on; the honour of three nations being at stake.

Nothing worthy of notice transpired until the 28th, when we thought we were going to have another Alma job. We began to get ready; artillery and cavalry were ordered to the front. The enemy got a slight taste of the Scots Greys; a few prisoners being captured. The Rifles got a few pop-shots at them; but it turned out afterwards that it was the reargaurd of the enemy.

A number of things were picked up by our people, but the affair ended in smoke; they evidently did not mean to try to oppose our advance—they had once attempted it, and wanted no more of it; so the following day we marched on without interruption to the nice little village of Balaclava. We had little or no trouble in taking it; the Russians, however, made a slight show of resistance, for the sake of honour.

The Rifles advanced, we supporting them. A few shots were fired; but as soon as one or two of our ships entered the harbour, and gave the old castle a few shots, they gave in, and our people at once took possession. The harbour was speedily filled with our shipping. Our men managed to pick up a few old hens and a pig or two, which came in very handy for a stew; and we got some splendid grapes and apples. Next day we moved up to the front of Sebastopol, whither other divisions had gone on before us. The siege guns were soon brought up, manned by Marines and Jack Tars, and we quickly round out that we had a nice little job cut out for us.

We must acknowledge that the enemy proved themselves worthy defenders of a fortress; they worked night and day to strengthen the lines of forts, huge batteries springing into existence like mushrooms, and stung us more than mosquitoes. It was evident to all that if the Allies wanted Sebastopol they would find it a hard nut to crack; that it would be a rough picnic for us. Sir George Brown might well say, that the longer we looked at it the uglier it got. The white tower was knocked all to pieces very quickly, but huge works were erected all around it, and called the Malakoff. We found it no child's play dragging heavy siege guns up from Balaclava, but it was a long pull and a strong pull, up to our ankles in mud which stuck like glue.

Often on arrival in camp we found but little to eat, hardly sufficient to keep body and soul together; then off again to help to get the guns and mortars into their respective batteries, exposed all the time to the enemy's fire, and they were noways sparing with shot and shell. We would have strong bodies in front of us, as covering parties and working parties; often the pick and shovel would have to be thrown down, and the rifle brought to the front. Sometimes we would dig and guard in turn; we could keep ourselves warm, digging and making the trenches and batteries, although often up to our ankles in muddy water.

All our approaches had to be done at night, and the darker the better for us. As for the covering party, it was killing work laying down for hours in the cold mud, returning to camp at daylight, wearied completely out with cold—sleepy and hungry; many a poor fellow suffering with ague or fever, to find nothing but a cold bleak mud tent, without fire, to rest their weary bones in; and often not even a piece of mouldy biscuit to eat, nothing served out yet. But often, as soon as we reached camp, the orderly would call out, "Is Sergeant G. in?"

"Yes; what's up?"

"You are for fatigue at once."

Off to Balaclava, perhaps to bring up supplies, in the shape of salt beef, salt pork, biscuits, blankets, shot or shell. Return at night completely done up; down you go in the mud for a few hours' rest—that is, if there was not an alarm. And thus it continued, week in and week out, month in and month out. So much for honour and glory! The enemy were not idle; they were continually constructing new works, and peppering us from morning: until night. Sometimes they would treat us to a few long-rangers, sending their shot right through our camp. And we found often that the besiegers were the attacked party, and not the attacking. Our numbers began to get very scanty—cholera was daily finding its victims. It never left us from the time we were in Turkey. It was piteous to see poor fellows struck down in two or three hours, and carried off to their last abode.

Nearly all of us were suffering more or less from ague, fever, or colds, but it was no use complaining. The doctors had little or no medicine to give. Our poor fellows were dropping off fast with dysentery and diarrhoea; but all that could stand stuck to it manfully. We had several brushes with the foe, who always came off second best. The Poles deserted by wholesale from the enemy, some of them would turn round at once and let drive at the Russians , then give up their arms to us, shouting "Pole, Pole!" We knew well that the enemy were almost daily receiving reinforcements, we had, as yet, received none. We were almost longing to go at the town, take it or die in the attempt to hoist our glorious old flag on its walls.

Then the nights began to get very cold, and we found the endless trench work very trying, often having to stand up to our ankles and sometimes knees in muddy water, with the enemy pounding at us all the time with heavy ordnance, both direct and vertical, guns often dismounted and platforms sent flying in all directions. Our sailors generally paid the enemy out for it. The Russians often fought with desperation but moral strength in war is to physical as three to one. Our men had handled the enemy very roughly more than once since the Alma, and they were shy at coming to close quarters, unless they could take us by surprise.

Thus things went on day after day, until the morning of the 25th October, 1854, when we awoke to find that the enemy were trying to cut off our communications at Balaclava, which brought on the battle. I was not engaged, but had started from camp in charge of twenty-five men on fatigue to Balaclava, to bring up blankets for the sick and wounded. It was a cold bleak morning as we left our tents.

Our clothing was getting very thin, with as many patches as Joseph's coat. More than one smart fusilier's back or shoulder was indebted to a piece of black blanket, with hay bound round his legs to cover his rags and keep the biting wind out a little; and boots were nearly worn out, with none to replace them. There was nothing about our outward appearance lady-killing; we were looking stern duty in the face. There was no murmuring, however; all went jogging along, cracking all kinds of jokes. We could hear the firing at Balaclava, but thought it was the Turks and Russians playing at long bowls, which generally ended in smoke. We noticed, too, mounted orderlies and staff officers riding as if they were going in for the Derby. As we reached the hills overlooking the plains of Balaclava, we could see our cavalry formed up, but none of us thought what a sight we were about to witness. The enemy's cavalry in massive columns were moving up the valley; the firing was at times heavy. Several volleys of musketry were heard.

My party was an unarmed party, hence my keeping them out of harm's way. One column of the enemy's cavalry advanced as far as we could see to within half-a-mile of our people, who were a handful compared with the host in front of them. It was soon evident our generals were not going to stop to count them, but go at them at once. It was a most thrilling and exciting moment. As our trumpets sounded the advance, the Greys and Inniskillings moved forward at a sharp pace, and as they began to ascend the hill they broke into a charge. The pace was terrific, and with a ringing cheer and continued shouts they dashed right into the centre of the enemy's column.

It was an awful crash as the glittering helmets of the boys of the Green Isle and the bearskins of the Greys dashed into the midst of levelled lances with sabres raised. The earth seemed to shake with a sound like thunder; hundreds of the enemy went down in that terrible rush. It was heavy men mounted on heavy horses, and it told a fearful tale. A number of the spectators, as our men dashed into that column, exclaimed, "They are lost! They are lost!" It was lance against sword, and at times our men became entirely lost in the midst of a forest of lances. But they cut their way right through, as if they had been riding over a lot of donkeys. A shout of joy burst from us and the French, who were spectators, as our men came out of the column. It was an uphill fight of three hundred Britons against five thousand Muscovites. Fresh columns of squadrons closed around this noble band, with a view of crushing them; but help was now close at hand.

With another terrible crash, and with a shout truly English, in went the Royal Dragoons on one flank of the column; and with thrilling shouts of "Faugh-a-Ballagh," the Royal Irish buried themselves in a forest of lances on the other. Then came thundering on the Green Horse (5th Dragoon Guards), and rode straight at the centre of the

THE CHARGE OF THE LIGHT BRIGADE

enemy's column. The Russians must have had a bad time of it. At a distance, it was impossible to see the many hand-to-hand encounters; the thick overcoats of the enemy, we knew well, would ward off many a blow. Our men, we found afterwards, went in with point or with the fifth, sixth, or seventh cuts about the head; the consequence was, the field was covered pretty thickly with the enemy, but hundreds of their wounded were carried away. We found that they were all strongly buckled to their horses, so that it was only when the horse fell that the rider was likely to fall.

But if ever a body of cavalry were handled roughly, that column of Muscovites were. They bolted—that is, all that could—like a flock of sheep with a dog at their tails. Their officers tried to bring them up, but it was no go; they had had enough, and left the field to Gen. Scarlett's band of heroes. However that gallant officer escaped was a miracle, for he led some thirty yards right into the jaws of death, and came off without a scratch. The victorious brigade triumphantly rejoined their comrades, and were received with a wild burst of enthusiasm. It would be well if we could now draw the curtain and claim a glorious victory. The French officers were loud in their admiration of the daring feat of arms they had just witnessed Many of them said it was most glorious. Sir Colin Campbell might well get a little excited, and express his admiration of the Scots Greys.

This old hero rode up to the front of the Greys with hat in hand, and exclaimed with pride: "Greys, gallant Greys! I am past sixty-one years; if I were young again, I should be proud to be in your ranks; you are worthy of your forefathers." But, reader, they were not alone. It was the Union Brigade, as at Waterloo, that had just rode through and through the enemy, and drew the words from Lord Raglan, who had witnessed both charges: "Well done, Scarlett!" The loss of this noble brigade was comparatively trifling taking into consideration the heavy loss they inflicted upon the foe. My readers must know that the Union Brigade was composed of one English, one Irish, and one Scotch regiment; so that it was old England, ould Ireland, and Scotland forever!

The Gallant Union Brigade

The Charge of the Light Brigade.

But we now come to where someone had blundered. The light cavalry had stood and witnessed the heroic deeds of their comrades, the heavies. Had we had an Uxbridge, a Cotton, or a Le Marchant at the head of our cavalry, not many of the enemy's heavy column, which had just received such a mauling from the heavy brigade, would have rejoined their comrades. The light cavalry would have been let go at the right time and place, and the enemy would have paid a much heavier price for a peep at Balaclava. The noble Six Hundred had not to wait much longer. They were all on the lookout for something. It comes at last. A most dashing soldier, the late Captain Nolan, rode at full speed from Lord Raglan with a written order to the commander of our cavalry, the late Lord Lucan. The order ran thus:—

> Lord Raglan wishes the cavalry to advance to the front, and try to prevent the enemy carrying away the guns. Troop of horse artillery may accompany. French cavalry is on your left. Immediate.
>
> (Signed) R. Airey.

Anyone without a military eye will be able to see at a glance that it was *our guns* (from which the Turks had run away), our commander wished the cavalry to retake from the enemy. It could have been done without much loss, as Gen. Sir G. Cathcart was close at hand with his division. The honest facts are these: The intrepid Nolan delivered the order to Lord Lucan for the cavalry to attack "immediately." Mind this was not the first order our commander had sent to the commander of our cavalry. The former order ran thus:

> Cavalry to advance and take advantage of any opportunity to recover the heights; they will be supported by the infantry, which have been ordered to advance on two fronts.

What heights? Why, the heights on which our spiked guns are, that the Turks had bolted from. It must have been very amazing to our commander that his orders had not been obeyed, although some thirty-five precious minutes had elapsed. From the high ground he could see that the enemy were about to take our seven guns away in triumph, hence the order "immediately." The commander of our cavalry evidently lost his balance with the gallant Nolan, as we find from authentic works upon the war. Lord Lucan, who was irritable, to say the least of it, said to Nolan, "Attack, sir, attack what? What guns, sir?"

"Lord Raglan's orders," he replied, "are that the cavalry should attack immediately."

Nolan, a hot-blooded son of the Green Isle, could not stand to be snapped at any longer, and he added, "There, my Lord, is your enemy

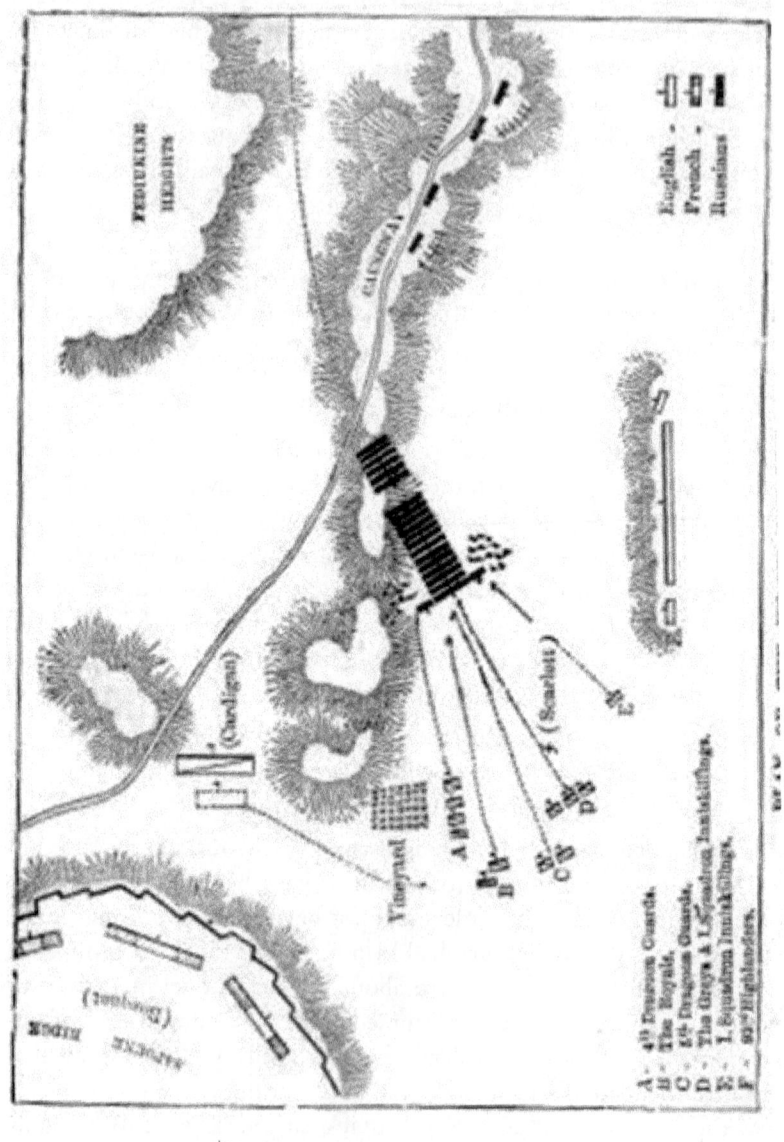

PLAN OF THE HEAVY CAVALRY CHARGE

and there are your guns." The order was misconstrued, and the noble Six Hundred were launched into the valley of death. Poor Captain Nolan was the first that fell. But they and he shall live renowned in story.

Thus far I had been an eyewitness of one of the noblest feats of arms that ever was seen upon a battlefield. It spoke volumes to the rising generation. Go and do likewise. Never say die. A brave man can die but once, but a cowardly sneak all his life long. It told the enemy plainly the metal our cavalry were made of. They said that we were red devils at the Alma; it must be acknowledged that they got well lathered then, and now the Union Brigade of heavy horse had shaved them very roughly. As for the Light Brigade, with sickness, disease, a strong escort for our commander-in-chief, and mounted orderlies for the different generals, it hardly mustered the strength of one regiment on an Indian footing. There was a lot of excitement on the hill-side when we found the Light Brigade was advancing, first at a steady trot, then they broke into a gallop. Their noble leader, the Earl of Cardigan, might well say, "Here goes the last of the Cardigans!"

Someone (an officer) said, "What on earth are they going to do? Surely they are not going to charge the whole Russian army? It's madness." But, madness or not, they were simply obeying an order. And this noble band pressed on towards the enemy, sweeping down the valley at a terrific pace in all the pride of manhood. Every man's heart on that hillside beat high. "They are lost! they are lost!" burst from more than one spectator. The enemy's guns, right, left, and front, opened upon this devoted band. A heavy musketry fire was likewise opened; but still they pressed on. The field was soon strewn with the dead and wounded. It was a terrible sight to have to stand and witness, without the power of helping them.

The excitement was beyond my pen to express. Big briny tears gushed down more than one man's face that had resolutely stormed the Alma. To stand and see their countrymen rushing at a fearful pace right into the jaws of death was a most exciting scene to stand and witness. The field was now covered with the wreck of men and horses. They at last reached the smoke. Now and then we could hear the distant cheer and see their swords gleaming above the smoke, as they plunged into one of the terrible batteries that had swept their comrades down. An officer very kindly lent me his field glass for a short time. The field presented a ghastly sight, with the unnatural enemy hacking at the wounded; some trying to drag their mangled bodies from the awful cross-fires, but a few escaped the bloodthirsty Cossack's lance.

We could see the enemy formed up to cut off all retreat; but it was now do or die. In our fellows went, with a ringing cheer, and cut a road through them; and now to our horror, the brutish enemy opened their guns with grape upon friend and foe, thus involving all in one common ruin, and the guns again opened on their flanks. It was almost miraculous how any of that noble band escaped. Our gallant allies, the French, had witnessed the heroic deeds of the Light Brigade, and now the *Chasseurs* went at the enemy in a most dashing manner to help to rescue the remains of such a noble band. The chivalrous conduct of our allies, the French, on this field will always be remembered with gratitude; they had ten killed and twenty-eight wounded.

This was the only field on which our cavalry were engaged during the campaign. At the Alma, a few squadrons were on the field, but not engaged. At Inkermann a portion of the cavalry were formed up; they then would have had a chance if the enemy had broken through the infantry. As far as the siege was concerned, they only did the looking-on part. Our gallant allies, the French, admired much the conduct of our cavalry, both heavy and light. General Bosquet said that the charge of the heavies was sublime; that of the Light Brigade was splendid; "but it was not war."

We have not the slightest hesitation in asserting that the Light Brigade was sacrificed by a blunder. It is but little use trying to lay the blame on the shoulders of poor Captain Nolan; had he lived the cavalry would have gone at our guns and recaptured them, or had a good try for it. It was Lord Lucan, and no one else, that ordered the charge. To say the least of it, it was a misconception of an order. But I am confident that Old England will long honour the memory of the noble Six Hundred.

My readers will please remember that my party was unarmed, hence my keeping out of harm's way. Had we been armed, I should most likely have gone down the hill at the double, and formed up on the left of the thin red line—the 93rd Highlanders. Shortly after the sanguinary charge of the Light Brigade I moved forward as fast as I could. On arriving at Balaclava I found the stores closed up, and the assistant quarter-master-general ordered me to take my party on to the field, to assist in removing the wounded, as far as it lay in my power.

Off I went at once. I found the cavalry still formed up. The Light

Brigade were but a clump of men! Noble fellows, they were few, but fearless still. I was not allowed to proceed further for some time, and I had the unspeakable pleasure of grasping more than one hand of that noble brigade. There was no mistaking their proud look as they gave me the right hand of fellowship. A sergeant of the old Cherry Pickers, who knew me well, gave me a warm shake of the hand, remarking, "Ah! my old Fusilier, I told you a week ago we would have something to talk about before long."

"But," I replied, "has there not been some mistake?"

He said, "It cannot be helped now; we have tried to do our part. It will all come out some day."

My men carried a number of the Heavies from the field to the hospitals; then I got my store of priceless blankets, and off we plodded through the mud back to camp. We had something to talk about on our way home. Our gallant allies, the French, were in high glee, they could hardly control themselves. As soon as they caught sight of us, they commenced to shout "*Bon Anglais, Bon Anglais!*" and so it continued until I reached our camp. But exciting and startling events now rapidly succeeded each other: the victorious cavalry had hardly sheathed their swords, after their conflict with the enemy, when about ten thousand, almost maddened with drink and religious enthusiasm, took another peep at our camp next day, supported by some thirty guns. They were driven back into the town quicker than they came out. This was afterwards called Little Inkermann, and was a stiff fight while it lasted.

CHAPTER 5

The Inkermann Battles

But I have something else in store. Our turn came next day, 26th October—Little Inkermann, as our men named it. About midday the enemy came out of the town in very strong columns, and attacked us just to the right of the Victoria Redoubt; the fighting was of a very severe nature. The 2nd Division, under Sir De Lacy Evans, received them first; and a part of the Light Division had a hand in it. The enemy made cock-sure of beating us and brought trenching tools with them, but were again doomed to be disappointed. We were hardly prepared for them; but soon collected ourselves, and closed upon them with the bayonet, when, after some hard fighting, they were hurled from the field. They paid dearly for a peep at our camp, leaving close upon 1000 dead and wounded.

They retired much (quicker than they came, with our heavy guns sweeping them down by scores, and cutting lanes through their columns. Our artillery on this occasion did great execution, whilst a continuous rain of Minie rifle balls mowed their ranks like grass, and for the finishing stroke they got that nasty "piece of cold steel;" our huge Lancaster guns simply killed the enemy by wholesale.

General Bosquet kindly offered assistance, but the reply of our commander was, "Thank you, General, the enemy are already defeated, and too happy to leave the field to me."

The attack of the 26th was nothing more nor less than a reconnaissance in force, preparatory to the memorable battle of Inkermann; but it cost them heavily, while we also lost a large number of men. On this field the brutal enemy distinguished themselves by bayoneting all our wounded that the picquets were compelled to leave behind in falling back for a short distance. The stand made by the picquets of the 30th, 55th, and 95th on our right was grand, for they retired disputing every stone and bush that lay in their way. The following morning our commander, under a flag of truce, reminded the Russian chief that he was at war with Christian nations, and requested him to take steps to respect the wounded, in accordance with humanity and the laws of civilized nations.

Nevertheless, the remonstrance did not stop their brutality. A few days later, on the memorable field of Inkermann, the Russians murdered almost every wounded man who had the misfortune to fall into their hands. Whilst the picquets were holding on with desperation, the Royal Fusiliers and portions of the Royal Welsh, 33rd Duke's Own, and 2nd battalion Rifle Brigade, went with all speed to the five-gun battery, to reinforce our picquets there, and a portion of us were directed to the slopes of the White-house ravine. We had just got into position when we observed one of the enemy retiring towards Sebastopol with a tunic on the muzzle of his rifle belonging to one of the Fusiliers, who was on fatigue in the ravine cutting wood when the attack commenced.

Having nothing to defend himself with, he had to show his heels. One of the Rifle Brigade at once dashed off shouting that the tunic should not go into the town. As the Rifleman neared the Russian he turned and brought his rifle to the present. John Bull immediately did the same. As luck would have it, neither of them were capped. They closed to box, the Briton proving the Russian's superior at this game, and knocked him down, jumping on the top of his antagonist: but the Russian proved the strongest in this position, and soon had the Rifleman under. We watched them, but dared not fire. A corporal of the Rifles ran as fast as he could to assist his comrade, but the Russian drew a short sword and plunged at our man, and had his hand raised for a second. The corporal at once dropped on his knee and shot the Russian dead. Our men cheered them heartily from the heights.

They were both made prisoners of by an officer, and in due course brought before the commander of our forces, who made all enquiries into the case, and marked his displeasure with the young officer by presenting £5 to the gallant Rifleman for his courage in not allowing the red coat to be carried into Sebastopol as a trophy, and promoted the corporal to sergeant for his presence of mind in saving the life of his comrade. No end of dare-devil acts like the above could be quoted, for the enemy always got good interest for anything which they attempted.

Our numbers were now fast diminishing from sickness and hardship; our clothing began to get very thin; we had none too much to eat, and plenty of work, both by night and by day, but there was no murmuring. We had as yet received no reinforcements; though the enemy had evidently been strongly reinforced. Day after day passed without anything particular being done except trench work. Our men went at it with a will—without a whimper—wet through from morn till night; then lay down in mud with an empty belly—to get up next morning, perhaps, to go into the trenches and be peppered at all day; to return to camp like drowned rats, and to stand to arms half the night.

The following letter was written from the:

Camp before Sebastopol,
October 27th, 1854.

My Dear Parents,

Long before this reaches you, you will have heard that our bombardment has proved a total failure; if anything, we got the worst of it. The French guns were nearly all silenced, but our Allies stuck to us well. But you will have heard that we have thrashed the enemy again, on two different fields. On the 20th inst., they attacked our position at Balaclava, and the people that we are fighting for (the Turks,) bolted, and let them take our guns. Our cavalry got at them—it was a grand sight, in particular the charge of the Heavy Brigade, for they went at them more like madmen than anything that I can explain; the Greys and Enniskillens (one a Scotch and the other an Irish regiment) went at them first, and they did it manfully.

They rode right through them, as if they'd been a lot of old women, it was a most exciting scene. I hear that the Light cavalry have been cut to pieces, particularly the 11th Hussars and the 17th Lancers. The rumour in camp is that someone has been blundering, and that the Light Cavalry charge was all a mistake; the truth will come out some day. The mauling that our Heavy Cavalry gave the enemy they will not forget for a day or two. I was not engaged in fighting, but simply going down to Balaclava on fatigue. You will most likely see a full account of the fight in the papers, and I feel that you will be more interested in our fight, which we had yesterday (the 26th.) What name they are going to give it, I do not know. It lasted about an hour-and-a-half, but it was very sharp.

The 2nd and Light Divisions had the honour of giving them

a good thrashing, and I do not think they will try their hands at it again for a little while. We had not much to do with it; it was the 30th, 41st, 49th, and 95th that were particularly engaged, and they gave it them properly. We supported them; the field was covered with their dead and wounded—our Artillery simply mowed them down by wholesale. The Guards came up to our assistance, but they were not engaged more than they were at Balaclava. We charged them right to the town. I heard some of our officers say they believed we could have gone into the town with them; but our noble old commander knew well what he was about.

I mean Sir De Lacy Evans, for he commanded the field. You must excuse this scrawl, as I must be off; I am for the trenches tonight. It is raining in torrents, so we are not likely to be short of water; but I am as hungry as a hunter. Don't be uneasy; thank God I am quite well, and we must make the best of a bad job. As long as we manage to thrash them every time we meet them, the people at home must not grumble—while they can sit by their firesides and smoke their pipes, and say we've beat them again. We begin to get old hands at this work now.

It is getting very cold, and the sooner we get at the town and take it, the better. It is immensely strong, and looks an ugly place to take, but we will manage it someday. The enemy fight well behind stone walls, but let us get at them, and I will be bound to say, that we will do the fighting as well as our forefathers did under Nelson and Wellington. Bye-the-bye, our sailors who man our heavy guns, are a tough and jolly set of fellows. I shall not finish this letter until I come off duty.

October 29th.

Well, I've got back to camp again. We have had a rough twenty-four hours of it; it rained nearly the whole time. The enemy kept pitching shell into us nearly all night, and it took us all our time to dodge their Whistling Dicks (huge shell), as our men have named them. We were standing nearly up to our knees in mud and water, like a lot of drowned rats, nearly all night; the cold bleak wind cutting through our thin clothing (that is now getting very thin and full of holes, and nothing to mend it with.) This is ten times worse than all the fighting. We have not one ounce too much to eat, and, altogether, there is a dull prospect before us. But our men keep their spirits up well, although we are nearly worked to death night and day.

We cannot move without sinking nearly to our ankles in mud. The tents we have to sleep in are full of holes; and there is nothing but mud to lie down in, or scrape it away with our hands the best we can—and soaked to the skin from morning to night (so much for honour and glory). I suppose we shall have leather medals for this one day—I mean those who have the good fortune to escape the shot and shell of the enemy, and the pestilence that surrounds us.

I will write as often as I can; and if I do not meet you any more in this world, I hope to meet you in a far brighter one. Dear mother, now that I am face to face with death, almost every day, I think of some of my wild boyish tricks, and hope you will forgive me; and if the Lord protects me through this, I will try and be a comfort to you in your declining days. Goodbye, kind and best of mothers. I must conclude now. Try and keep up your spirits—

And believe me ever
Your affectionate son,
T. Gowing,
Sergeant, Royal Fusiliers.

The Battle of Inkermann.

On the morning of the 5th November the enemy attacked us in our trenches in broad daylight. Our heavy guns gave it them prettily, and mowed down their dense columns by wholesale; but still they came on, until they felt the bayonet. Then, after some stiff fighting, which lasted more than an hour, they were compelled to beat a hasty retreat, our heavy guns sweeping lanes through them, and we plying them with musketry both in front and flank. We found they could run well, only too glad to get under cover. A sortie has no chance of success unless the besieging army can be taken by surprise; but no doubt this attack was made in order to distract our commander's attention from the vital point.

The ever-memorable battle was then raging on our right rear, and by the shouts of the combatants and the tremendous firing, we knew that something very serious was going on, so as many of us as the general could spare were ordered to march as fast as our legs could carry us to the assistance of our comrades, then at the dreadful fight raging at Inkermann. As we had just drubbed the enemy terribly, our blood was up, but we were hungry: many of us had had nothing to eat for twenty-four hours, and were wet through to the skin. They say an Englishman will not fight unless his belly is full; that's all bosh: let him once be roused, and you will soon see whether he will or not. Well, to the field we went, and the sights were something horrible, but there was not a desponding voice; the fog was so dense that at times we could not see twenty yards.

Our men were falling very fast, for the enemy were in overwhelming strength, particularly in guns. But it is impossible to disguise the fact that the crafty Muscovites in the darkness and fog had stolen a march upon our commanders; that the Allies were taken completely by surprise; and that only the intrepidity of the picquets of the Light and Second Divisions saved the entire Allied Armies from an overwhelming disaster. We can now say without boasting that the heroic conduct of a mere handful of Britons were, and are to this day, the admiration of all. The determined rushes of the Muscovites were hurled back time after time. Their princes boasted that they would drive us all into the sea. So they would, perhaps, if weight of numbers could have done it; but that nasty piece of cold steel stood in the way.

At this critical moment the startling intrepidity of the sons of Albion, side by side with the heroic boys of the green isle, came out in all its native splendour, to shine by the side with that displayed at Trafalgar, Albuera, and Waterloo. Their deeds are today stimulating their descendants on the banks of the Nile, and will do till the end of time, or as long as we have an enemy to face, whether they are to be found on the burning plains of Egypt or the frontiers of Afghanistan. The queen of weapons was used with deadly effect, the drunken massive columns of the enemy were pitched over the rocks by men who might die but never surrender, and who had a strong objection to a watery grave. Our highest martial interest, honour, was at stake; but, reader, it was safe withal, from our much-respected commander-in-chief to the drummer-boy. They had all made up their minds to conquer or to die. Children yet unborn will exclaim "all honour to that band of heroes."

The odds were heavy, but from the brutes we had to face we had no mercy to expect. Our Fourth Division—composed of the following regiments, the 20th, 21st, 57th, 63rd, 68th, and 1st Batt. Rifle Brigade, under Cathcart—fought at a disadvantage, having been armed with the old Brown Bess musket, against the Needle-Rifle which the enemy were armed with. Our weapons were almost as much use as

The Battle of Inkermann

a broomstick. Yet with all these disadvantages we smote the enemy with a terrible slaughter, and there was seen again with what majesty the British soldier fights. Our loss was heavy: three generals fell and every mounted officer, but our men fought to the bitter end, and stood triumphant on the rocky ridge, cheering for victory—the unconquerable heroism of the handful of men we knew would set the church-bells of old England ringing and clashing for victory, and give schoolboys a holiday.

All regiments vied with each other, as the following will prove:— At the Alma and Balaclava we had fought for victory; but at the fight that was now raging, a mere handful of Britons were contending for very existence, for to be beaten here meant an ignominious death at the hands of a lot of fierce brutes, mad with drink—Dutch courage had to be poured into them to make them face our ranks. The drunken yells of their massive columns were answered by volley after volley at point-blank range, and then, with a clear and distinct cheer for old England, we closed upon them with the bayonet, and stuck to them like wax until they were hurled from the field.

We had no supports or reserves, but every man, as fast as he could reach the field, went straight at them, with a shout that seemed to strike terror into them; and so the fight went on, hour after hour. In many parts of the field it was a horde of half-drunken madmen attacking cool and collected Britons, determined to conquer or die. Our Guards were the admiration of the whole army; their deeds at Inkermann will never fade. Led by His Royal Highness the Duke of Cambridge, they repeatedly buried themselves in the Russian columns, as cheer after cheer went up in defiance to the enemy's unnatural yell.

The Guards, all must admit, set a glorious example, for if they had to die, they acted upon the old 57th motto, *Let us die hard*. The daring, courage, and obstinacy of our Guards was grand; the terrible odds that they faced on this field puts Hougoumont in the shade, and ranks beside the unconquerable heroes of Albuera, fully justifying their high prestige in the army.

Some who read this may think that I am an old Guardsman—so I am; I had the pleasure of guarding the honour of our beloved Isle, in the 7th Royal Fusiliers. But, I wish to give honour where honour is due. The 7th, however, were not behind when hard fighting had to be done. One of our Majors—a Norfolk hero—Sir Thomas Troubridge, although he had both his feet shot away, would not give in, neither would he allow himself to be carried off the field, but continued fighting to the end. When he was lying apparently bleeding to death, with both his stumps resting upon a gun-carriage, he called upon us to "shift those fellows with the bayonet," animating us by voice and gesture. Although the poor man could not lead us, he could cheer us on. And on we went with an irresistible rush, and routed them then and there. On one occasion after he was wounded, he called upon us not to forget our bayonets, adding, "They don't like cold steel, men." Neither did I.

It was here that I received two bayonet wounds, one in each thigh, and would most likely have been despatched, but that help was close at hand, and the fellows who wounded me fell at once by the same description of weapon, but not to rise again and write or talk about it. Revolvers and bayonets told heavily that foggy morn, and when our men were short of ammunition, they pitched stones at the enemy. My legs were quickly bandaged, and after giving the enemy a few parting shots at close quarters, which must have told upon their crowded ranks, I managed to hobble off the field, using my rifle and another I picked up as crutches. We could spare none to look after the wounded; it was every man for himself.

After hobbling some distance out of the range of fire, I lay down, for I could get no further without a little rest. Our allies, the French, were then coming up to our assistance in a right mood for fighting. The *Zouaves* passed me with a ringing cheer of "*Bon Anglais*" and "*Vive l'Empereur*," repeated over and over again. A mounted officer of rank, who was with them, stopped and asked me a number of questions in good English. He turned and spoke to his men, and they cheered me in a most lusty manner. The officer kindly gave me a drink out of his flask, which revived me considerably, and then, with a hearty shake of the hand, bade me goodbye, and passed on into action, shouting out something about the enemy walking over his body before he would surrender.

Thus was Waterloo and Trafalgar avenged, by the descendants of the vanquished advancing with rapid strides and a light heart, but with a strong arm, to assist the sons of Albion in one of the most unequal and bloody contests ever waged. Let us hope that the blood then spilt may have cemented forever the friendship between the two nations who are so near neighbours. The French fought in a most dashing manner, side by side with us, till the enemy were driven from the field. The Russian officers fought with desperation, though their men hung back unless almost driven to it.

But the reader must remember our men and the *Zouaves* plied the queen of weapons with terrible effect, and all met the enemy with an unconquerable energy, while we often stimulated each other by asking—what would they say of us in England?

But I could do no more; I had done all I could, and now had to remain and take my chance of being killed by a stray shot. It was hard work to lie there for upwards of an hour-and-a-half in suspense. I felt as if I should like to be at them, for a little satisfaction; but I had to lie passive.

I am proud to record that no regiment on that memorable field could take the shine out of the gallant old 7th Fusiliers. I lay on the field bleeding, when I heard the welcome shout of victory; I was shortly afterwards attended to, and carried to hospital, there remained for a day or two, and was then sent on to Malta, to be patched up ready for another go in at them.

The enemy's loss was exceedingly heavy; twenty thousand men is the estimated loss of the Russians, in their endeavours to take the Heights of Inkermann on that memorable Sunday, 5th November, 1854. The carnage was something frightful, as our close point-blank fire had told heavily upon the enemy's columns. Our total strength on the field was about nine thousand, upwards of one third of whom fell killed or wounded; while of the six thousand French who came to help us, they lost seventeen hundred. But the enemy were completely routed, and England confessed that every man that foggy morn had done his duty. We had been fighting against heavy odds, and men armed with as good weapons as ourselves, while they were wrought up to a state of madness or desperation with drink.

Inkermann will not admit of much description, particularly from one who was in the thick of it. The fighting all day on that awful Sabbath was of a furious character. The bayonet was the chief weapon, and the Minié rifle balls told heavily upon the crowded ranks. To sum it up in a few words, every man had to, and did tight, as Britons ought to do when the honour of the nation is at stake. The best of generals might have lost such a fight as Inkermann,—none could direct, for the fog was so dense that one could not see, at times, twenty yards. On came the Russian columns, but they had to go back time after time much quicker than they came.

The bayonet was used with terrible effect by all regiments. The enemy, driven on by their brave officers, had to and did literally climb over the heaps of their slain countrymen and ours, to renew this bloodthirsty contest, but they were met by British cold steel, and were hurled or pitch-forked from the field. We might appropriately say of a number of the brave men who fell on that field in the hour of victory—

That nothing in their life
Became them like the leaving it.

We had proved, in a hundred fights, that no enemy could resist our men. But at Inkermann, victory hung in the balance, and our weak Battalions had to resist the enemy's heavy columns bayonet to bayonet. It was Greek meeting Greek, for a number of most determined encounters were maintained against very heavy odds; and as often as the Russian Infantry charged us, our people met them with that never-failing weapon. The 41st and 49th regiments held the Sandbag Battery, and were fairly mobbed out of it by the overwhelming numbers of the enemy, who were exulting in their victory with yells of triumph, when up came the Guards, and in they went with a cheer and a rush that told heavily upon the foe.

The Russians, except the dead and dying, were literally lifted out of the battery and its vicinity, by these gallant regiments. Our army may well be proud of its present commander-in-chief, for it was His Royal Highness himself who led these unconquerable men. Fresh draughts of *"Rackie"* had to be issued to the legions of Russia, in order to make them face us again. All was done that could be devised by the enemy, in order to fasten victory to their standards. Holy Russia was represented on the field by the two Imperial Grand Dukes, sons of their sacred chief, and the soldiers were taught that they must, as true Russians, die for their holy *Czar*, the glory of conquering in the presence of his children, even at the expense of life, would open the gates of heaven to them (?) They were repeatedly urged on to the attack, and as often driven back. The 41st fought like tigers, to gain time for their comrades to come up.

The grey-coated battalions of the enemy were now on the right, on the left, and in front of us, but there was not a desponding voice in our ranks. The Duke of Cambridge was requested to retire a little out of the immediate reach of the murderous musketry fire. But—"No; I will, when these fellows are shifted," was the reply. It was well that the French came up when they did. Our men were gradually being crushed in some parts of the field, but showing the enemy a most determined front. It was at this juncture that His Royal Highness set so animating an example; and the French coming up to our assistance, again the hosts of Russia had to retire. About this time a cry was raised that the ammunition was running short.

Sir G. Brown, exclaimed—"Then there is nothing for it but the bayonet: *at them, my lads.*" And at them we went; and they had to go back, although their Princes boasted that they would put us all into the sea. It was a great pity we had not the 42nd, 79th, and 93rd Highlanders with us, for we knew well they would have left their marks upon the enemy, under the guidance of their old Commander, Sir Colin Campbell, but they had to watch Balaclava. We lost a great number of officers, and at the close of the day the 4th division was commanded by a captain. But on that memorable field if there was one corner hotter than another, the Guards had it.

At one time they were completely surrounded by the assailing multitudes, and the dense fog prevented them from seeing anything but the foes all round. Shoulder to shoulder, with a ringing cheer, they cut their way out; shouting, "Keep to the colours." It was a bloody contest; but this little band—now reduced to about 700 unwounded men, showed the enemy an undaunted front. The 20th was sent to help them. They staggered under the murderous fire that met them. This battery had now become more like a slaughterhouse than anything else. The Guards went at them again, and routed the Russians out of it. At the 5-gun battery the fighting was desperate, but the enemy never got into it to live, Inkermann may well be called the soldiers' fight, for at times the fog was so thick that we could not see friend from foe.

Our men, however, managed to find the Russians, and then "shift" them. Except Trafalgar and Waterloo, no battle fought by the British since the invention of powder has called forth such exultation. And still the word "Inkermann" stimulates the warlike enthusiasm of every Briton, and the rising generations will recall with rapture the name of some distant relative and exclaim, "He fought and fell at Inkermann," while with manly pride they feel that they have sprung from fathers whom the nation at large delights to honour. The Alma, and Balaclava awakened the war-spirit—that indomitable spirit that lies latent in the breast of every Briton. The news of victory at these places set the church bells ringing; but the victory by a mere handful of men on the heights of Inkermann, went through every Briton like an electric shock; and thousands at once volunteered to defend the flag, side by side with the heroic sons of France.

In our most remote colonies, the people of British extraction exulted at the tidings of Inkermann. In all our large cities—London, Manchester, Leeds, Sheffield, Birmingham, Norwich, Nottingham, &c., in the workshops, in the furnace-rooms, at the forges, in the meanest tap-rooms, in the most remote village taverns, in the hills of Scotland, and the bogs of Ireland—all were proud they were united Britons, and of the same stock that had just hurled the armies of Russia, although in overwhelming numbers, from the heights of Inkermann.

My young readers must bear in mind that this battle was not fought by men who were well fed, well clothed, or well housed, nor by an army that was well prepared; but, on the contrary, by men who were, so to speak, half starved, clothed in rags, and exposed to all the inclemencies of a rigorous climate, whilst they were attacked by hordes of men confident of victory, whose feelings had been wrought to madness by stimulants and priest-craft. At one time victory trembled in the balance; some of our guns were in the hands of the enemy, and the gunners had been all shot or cut down. But the boys of the Emerald Isle were close by. The 88th Connaught Rangers and the 49th went at them; and recaptured the guns.

The advance of our Guards at the Sandbag, or 2-gun battery, was grand, and surely it could be said of them, "Nothing could stop that astonishing Infantry." No sudden burst of undisciplined valour, no nervous enthusiasm weakened their order; their flashing eyes were bent upon the dark masses in their front; their measured tread shook the ground; their ringing cheer startled the infuriated columns of the enemy, as their bayonets were brought down to the charge; and, led by a grandson of a king—H.R.H. the Duke of Cambridge—in they went, shoulder to shoulder, and the enemy with all their boasted strength, were driven down the hill.

At the Alma and Balaclava, when the enemy had gained a temporary success, they behaved in a most barbarous manner to our wounded; sometimes their officers set them the example by plunging their swords into the helpless. At Inkermann, they outstripped all their former deeds of assassination. Mercy they did not seem to understand when once our poor fellows were in their clutches. But yet our men, I am happy to record, would not retaliate, except in so far as that, after the battle was over, their wounded were left to lie, while ours were removed from the field; but those who were alive next morning were then attended to, and taken to our hospital tents.

Such are the horrors of war. Our loss had been heavy: there were killed 4 generals, 50 officers, 42 sergeants; total killed, wounded, and missing, 2700, exclusive of the French loss, and that was heavy for the numbers engaged. The whole French army were loud in their expressions of admiration of the British, their exultation seemed to be beyond all bounds, for our deeds had put Alma and Balaclava in the shade, and cast a fresh lustre upon our glorious old Standard.

They looked at us in wonderment, for they knew well the odds we had fought against, hour after hour. And, I have not the slightest doubt, some of their old officers thought of our forefathers who had so often fought them, and never once met them but to give them a good sound thrashing. As Napoleon said, we had often been beaten, but would not give in; we would stick to them like a good bulldog, and worry them out. Reader, such was Inkermann.

The aspect of the field was awful—dead and dying mutilated bodies in all directions. Many of our men had been wounded frequently with shot and bayonet; others were cut limb from limb, and yet a spark of life remained. Many had perished by the bayonet and it was noticed that but few had fallen with one thrust. In and around the 2-gun battery the sights were sickening. Our Guardsmen, and 41st, 47th, and 49th, lay locked in the arms of the foe with their bayonets through each other—dead. Some of our officers and men were found dead, with no fewer than twelve or fifteen bayonet wounds; the appearance of the poor fellows who had been thus tortured was painful. To describe the scene would be impossible—the result of eight hours' hand-to-hand conflict—it was horrible to look upon.

Scarcely did any field in the whole Peninsula war present, as the result of conflict, such a murderous spectacle as the terrible sights that now lay before us. There were literally piles of dead, lying in every posture that one could imagine; I may say that there were acres of defaced humanity—ghastly wounds from sword, bayonet, grape, and round shot; poor fellows literally shattered—and yet with life still in them. Others lay as if they had been asleep—friend and foe mixed together. In some parts of the field our men lay in ranks as they had stood; and the enemy in columns, one on the top of the other. The Russian Guardsmen lay thick all over the field. Upwards of 2000 dead were found belonging to the enemy. Just outside the 2-gun Battery the wounded were numerous, and their groans were pitiful; while cries of despair burst from the lips of some as they lay, thinking perhaps of wives and helpless little ones far away.

The Russian dead were buried in large pits by themselves; and our people and our gallant allies, the French, were laid side by side. For hours during that dreadful night of woe and victory, the wailing of a poor dog—which had followed his master—could be distinctly heard. The faithful creature had found his master's body, and he pierced the night air with his lamentations.

Such was the field of Inkermann. That was keeping up Gunpowder Plot with a vengeance.

The letter I sent to my parents on this occasion was as follows:—

Camp before Sebastopol,
November 6th, 1854.

My dear Parents,

Long before this reaches you, you will have seen the account of our glorious battle of the 5th (yesterday). It was a terrible fight. I was in the trenches when it commenced. We had a shy at them there, and sent them back much quicker than they came out. A number of us then marched on to the field of Inkermann. The fight was raging when we got there; and the fog was so dense that we could not see what we were doing, or where to go. Our poor fellows soon began to drop.

We were wet through to the skin, and as hungry as hunters. We were ordered to the Five-Gun Battery, to support our comrades. Sir Thomas Troubridge was in command, and it took all our time to hold our own.

What a gunpowder plot! but, above all, what a Sunday! I thought, dear father—I thought of you, and what you were most likely doing. It's no use my trying to hide or cloak matters up—you will see this is not my handwriting—they have managed to hit me at last; but you must not be alarmed; I am not half so badly hit as some of my poor comrades are, so keep up your spirits. I am in good hopes of getting over this; and, if it should please the Lord to spare me, to be a comfort to you in your declining days.

Do not answer this, as a number of us are to be sent down to Scutari. Will write as soon as I can.

Do, dear parents, try and keep your spirits up; and I know you will not forget me at the Throne of Grace. I will try and give you, at some future day, a full account, as far as I could see, and from what I can find out from my comrades. Will write as soon as I can. Cheer up! I'll warm them up for this, if ever I get a

chance. My kind love to poor mother, brothers, and sisters.
Believe me, dear Father,
> Your affectionate son,
> > T. Gowing,   Sergeant, Royal Fusiliers.

The following is a copy of a letter addressed to Field-Marshal Lord Raglan, by command of Her Most Gracious Majesty, on receipt of the news of the victory at Inkermann:—

> Her Majesty is desirous of expressing her gratitude for the noble exertions of the troops in a conflict which is unsurpassed in the annals of war for persevering valour and chivalrous devotion. The strength and fury of the attacks, repeatedly renewed by fresh columns with a desperation which appeared to be irresistible, were spent in vain against the unbroken lines, and the matchless intrepidity of the men they had to encounter. Such attacks could only be repulsed by that cool courage, under circumstances the most adverse, and that confidence of victory, which have ever animated the British Army. The banks of the Alma proved that no advantages of position can withstand the impetuous assault of the Army under your command. The heights of Inkermann have now shown that the dense columns of an entire army are unable to force the ranks of less than one-fourth their numbers in the hand-to-hand encounters with the bayonet which characterized this bloody day.
> Her Majesty has observed with the liveliest feeling of gratification the manner in which the troops of her ally, the Emperor of the French, came to the aid of the divisions of the British Army engaged in this numerically unequal contest. The Queen is deeply sensible of the cordial co-operation of the French commander-in-chief, General Canrobert, and the gallant conduct of that distinguished officer, General Bosquet; and Her Majesty recognizes in the cheers with which the men of both nations encouraged each other in their united charge, proofs of the esteem and admiration mutually engendered by the campaign and the deeds of heroism it has produced.
> The Queen desires that your lordship will receive her thanks for your conduct throughout this noble and successful struggle, and that you will take measures for making known her no less warm approval of the services of all the officers, non-commissioned officers, and men, who have so gloriously won, by their

blood freely shed, fresh honours for the Army of a country which sympathises as deeply with their privations and exertions as it glories in their victories and exults in their fame. *Let not any private soldier in those ranks believe that his conduct is unheeded. The Queen thanks him. His country honours him.*

Her Majesty will anxiously expect the further despatch in which your lordship proposes to name those officers whose services have been especially worthy of notice. In the meantime I am commanded by Her Majesty to signify her approbation of the admirable behaviour of Lieut.-General Sir George Brown, and her regret that he has been wounded in the action. Her Majesty has received with feelings of no ordinary pleasure your lordship's report of the manner in which Lieut.-General His Royal Highness the Duke of Cambridge distinguished himself. That one of the illustrious members of her royal house should be associated with the toils and glories of such an Army is to the Queen a source of great pride and congratulation.

To Major-General Bentinck, Major-General Codrington, Brigadier-Generals Adams, Terrens, and Buller, your lordship will be pleased to convey the Queen's sympathy in their wounds, and thanks for their services. To the other officers named by your lordship I am directed to express Her Majesty's approbation. The gallant conduct of Lieut.-General Sir de Lacy Evans has attracted the Queen's especial thanks. Weak from a bed of sickness he rose at the sound of the battle, not to claim his share in prominent command, but to aid with his veteran counsel and assistance the junior officer upon whom, in his absence, had devolved the duty of leading his division.

Proud of the victory won by her brave army—grateful to those who wear the laurels of this great conflict—the Queen is painfully affected by the heavy loss which has been incurred, and deeply sensible to what is owing to the dead. Those illustrious men cannot indeed receive the thanks of their sovereign, which have so often cheered the soldier in his severest trials; but their blood has not been shed in vain. Laid low in their grave of victory, their names will be cherished for ever by a grateful country, and posterity will look upon the list of officers who have fallen as a proof of the ardent courage and zeal with which they pointed out the path of honour to their no less willing followers.

The loss of Lieut.-General the Honourable Sir George Cathcart is to the Queen and to her people a cause of sorrow which even dims the triumph of this great occasion. His loyalty, his patriotism, and self-devotion, were not less conspicuous than his high military reputation. One of a family of warriors, he was an honour to them and an ornament to his profession. Arrived in his native land from a colony to which he had succeeded in restoring peace and contentment,, he obeyed at a moment's notice the call of duty, and he hastened to join that army in which the Queen and his country fondly hoped he would have lived to win increased renown.

The death of Brigadier-Generals Strangways and Goldie has added to the sorrow which mingles in the rejoicing of this memorable battle. The Queen sympathises in the loss sustained by the families of her officers and soldiers, but Her Majesty bids them reflect with her, and derive consolation from the thought, that they fell in the sacred cause of justice, and in the ranks of a noble army.

I have the honour to be, my lord.
        Your lordship's obedient, humble servant,
                    Newcastle.
To Field-Marshal Lord Raglan, K.C.B., and C.

As a further mark of Her Most Gracious Majesty's approbation of the heroic, matchless gallantry displayed on that memorable field, the following Royal Warrant was issued:—

The Queen has been pleased to command that, as a mark of Her Majesty's recognition of the meritorious services of the non-commissioned officers of the Army, under the command of Field-Marshal Lord Raglan, in the recent brilliant operations in the Crimea, the Field-Marshal shall submit, through the General Commander-in- Chief, the name of one sergeant of each regiment of cavalry, of the three battalions of Foot Guards, and of every regiment of infantry of the line, to be promoted to a cornetcy or ensigncy for Her Majesty's approval; and, with the view to render immediately available the services of these meritorious men. Her Majesty has directed that the Field-Marshal do appoint provisionally, and pending Her Majesty's pleasure, the sergeants so recommended to regiments in the Army under his command; and Her Majesty has further been graciously pleased to signify her intention that, on the several recommendations receiving Her Majesty's approval, the commissions shall in each case bear date the 5th of November, 1854.

A FEW WORDS ABOUT A NORFOLK HERO AT INKERMANN.

Of all the brave men who fought at Inkermann, none could surpass Sir Thomas Troubridge. It is but little use trying to pick out this or that regiment, for on that memorable field there were no supports or reserves; every man was in the fighting line, and it was "conquer or die." One in the thick of the fight could not see much, but I simply know that none could take the shine out of the old Fusiliers. And with such men as Colonel Lacy Yea, Sir Thomas Troubridge, Captain Shipley, Lord R. Brown, Mr. Jones, and a few others, our men would have gone through fire and water. Sir Thomas Troubridge was the admiration of all, for, though terribly wounded, he would not allow himself to be removed from the ground until victory had declared itself for the sons of Albion, but remained, with the bravest fortitude, encouraging his men to "fight it out."

He would now and then call out, "Fire away, my lads; give them the steel if you get a chance; stick to them my men." It was a sergeant named Laws, (a Norwich man), who ran for a doctor to attend upon him; but his resolute spirit did not forsake him. No, he would rather die on the field, at his post with his fusiliers, than be carried to a place of safety. And his noble conduct had a wonderful effect upon the men, for everyone would have died rather than forsake him—such a gallant soldier.

At the Alma his conduct was the admiration of all who could see him, for he was often in front of us, encouraging us; but he escaped that fiery ordeal without a scratch, to fall, with both feet gone, on a more glorious field. Like a number of the bravest of the brave, he was a good living man, and was prepared for anything. He was as true as steel; an honest, upright, truthful, fearless, good man, gifted with a clear, comprehensive mind, and every inch a Fusilier.

Note referred to at the beginning of the chapter
THE FIRST TO LAND IN THE CRIMEA.

I do not wish to be partial, but to give honour where honour is due. There have been doubts expressed as to which regiment landed first on the enemy's shore in the Crimea, on the 14th September, 1854. I will claim that honour for the 7th Royal Fusiliers; and, further, for that noble hero the late General (then Major) Sir Thomas St.

Vincent Cochrane Troubridge, Bart. Sir Thomas sprang from a family of tried warriors, his father being right hand man to the immortal Nelson, at St.Vincent, the Nile, and Trafalgar. The following letter will, I hope, dear up all doubts as to who first landed.

Viceregal Lodge, Dublin,
April 17th, 1856.

My Dear Sir,

As doubts have been expressed as to which regiment landed first in the Crimea, I therefore think it only an act of justice to inform you that a company of the 7th Fusiliers, under Major Sir T. Troubridge, was in my boat; and that the only boat near us was one belonging to, I think, the Sanspareil, and having Rifles on board. Sir G. Brown had previously landed with Captain Dacres, R.N. I may say that mine were the first troops landed in the Crimea. I write this that you may do justice to a regiment that I have long known, and that is second to none in the British Army.

I remain, my dear Sir,
Truly yours,
C. Vesey,
Com R.N., and A.D.C.

Chapter 6

Malta & Back to the Front

As soon as it came to my turn I was attended to, and my wounds dressed and bandaged. I remained for two days, and then a number of us were sent to Scutari. We were taken down to Balaclava on mules, some of them lent by our chivalrous allies the French. We got a good shaking, but eventually found ourselves on board an old steamer. It was a horrible scene—poor fellows having every description of wound; and many died before we left the harbour. We were packed on board anyhow,—to live or die; and away we went. The sea was rather boisterous, and, I can assure the reader, I was not very comfortable, with poor fellows dying fast all around me. There were not sufficient medical officers to look after fifty men, much less three or four hundred.

I would here ask the reader to try and picture to himself a ship rolling and tossing about at sea with such a freight. The sight was heart-rending. Many of our poor fellows had had not the slightest thing done for them since they were wounded on that bloody field. They had fought and helped to uphold the honour of their country, and were now left to die in agony, and— oh! horror of horrors!—their poor mangled bodies were infested with vermin. I could give particulars that would cause the blood of the reader to curdle in his veins and shock his credulity, but I forbear.

Enough has been said, surely, to afford a sufficient condemnation of British management! Yet in spite of these facts, which were too patent to be kept from them, thousands upon thousands of the youth of the three kingdoms were burning to join their countrymen at the seat of war. On behalf of the British army I demand fair treatment for the men who are willing to risk their lives in the service of their country. Horses and even dogs received far more attention and better treatment during that trying campaign than the poor sick and wounded men. I say that what is needed is some system of organization that shall render impossible the repetition of such inhumanities as disgraced the Crimean campaign. Let men of brains, and with human hearts in their bosoms, be appointed to devise such a system, and I am certain my fellow-countrymen will grudge no expense in making it effective. Our doctors worked like horses, but they could not do impossibilities; six times the number could not have done the work—but the fault did not rest with them.

After being tossed about for some four or five days, we reached Scutari, to find it so full of sick and wounded that we were not allowed to land, and on we had to go to Malta. Describe the scene between decks I could not. Men were on all sides shrieking with pain, some were lying in a state of putrefaction, others in a morbid state, and some were being carried up on deck, to be consigned, wrapped in a blanket, to a watery grave.

At last we reached our desired haven, Malta, and were taken ashore as quickly as possible. Many an eye was wet with tears; the good people did all that lay in their power for us, and we could see pity beaming upon every countenance. We found the Maltese a kind-hearted people. On to the hospital we went, were at once put to bed, and attended to by kind motherly hands, that did all that was possible to soothe us. Nothing could exceed the kindness of all those who had anything to do with us. In one month I was on my feet again, convalescent, and with plenty of good nourishment I soon began to gather strength; and in the early part of January, 1855, wanted to be off again, to have a little satisfaction, but I had to remain another month.

I wrote to my parents from Malta, under date as follows:—

December 21st, 1854.

Once more a line from your rough but affectionate son. Your letters have all duly reached me. I am happy to inform you that I am getting on capitally. I have the best of attention; and, what's more, a pretty young lady for my nurse. You know, father, that soldiers have an eye to pretty girls; but woe be to the man who would attempt to molest one of these dear creatures, for they are worth their weight in gold. I am able to stand up, I am happy to inform you; but I must not let my nurse see me, or the doctor would eat me.

We found that the nation's heart was bleeding for her soldiers and sailors—a grateful country was roused by the before unheard-of privations and sufferings and the heroic stand that her sons were making. All, even our enemies, were compelled to admire the daring devotion and courage displayed by a mere handful of men, at the heights of Alma; all were compelled to applaud the conduct of our soldiers on the plains of Balaclava; and the stand made at Inkermann will be the theme of admiration for ages to come. England and the world admitted that every man had nobly done his duty, and that the conquerors on Inkermann's Heights had every whit the courage and daring of their forefathers.

I was now well able to take my walks abroad and have a good look at all the sights and scenes of Malta, and there are some grand sights to be seen—the Church of St. John, I suppose, is one of the grandest in the world. Then I used to wander around the vast fortifications day after day. Accounts kept coming in from the seat of war. We heard that our poor fellows were dying fast of starvation and cold; death was, in fact, raging through the camp at a fearful pace, and yet our men stuck to it. From letters I received from the front, it appeared the storm that had struck the Crimea had swept away nearly all our poor fellows' tents, and they had to get into caves in the rocks, and do the best they could on that terrible 14th November, 1854. The ship *Prince*, with winter clothing for the whole army, had gone down just outside the harbour of Balaclava—all hands perished; and a number of other ships shared the same fate.

The cold was something terrible, men were frost-bitten, daily losing fingers and toes, and undergoing such sufferings as no tongue or pen can describe. In December, 1854, and January and February, 1855, our poor fellows were dying like rotten sheep for want of the common necessaries of life—they had little or no food, hardly sufficient clothing to cover their nakedness, the tents were full of holes, and they had nothing but mud to lay their weary bones m, with the thermometer far below freezing point. Then, too, they often had to fight with desperation to hold their own. So, upon the whole, there was not a very bright prospect before me.

Regiments and drafts kept passing on for the front, and I was longing to have a slap at them once more, just by way of getting out of debt; so, towards the end of February, 1855, after I had made some splendid purchases in the way of good blankets, 2 dozen good flannel shirts, 2 dozen *ditto* drawers, 2 dozen warm gloves for my comrades, a good supply of flannels for myself, and a brace of revolvers, off I went once more to fight for Old England, home, and glory. These facts were communicated to my parents, in the following letter:—

Malta, Feb, 11th, 1865.

My Dear Parents,
I do not think I shall be here much longer. A number of us are ready for them again, and I have a debt to pay off, but at your request will not run my head into danger more than I can avoid; out I hope the Lord will give me strength of mind and of body to do my duty; for, father, I do believe I am a true-born Suffolk man, for I could not bear the thought of skulking. If ever I fall, I hope it will be with my face to the foe, and that after I have got out of debt—for I should not like to owe them anything. I never yet told you that two of them came at me at Inkermann, and that was not fair, taking into consideration they could see that I was engaged at the time with a huge monster.

Never mind; thank God I have got over that, and am ready for them again. I hope my next letter will be from the interior of Sebastopol. The French appear to mean business; hardly a day passes but ships laden with them put in here for coal. A number of their Imperial Guards landed here a few days ago. There were four or five of us out for a walk; and when it was explained to them that we had all been at the Alma, and were wounded at Inkermann, you would have thought they had gone mad; they embraced and kissed us over and over again, and shouted '*Bon Anglais, Bon Anglais!*' and '*Vive l'Empereur!*' until further orders. I thought it was a great pity we did not understand each other—we had two interpreters—and I can tell you that they had quite enough of it; but as far as I could see, the very name of Inkermann was enough for three or four cuddles; and although I did not like to be kissed by a man, I had to put up with it. They are fine looking men; a great many of them are much taller than I am (six feet), and, if they get a chance, will most likely leave their mark upon the Russians. At all events, they will soon have a peep at them, and will find them ugly customers to deal with. Well, we parted with our friends on the best of terms, but we had to put up with another good squeeze.

I must tell you I have been marketing. I have bought all sorts of warm clothing for my comrades, for I find it is needed; they found the cash. I have got a good revolver for myself, and am off tomorrow. I do not wish to boast; but, come what will, I will never bring disgrace upon our old county—dear old Suffolk, that gave me birth—or upon Norfolk, that brought me up. Remember, dear father, Norfolk can boast of Nelson.[1] Keep up your spirits, dear parents; all's well that ends well. Will write as soon as I can. Goodbye, and God bless you.

Believe me, as ever.

Your affectionate son,

T. Gowing, Sergeant,

Royal Fusiliers.

We had a jolly time of it all the way up, plenty of the good things of this life on board. What a difference! what a contrast to the voyage down! We had forgotten all our pains and sorrows, and were once more on the way to assist our comrades in subduing the haughty Muscovites. We knew well that in all probability few of us would ever see our dear old home again, or those who were near and dear to us. But we had to look stern necessity in the face. It was a call to duty that we were obeying, and for "England's home and beauty" we would go forward, let the consequences be what they might. Many an aching mother's heart was following our every movement.

The scenes that we had already passed through were enough to melt more than one Absolom's heart, and set him thinking, first, of an endless eternity, and then of a fond and almost broken-hearted mother at home. But duty, stern duty, must be done, and done well, *for England expects that every man will in the hour of need do his duty*. It was still very cold, but we had plenty of clothing and wanted for nothing. We had some splendid sights going through the Dardanelles. Constantinople looked grand; but we were not allowed to disembark, though we stayed there for a time to take in coal; then away we went. We met some of our poor fellows coming from the front. We found the Black Sea very rough, in fact, rolling mountains high, but our gallant old ship dashed on; we had another in tow, but lost her—the cable broke in the night, and she had to look out for herself.

We reached the snug little harbour of Balaclava on the morning of the 8th March, 1855, and, as usual, found it crammed with shipping. We had to remain outside, until our captain obtained permission to enter, then in we went and landed; at once marching to the front to the old Light Division, and I again found myself in the midst of old chums—but what an alteration! Poor half-starved miserable-looking creatures, mere wrecks of humanity, but still with that unconquerable

---

1. Now she can boast of other heroes—to wit, Troubridge, of Inkermann; Windham, of the Redan; Wilson, of Delhi; and another Wilson, of El Teb.

look about them, so that it was a pleasure to do anything for them. I had a treat in store for my company. I asked and obtained leave to go to Balaclava the following day, telling the captain what I had brought for the men. I took six men with me and loaded them with some of the good things I had purchased, and away we went back again.

We had to plough through mud nearly all the way up to our ankles; and when I came to open the packages and distribute the goods, I got many a "God bless you. Sergeant." A flannel shirt and drawers were worth their weight in gold. I did not lose a man out of my tent after I rejoined, except from the enemy's fire; the flannel kept the cold out; the men were always cheerful and I could do anything I liked with them—they were a brave set of fellows. Let our men have but fair treatment, and I have not the slightest hesitation in saying, that they would, if well officered, shake the biggest bullies on the Continent out of their boots, and chase them off any field.

The loss of the *Prince*, on the evening of the 14th November, 1854, just outside the harbour of Balaclava, was the cause of thousands of poor fellows coming to an untimely end; for, in addition to an enormous supply of everything that could be thought of to combat the foe with, such as small-arm ammunition, shot and shell of all sizes, &c., she had on board for the army the following:—

Woollen coats or frocks	53,000
Pairs of worsted socks or stockings	33,000
„ lamb's wool socks or stockings	2,700
„ drawers—lamb's wool	17,000
Good blankets (single)	16,000
„ *palliasses* (single, for hospitals)	10,000
„ rugs (single)	3,750
„ cloaks, well lined with flannel	2,500
Pairs of boots (ankles)	12,880
„ shoes, for hospitals	1,000

Eight other ships were also lost, with nearly all hands on board, that night. The value of their freights has been estimated at £1,500,000. But the value of the stores and outfits for the army was incalculable. From that date the deplorable condition of the army commences. Yet there were thousands of tons of stores lying at Balaclava, rotting. The commissariat had completely broken down. All that was wanting, was someone with a head on to put things straight—all was higgledy-piggledy and confusion. The cavalry horses, that had cost an enormous amount, sank up to their knees in mud at every step, until they dropped exhausted; and all the way from the camp to Balaclava were to be seen dead horses, mules, and bullocks in every stage of decomposition. And our poor fellows, who had fought so well at the Alma, Balaclava, and the two Inkermanns, were now dying by hundreds daily. The army was put upon half rations, *viz*:—half-a-pound of mouldy biscuit, and half-a-pound of salt junk (beef or pork); coffee was served out, but in its raw green state, with no means of roasting it.

No wood or firing was to be had, except a few roots that were dug up. Men would come staggering into the camp from the trenches soaked to the skin and ravenously hungry, when a half-pound of mouldy biscuit would be issued, with the same quantity of salt junk, so hard that one almost wanted a good hatchet to break it. The scenes were heartrending. The whole camp was one vast sheet of mud, the trenches in many places knee deep; men died at their posts from sheer exhaustion or starvation, rather than complain, for if they reported themselves sick the medical chests were empty. And amidst all these privations the enemy kept peppering away at them.

A bright but melancholy proof was then given of what Britons will endure before they give up. But, perhaps, one of the most mortifying pills that our poor fellows had to swallow was the knowledge that, although they were dying by wholesale for the want of shelter, clothing, and food, the huts had arrived in safety at Balaclava, or were floating about the harbour and being stolen by those handy little fellows, the *Zouaves*, to make firewood of; the overcoats lay in lighters; while food and nourishment, and every comfort that could be thought of by a kind-hearted people—such as potted meats of all descriptions, ground coffee, preserved soups, good thick warm flannel shirts, comforters knitted by ladies at home, flannel drawers, and good fustian jackets, water-proof coats and leggings, and tobacco in tons—were rotting in the harbour or stacked up upon the shore.

A few men who were stationed at or near Balaclava got the lion's share. The Guards had not much to complain of after they were sent down to Balaclava, for they were in clover—little or nothing to do—and if they did not exactly live upon the fat of the land, they ought to have done so. As for the unfortunate divisions that had, day after day and night after night, to face the foe in the trenches, hardly an officer, or man but was suffering from diarrhoea or dysentery. And, to make things worse, medicine could not be had. Some of our regimental doctors actually begged the chief medical authorities, for humanity's sake, to let them have some medicine for diarrhoea or fever; but, no! the answer was "We have none."

"Have you any medicine for rheumatism?"

"No I we have none."

Thus, our fellow-countrymen were left to die, whilst tons of medicines of all descriptions were close at hand, floating in the harbour of Balaclava! But I must be honest, and say plainly that a vast deal of the sickness was brought on by the men themselves by excessive drinking. We were allowed three (and sometimes four) drams of the best rum daily; but from the manner in which it was issued it would not intoxicate the men, for it was divided into three or four parts, and in camp it was mixed with lime juice. But there were hundreds not satisfied with that, who would go anywhere and do anything to get more; and then in all probability fall down, and, if not noticed by someone, the extreme cold soon settled up their account—*frostbitten or frozen to death*.

Thus, it was not all the fault of the authorities. The whole army was in rags and filth, and half frozen in the trenches in front of the enemy. Not one, but hundreds, were stricken down by starvation. They were only about eight miles from plenty, and yet were dying of hunger; there were clothing and medical stores in ship-loads, but no organization. And yet, with all this wretchedness, our men fought with undaunted bravery whenever the enemy attempted to trespass upon the ground they were told to hold.

In January, 1855, after thousands had died, the warm clothing was served out, but blankets were still short. And—would you believe it, reader?—when men who had died in hospital were taken to their last abode rolled up in a blanket, on arrival at the grave or pit, the unfortunate dead, perhaps a loving son of some poor heart-broken mother, was rolled out of the blanket into his grave in a state of nudity, and at once covered up with a few shovels-full of earth, *the blanket being brought back and washed, and becoming the property of one who had helped at the interment.* I knew of a very painful case.

One of our sergeants named G———s, had buried two poor fellows on a cold bleak morning in the month of January, 1855, but through some mistake had left them in their blankets. On returning to camp he met our colonel, who inquired what he had been doing; and when the poor fellow said that he was returning from the cemetery, and that he had just interred two men, the colonel roared out—"Then where are the blankets. Sir; go back and get them, and parade them before me when washed." A kinder-hearted man, or a braver soldier than our commander never faced the foe; but orders must be obeyed. Some regiments were reduced to a single company, and had to be sent out of the field, yet had not suffered much from the enemy. The Guards left home 2,500 strong, and reinforcements amounting to 1500 had joined them; but by the end of 1854 they could only muster about 900 fit for duty.

Lads were sent out and died almost as soon as they landed; one night in the trenches was quite enough for them—they either crawled back to camp and died, or were sent home again, or to Scutari or Malta. A number of poor fellows were almost daily sent down to Balaclava on litters—one on either side of a mule—they formed a ghastly procession; many died before they reached the port. Death was stalking all over our camp, on every side was cholera in its worst form, dysentery, diarrhoea, rheumatism, catarrh, and scurvy. Men were positively forbidden to take off their boots, as it was found impossible to get them on again; while some might be seen limping about the camp in the snow (two or three feet deep) with no boots of any sort; others with boots up to their knees, which they had borrowed from some dead Russian.

Some of our critics (newspaper correspondents) were at a loss to find out to what regiment a man really belonged, or even what nation, as during the worst part of the winter no two men were dressed alike. Some had hay bands bound round their legs, others had long stockings outside their rags or trousers, some had garters made from old knapsacks, others had leggings made from sheep skins, bullocks' hides, buffalo hides, horse hides—anything to keep the extreme cold out. Some had got hold of a Russian officer's overcoat, which was almost a load to carry. As for Joseph's coat of many colours, I do not think it would have taken a prize for patchwork by the side of some of our men's clothing. They say patch beside patch looks neighbourly, but our men's coats were nothing but rags tacked together.

As for head dress some had mess-tin covers that could be pulled down well over the ears; others had coverings for the head made out of old blankets four or five times doubled. Yet there was but little murmuring so long as the men could get sufficient to eat, and in the midst of all their troubles they were loyal to the backbone, and would sing aloud "God save the Queen."

Some of their beards and moustaches were almost two feet long, and sometimes these were so frozen that they could not open their mouths until they could get to a fire and thaw them. As the reader may imagine, they were a queer-looking lot; but nothing but death could subdue them. They were not very *"illigant"* in their appearance, but one could read in their countenances that they meant death or victory. During January, 1855, the men were informed that Her Most Gracious Majesty had been pleased to grant a medal with three clasps for the Crimean campaign, thus—one for Alma, one for Balaclava, and one for Inkermann. Little Inkermann was not named; and some of the officers, non-commissioned officers, and men, who had fought there, were not at all satisfied. Some of our men inquired what we were to get for the town.

Why, a star, of course! A *crack of the head more likely*. This was in January, 1855; we little dreamt then that we should have nine months' more continuous fighting before Sebastopol fell, and that much more of the best blood of Britain was to be spilt long before then. I have often thought since that my getting those two nasty pokes at Inkermann was the means, in the hands of God, of saving my life; for I thus escaped the hardships of the months of November and December, 1854, and January and February, 1855.

During my absence from the camp there was not much fighting going on, except at the "ovens," as our men called them; for the enemy could not stand the intense cold any more than our men; though they had the best of us, as they had good shelter huts until our guns knocked them about their ears.

CHAPTER 7

Night Attack

Our heavy guns still kept at it. I soon found my way into the trenches again, and had a very narrow escape, not of being wounded, but of being "taken in and done for," or killed on the spot. In the dark, after posting some sentries, I took a wrong turn and went almost into the midst of the enemy. They could have shot me; but just then, I am sorry to say, we had a number of men deserting to the enemy, and I believe they thought I was one of that class, but they soon found out their mistake, for I was off as fast as my legs could carry me in the opposite direction. As need scarcely be remarked, I did not wait to look behind me until I got close up to our own people, then I turned about and faced them.

That night I met for the first time that noble-minded man, Captain Hedley Vicars. He and I had a long chat in the trench. Although I had heard of him, I had not until then known him personally. He was under the impression this was my first time in front of the enemy, as I told him I was nearly taken prisoner; but when I informed him I had been present at the Alma, Balaclava, and Inkermann, and was wounded at the latter battle, he was quite astonished. He was very affable and kind, and his men seemed to be very fond of him. He appeared to be one of those cool determined men that are sure to win the respect of all classes, and will lead men at anything.

As far as I could see, he had not a bit of pride about him. I soon found that he was a Christian, and was not ashamed of his Master. The light that had been planted in him he could not hide under a bushel, for his whole conversation was of redeeming love, and how he had been plucked *as a brand from the fire*, when afar off from God by wicked works. What a soldier! I told him about my comrade at the Alma. "Well, Sergeant," he said, "the Lord's time is the right time;

who is the best off now, you or he?" He then asked me a number of questions about better things; I do not think I ever met such a man. His men seemed to be devotedly fond of him. I spent some time with him next day, as the 97th touched our right, the left of their detachment meeting the right of ours. He invited me to his tent for that night for prayer, as he told me a few who loved the Lord met there as often as they could. I did not profess anything at the time, but was going against light and knowledge. I went once and only once, before he was killed.

This subject is referred to at greater length in my next letter home, which was as follows:—

Camp before Sebastopol,
March 15th, 1855.

My Dear Parents,
Once more a few lines from this miserable camp—mud! mud!! Mud!!! We arrived here on the 8th, and at once marched up to the front; a number of my poor comrades I hardly knew—what a change! The old Fusiliers, once one of the finest corps in our service, now poor half-starved, miserable-looking wrecks of humanity. The older hands had still that unconquerable look about them, that it would be far cheaper for the enemy to build a bridge of gold for them to pass over, than to try and take them prisoners.

We have plenty of work in the camp; and 'tis bleak, cold work in the trenches, standing up to our ankles in mud and water, with hardly sufficient food to keep body and soul together; as for the fighting, we never hear one word of murmuring about that. I came off the trenches last night; we had a brush at the enemy, but it was soon all over: our people were ready for them, and gave them a warm reception. I met with a captain of the 97th (Vicars). He is, I do believe, a thorough Christian man. We had a long chat together. He appears to be a general favourite with his men. He held a prayer-meeting in the trench yesterday morning, and got as many men around him as he could. I like him very much. I do wish he belonged to us (the Fusiliers, I mean); he appears a good, earnest man, and not at all backward in standing up in his Master's name, trying to

Extol the stem of Jesse's rod,
And crown Him Lord of all,

in this cold, bleak corner of the earth; but yet a most determined soldier for his country. Some of his sergeants told me yesterday morning that he had used his good sword the night previous about some of the enemy, and they did not think the doctors would be of much use after he had done with them. The noble captain invited me to his tent, and I spent, I am happy to say, a comfortable hour with him. I do not know when this town will be taken, there is a lot of rough fighting to be done yet. I must conclude, with love to all; it is very cold to handle the pen. Pray for me, and God bless you all.

Believe me, ever
    Your affectionate son,
      T. Gowing,
        Sergeant, Royal Fusiliers.

I was with Captain Vicars once more in the trenches before that miserable night, the 22nd March. We had a lot of sickness in the camp, and duty was very heavy for those who could do it. The Old Light Division had been strengthened by the 34th to the 1st Brigade, and the 90th and 97th to the 2nd Brigade; but, with sickness and hardships, they, like ourselves, were not very strong—except in the head.

That 22nd March was a terrible night to be out in. We were nearly up to our knees in mud and water. It came on to blow and rain as hard as it fairly could. It was as dark as pitch, and in the midst of all—our plight was, I suppose, not bad enough—the enemy came out and attacked us, in both flanks and front. They came on pretending that they were French, and in the dark we could not see them; so that they were right in the midst of us before we could fire a shot. Talk about hard knocks,—they were served out that night as freely as ever they were. It was foot and fist, butt and bayonet, as hard as we could go at it; in fact, they could have it any way they liked: the fighting was desperate. The enemy came on in overwhelming numbers,—there were enough to eat us,—but we stuck to them with a death-like grip, until they were driven back.

We lost both our officers that night—Captain the Hon. C. Brown, and a Mr. Henry, who was a fine specimen of a British soldier. The former was killed, and the latter dangerously wounded. The news flew that Captain Vicars had fallen, and the men rushed in the direction in which it was said he was, and literally lifted the enemy from the field with the bayonet. Some of our men's bayonets were bent *like reaping-*

hooks next morning, which was a clear proof of the vehemence with which we had been at it. My letter will more fully describe that attack. The 97th were wrought up to a state of madness, to think that so kind and good an officer should fall by the hands of such fiends. The enemy were at last sent reeling from the field with our bayonets uncomfortably close to them. It was one of the most desperate attacks the Russians had made since the commencement of the siege, and the slaughter was in proportion; the bayonet was the chief weapon used, and, after poor Captain Vicars fell, it was used with a will and with a vengeance.

One Russian was caught trying to walk off with one of our small mortars; he was a huge monster, but some ten inches of cold steel, from a man named Pat Martin, stopped his career. Another, a Greek Priest, fired his revolver into our small-arm magazine, but luckily no harm was done. He was at once bayoneted; next morning he was seen to be a powerful fellow. Poor Captain Vicars was brought into the trench and placed upon a stretcher. He seemed quite cheerful, said he did not think it was much, and hoped soon to be able to go at them again. These were not, perhaps, his exact words, but the substance of them as nearly as I can remember. He was then sent home to camp, but before he had reached it his spirit had fled to him who gave it. He was ready.

Her Most Gracious Majesty had lost by that fatal bullet one of Britain's bravest sons; and all around the spot where poor Vicars had fallen it was evident the bayonet had done some terrible work.[1] The enemy let us alone for the remainder of the night, and next morning there was a flag of truce out. They had paid heavily for their intrusion, for in places they lay in heaps one on the top of the other. We were relieved next morning; and in the evening poor Captain Vicars was laid in his cold grave, together with other officers. We committed his body to the earth.

The 97th seemed to feel his loss keenly, and over his grave strong men wept like a lot of children who had lost a fond father, and then vowed they would revenge him the first opportunity.[2] The captain was a general favourite throughout the Light Division, for he used to go, when off duty, from regiment to regiment doing all he could to point

---

1. The total force engaged that night was about 1,500 men against 15,000;—the same number of unconquerable British soldiers that stood triumphant on the fatal hill of Albuera.
2. And that vow was kept not only by the 97th.

The night attack in the trenches when Hedley Vicars fell

poor thoughtless sinners to the Lamb of God.

The following is my letter describing the fighting of the 22nd:—

Camp before Sebastopol,
March 24th, 1855.

My Dear Parents,

I hardly know how to commence this letter. Since mine of the 15th, we have had a terrible fight. Thank God, I have been spared once more. I do think that I am out of their debt. To describe the fight adequately, would be impossible. I will try and do a little to it. A good strong party of us, under command of Captain the Hon. C. Brown, went into the trenches on the 22nd. It blew a perfect hurricane, with rain and sleet; it came down just anyhow. We were standing up to our ankles in mud and water, like a lot of half-frozen, half-drowned rats, when, about 10.30 p.m., the enemy attacked our Allies. It was as dark as the grave, and in fact, we could not see one yard in front of us. We had strong parties of the Light Division in our advanced works. The enemy got right in the midst of us before we knew anything of their whereabouts, and then we set to work with the bayonet.

It was charge and recharge, officers shouting to their men "This way, this way. Fusiliers!" "Come on, 90th!" "Now, at them, 97th!" We had to grope for them the best way we could, stumbling over friend and foe. Up and at them again. Officers fighting with desperation, shouting all the time, "Come on my lads, stick to them." Our captain was killed, and one of our lieutenants (a Mr. Henry) wounded. He was a man of about six feet two-and-a-half inches, and before he fell he let the enemy know what metal he was made of.

You remember a captain of the 97th, that I have spoken about (Captain H. Vicars, I mean): I am sorry to have to inform you that he received his death wound while nobly leading the 97th and us, shouting with all his might, "This way, 97th; come on. Fusiliers." Our men took a terrible revenge for his death. A number of our bayonets were bent like reaping-hooks next morning; and all around where that noble Christian fell, the enemy lay thick, one on the top of the other. They fought with desperation; but that never-failing weapon, the bayonet, was too much for them. They tried to blow up our small-arm magazine, but the fellow who made the attempt was at once despatched.

Captain Hedley Vicars, 97th regiment in the trenches

The sights next morning (the 23rd,) were awful. I do believe, for the time it lasted, it was worse than Inkermann: it was nothing but butt and bayonet, and some of our Lancashire boys did not forget to use their feet. Thank God, I got out of it without a scratch worth mentioning. I managed to lose my cap, a shot went through the collar of coat, and one through my trousers. We buried our officers last night, and there was hardly a dry eye when poor Captain Vicars was lowered into his grave. I feel confident that he has gone to that Home that is prepared for all those who are faithful to the end. This army has lost a cool, determined officer, and there is one Christian less in this sin-blighted world. He had won the affections of the whole Light Division.

The 97th might well be proud of him. It is only a few days since I was with him at one of his meetings; but, dear father, he is not lost, but gone before. He can now sing, with all his manly heart, while he views his glorious Master without a veil between. It is bitterly cold here at present, and I for one do wish they would let us go at the town. We know well that it will be a hard nut to crack, but it must be done, the honour of Old England and France is at stake, and take it we will some day. I do not wish you to publish my letters, for the simple reason that sometimes I speak a little too plainly, and it might hurt me; if anything should happen to me here, you can then please yourself. Take care of them all, as they may come in handy some day, if only to read to friends near and dear to us. I must conclude. Thanks for the papers.

  Believe me ever, dear Parents,
    Your most affectionate son,
      T. Gowing,
        Sergeant, Royal Fusiliers.

CHAPTER 8

Sebastopol

We had now some hard hitting almost every day or night. We commenced gradually to creep up to the doomed city—here a bit and there a bit, shots being continually exchanged. All the enemy's outworks had to be seized, and that was no child's play. The taking of their rifle pits was fearful work. It was all done with the bayonet, in the darkness of night. For the information of my non-military readers, I will just explain what rifle pits are. They are holes, large or small, constructed in various ways, and manned by crack shots, who tormented us considerably by picking off our artillery-men and the sailors manning our heavy guns; for if anyone showed his head above the parapets of the trenches he was almost certain to have a hole made in it.

The taking of these pits was, as I have said, fearful work, and was all done with the bayonet, no quarter being given or taken. This work is generally undertaken by volunteers from the various regiments that happen to be in the trenches at the time. I volunteered to form one of these "nice little evening parties,"—but I wished to go no more; yet, had I been ordered, I would have gone, for I had rather die a thousand deaths than be dishonoured.

In a few words I will try and describe the method of capturing rifle pits. About 100 or 150, sometimes 300 or 400, men would be formed up at the point nearest to the pits to be assailed, all hands sometimes taking off their accoutrements; at a sign from the officers who are going to lead, the men would creep over the top of the trench and steal up to the enemy on "all fours;" not a word is spoken, but, at a given signal, in they all go, and, in less time than it takes me to write this, it is all over—the bayonet has done its work; the defenders are all utterly destroyed or taken prisoners, while the pits are at once turned and made to face the enemy, or are converted into a trench. Therefore, with this sort of work going on, I think I am justified in saying that hard knocks were given and taken almost every night.

As far as the camp was concerned, things began to look much brighter. Thanks to the kind-hearted friends at home, we now had plenty of good food, and sickness was on the decrease. We had a few petty annoyances, such as being compelled to wear socks, and to pipe-clay our belts so as to make us conspicuous targets for the enemy. As for the fighting, we had plenty of that, but we managed to get over it, I think, as well as our forefathers had done. It was "give and take," but we generally contrived to let the enemy have "excellent interest."

The following letter, giving additional details of the fighting on March 22nd, may be of interest here:—

Camp before Sebastopol,
March 29th, 1855.

My Dear, Dear Parents,

In answer to yours of the 1st inst., I am happy to inform you that I am quite well, and in good spirits. I wrote you a long letter on the 24th descriptive of the attack on the 22nd. Truly it was an awful night, and a terrible fight we had. The attacking force, we find, were all picked men, most of them sailors. We hear that the Russians have got a new commander, and that he boasted he would compel us to raise the siege or drive us all into the sea; and I must say that they shaped well, for they came on manfully, but that nasty piece of cold steel stood in the way. I told you in my last about the death of poor Captain Vicars.

I do not believe that there was a man in the whole Light Division but would have died to save that noble soldier. When the news flew that Vicars had fallen it seemed to work upon our men, and they were wrought up to a state of frenzy; and with all the enemy's boasting, and with the overwhelming odds against us, we managed to shift them, and, so to speak, almost pitched them out of our batteries and trenches with the bayonet; and I should like to know what sort of a Briton he would be that would not follow such a man, such a two-fold soldier, as Captain Vicars.

One of the sergeants of the 97th told me that only a few hours before the attack this exemplary, noble Christian, was reading and expounding a portion of God's word to his men, and engaging in prayer with them, and shortly afterwards we find him calling upon these very men to follow him to death or to victory. My dear parents, you must not ask me such questions. I am bound to do my duty, I will not, if I am cut to pieces, bring disgrace upon Norfolk, that brought me up. We have only once to die, and if I am to fall in front of this town, let it be with my face to the foe. I do not wish to boast, but I think I am out of their debt.

I find the fellow that shot Captain the Hon. C. Brown was a Russian or Greek priest, and it was the same man that fired his revolver into our magazine, but a bayonet thrust stopped his little game, and extinguished his fanaticism.

I must tell you that we all received great praise, or soft soap, from Lord Raglan. I do not know exactly the united strength of those who took part in that fight, but the brunt of the fighting fell upon the 7th Royal Fusiliers, 34th, 77th, 88th, 90th, and 97th regiments. To explain the fight would be impossible—it was so dark. We did not fire much, all was left to the bayonet; but to say that this or that regiment did more than any other would be a piece of injustice. We had a handful, and although they were about ten to one, they found us one too many for them.

Whether it will be called a battle, or what our people are going to call it, I do not know; this I know, it has been a grand attempt at ducking us. We hear that the *Zouaves* fought like so many tigers, and although the odds were heavy against them, they routed the enemy off the field. I don't think I ever told you before, that they are not all Frenchmen that wear French uniforms. The *Zouaves* have a number of English and Irish mixed up with them—wild spirits that join them on account of the rapid promotion. You must try and keep your spirits up. I am as happy as the day is long, that is, when I have enough to eat. We must try and make the best of a bad job.

Nearly one-third of the Fusiliers are Norfolk men, and I will be bound they will hold their own, and I can tell you they are not the smallest men that we have. I must conclude, with love to all. Give my kind regards to all inquiring friends, and

    Believe me as ever, dear Parents,
        Your affectionate son,
           T. Gowing,
              Sergeant, Royal Fusiliers.

P.S.—Try and keep your spirits up, dear mother. I will come

home someday lop-sided, with honours, that is, if I do not get my head put under my arm.

T. G.

The Second Bombardment of Sebastopol.

On the morning of Easter Monday the camp was shaken by the commencement of the second bombardment. The French opened fire with some 350 heavy guns, and our people with about 220 guns and mortars. The enemy returned the fire with spirit, with some 600 of the heaviest guns and mortars, exclusive of their shipping. It was something grand, but awful; the ground seemed to tremble beneath the terrible fire. I was in camp, but felt compelled to go up to the Victoria Redoubt to have a look at it. The Russians frequently fired in salvoes, against both us and our allies.

This duel of artillery went on day after day, but it all ended in nothing, the enemy's works appearing to be as strong, after all this expense and loss of life, as before the bombardment commenced. As Sir G. Brown once said, the longer we looked at the place the uglier it got, and it would have to be taken in the old way, let the consequences be what they might; the bayonet must do what shot and shell could not. So our people set to work to creep up to the prize that for the first time had baffled all our united fire of artillery, and try the effect of cold steel. Every obstacle had to go down in order to enable us to get up to their works, and during the remainder of April and May we had some terrible fighting.

More rifle pits had to be taken, and the old Light Division sustained another heavy loss in Colonel Egerton, of the 77th, who had from the commencement of the Campaign proved himself one of Britain's truest sons. He fell dead at the taking of rifle pits, that were afterwards named Egerton's pits; he was one of the biggest men I ever saw in uniform. The old Pot-hooks (the 77th) fought in a most dashing manner, and although they had lost their colonel, their spirits were not damped, but they went at it with a will as conquerors.

The enemy tried hard that night to retake the pits, but it was no go; they were met with a fire that mowed them down by wholesale; they then got the bayonet. The 77th were backed up by a good strong party of the 33rd, and detachments of almost every regiment of the Light Division.[1] The fighting was of a most formidable and deter-

---

1. The 97th could be distinctly heard shouting: "Remember Captain Vicars, boys," "Stick to them;" and the officers shouting "Give it home, my lads."

mined character; but the pits remained in the hands of the conquerors of Alma, Balaclava, and the two Inkermanns. It would be impossible for me to describe all the different combats, but every inch of ground up to the town had to be dearly purchased by blood.

Nothing particular occurred to note now, except that a steady stream of men kept joining us, particularly French, and we had now a splendid army in front of the doomed city. Our men were burning to go at it, and take it or die in the attempt; but we had some more outworks yet to capture before we were to be let loose. From the early morning on the 7th of June, the French were passing through our camp on the way to the trenches. The Imperial Guards and *Zouaves* appeared in high spirits, and our men turned out and cheered them lustily; and when their new chief, Pelissier, with General Bosquet went by, you would have thought our people had gone mad.

General Bosquet was a great favourite with the entire army; and Pelissier was known to be a most resolute man. Our men cheered them heartily, throwing their caps in the air. The fire-eating Bosquet and his chief seemed to appreciate the reception they got from the old Light Division. As soon as the cheering had subsided a little, the two leaders stopped, and Bosquet called out, "Thank you. my men,"— then, with his hand up, to stop us from shouting—"We shall be at them before long, shoulder to shoulder, and then, my boys, stick to them." Our men cheered them until they were hoarse. Some of our officers turned out to see what was up, but the French had passed on.

Capture of the Mamelon and the Quarries.

We shortly afterwards fell in, and marched into the trenches. We knew well that there was something to be done, but things were kept very quiet. We mustered pretty strongly in our old advanced works. The French went at the Mamelon in a masterly style, column after column, and as fast as one column melted away, another took its place. We had a splendid view of it—it was grand—and we could distinctly see one of the *Vivandiers* on horseback, moving with the throng, and then dismount. We cheered them most heartily.

Our turn came at about 6.30. p.m., and away we went at the Quarries with a dash, the old 7th and 88th leading the van. It was England and Ireland side by side. The enemy might well look astonished, for our bayonets were soon in the midst of them. They were routed out of the Quarries; and our people set to work with pick and shovel as hard as men could work. But the enemy were no mean foe; they were armed with as good a weapon as ourselves, and were not going to submit to being shut up in the town, without giving some hard blows. They came on repeatedly, and tried to retake the position from us; but the old Fusiliers and Connaught Rangers, assisted by detachments of various regiments of the Second and Light Divisions, on each occasion sent them reeling back. At times we were hardly pushed, for we had no ammunition left, and had to do as we had done at Inkermann, *viz.*, pitch stones at them. I am not altogether certain that some of the 88th did not use their teeth—all is fair in love and war.

Both officers and men fought with desperation. It was resolved by all of us not to be beaten; but at times we were under such a fire of grape and musketry that it appeared impossible for anything to live. As far as I could see, all had made up their minds to die rather than turn their backs on the foe, and we had that night leaders who knew how to die but could hardly run. As far as the old 7th Fusiliers were concerned, we had some splendid officers—Mills, Turner, Waller, Jones, Fitzclarence, all courageous men, just the right sort to lead a storming party. Mr. Jones and Waller repeatedly led our men at the enemy during that sanguinary night.

At times all was confusion, uproar, and smoke. Dust and showers of stones flew like hail. It was hot work all night, but we meant to win or die. The hurrahs of our fellows told both friend and foe that our blood was up. If we were short of ammunition we had plenty of steel; we had a Wolseley with us and others as good, but nearly all our commanders bit the dust, dead or wounded. I had the honour of taking a man's name that evening for a most daring act, *viz.*, bringing a barrel of ammunition on his head across the open field, under a tremendous fire, throwing it at our feet, exclaiming, "Here you are, my lads, fire away," and then going back to get another. I had the pleasure of meeting him afterwards in India, with the cross upon his noble breast—"Gunner Arthur," But Arthur was not alone; two of our own men—Private Matthew Hughes and Corporal Gumley did exactly the same.

Hughes, smoking his old clay pipe all the time, exclaimed, "Keep it up, lads;" "Lend a hand, sir, to distribute these pills," addressing a young officer. The fighting all night was of a deadly character, but we had then got the Quarries, and were not going to let the enemy have them again. As for the Mamelon, it was "ding-dong hard pounding." Five times the French went at it. The fifth column was blown into the air to a man, guns, platforms, and all; and then, with maddening shouts, the gallant sons of France went at the ruins, and, in spite of the barbarous brutes, took them.

The *Zouaves* followed them up and went right into the Malakoff, where a great number fell, but it was not the intention to take or attempt to take that work. Our hands were full, we had all that we could do to maintain our position; but we found time to give our heroic Allies three times three, for they richly deserved it. All the enemy's attempts at retaking the Quarries were baffled, for some fourteen times they were hurled back with a terrible slaughter. We were now under good cover, the pick and shovel having been at it all night.

My letter home at this time was as follows:—

Camp before Sebastopol,
8th June, 1855.

My Dear Parents,

Once more a few lines to inform you that I am, thank God, still in the land of the living. We have had another regular go-in in front of this doomed city. The French were passing through our camp nearly all day yesterday, and we had a good idea that something was in the wind; they seemed all in good spirits, and we turned out and cheered them heartily, and their chiefs seemed to appreciate it. In the afternoon, I marched off with a strong party of our regiment; we had some wild spirits of officers with us, that would lead men at anything. We soon found out that they had a nice little job cut out for us—all their outworks had to be taken from them.

We were told off to take the Quarries; we had strong parties of the Light and 2nd Divisions with us, and about 5.30 p.m. the 7th Royal Fusiliers and the 88th Connaught Rangers, dashed at them. It was rough hard hitting, for about half-an-hour. It was a little piece of work well down. We routed the enemy but we had hard work to hold our own, for they came on repeatedly with strong columns, and tried to retake them from us. The fighting then became desperate, the bayonet was freely used on both sides, but although the enemy were three and four to one, they shrank back, and although their officer tried to lead them on, they could not be brought to a determined rush.

Thank God, I escaped once more, but it would be impossible for me to tell you how, only that a merciful God has been watching over me. We ran short of ammunition, and then we were in a nice mess; we used stones as we did at Inkermann, and as soon as they came close enough, we went at them with that ugly piece of cold steel. We proved them again to be cowardly beggars in the open field.

Oh! I do wish they would let us go in and finish them off, for with all this dillydallying we are daily losing a number of our best men, and the men that are being sent out to fill up the gaps are too young for this rough work, but they are mixed up with the older hands, and they stick to it well. I must tell you that our Allies, the French, went at the enemy in a masterly style, column after column, but I fear their loss has been heavy, as one entire column of about 2,000 men was blown into the air; we hear their loss amounts to upwards of 3,000 men. We have taken three noble positions from them, and I hope you will now soon hear news that will set the church bells of Old England ringing again for victory, as after the Alma, Balaclava, and Inkermann.

But, dear parents, who will live to tell the tale of the fall of this town, only One above knows. But when one comes to look at it seriously, it's terrible work; many a poor mother has to mourn a noble boy, that was hale and hearty yesterday morning. But there, we must not look at it in that light, or we could never do our duty. I know our loss must have been heavy, not much short of 800 killed and wounded. But the Light Division, as at the Alma, has borne the brunt of it. Camp life at present is very pleasant, we have now plenty to eat, and as much as we require to drink; and this I know, if anyone wants more fighting than we get, he is a glutton, for we are often at it from morning until night, and from night until morning, but no grumbling.

We will try and give Mr. Bull, some of these mornings, something to talk about. I see by the papers, that the people at home begin to find out that it's no disgrace to be a soldier. I hope you will excuse this short note, will write again if I am spared, in a few days. Trusting this will find you all enjoying the best of blessings. Goodbye, dear parents, and God bless you.

       I am, your affectionate son,
            T. Gowing,
              Sergeant, Royal Fusiliers,

Returning to camp next morning, we were thanked for our conduct by Lord Raglan, who promised to report all for the information of Her Most Gracious Majesty. We were heartily greeted by our comrades. Our loss had been very heavy. In killed and wounded the

Mamelon, Quarries, and Circular Trench had cost the Allies close upon 3,500 officers, non-commissioned officers, and men, but yet our people were full of hope; the enemy had lost all their outworks, and every inch of ground was hotly disputed. The Quarries were afterwards well named "The Shambles," for we daily up to the 8th September lost a number of men in them from the cross-fires of the enemy.

We had now some rough work. From the 7th to the 17th June it was one continual fight. We had a magnificent army around or in front of the south side of the town, and our men were burning to go and take it, or die. We had now been some nine months besieging the town, which had for that time defied the united powers of France, England, and Turkey, assisted by some 15,000 Sardinians. It is true the latter had nothing to do with the actual siege, but they took the place of our men or the French in guarding our communications. One great battle—Alma—had been fought to get at it, and two others had been fought in order to prevent the raising of the siege—Balaclava and Inkermann; and the civilized world were again asking when the last great *coup* would be made.

SEBASTOPOL AGAIN BOMBARDED.

On Sunday, the 17th June, 1865, the third bombardment of Sebastopol opened with a terrible crash, and from morning until night they kept it up as hard as they could load and fire; the very earth seemed to shake beneath the crash of guns. We all marched into the trenches full of hope that the grand and final struggle was about to commence. We thought we had come to the last scene in the great drama. The Old Fusiliers were told off for the post of honour. We were to lead the way. It was not the first time we had done it, and from the colonel downwards all seemed in good spirits; and on that memorable 18th June, the 40th anniversary of Waterloo, we were to combat side by side with our old enemy, and thus avenge that historic battle.

ATTACK BY THE ALLIES AND ITS BLOODY REPULSE.

At a given signal away went the French at the Malakoff with a ringing cheer of *Vive l'Empereur*, It was quite dark, for it was just about 2 a.m. The Malakoff looked like a vast volcano, with a continual stream of men going at it. At another signal off we went at a rapid pace, with our colonel in front, sword in one hand and revolver in the other; they let us get well out into the open so that we had no cover, and then, reader, such a fire met us that the whole column seemed to melt away. Still on we went, staggering beneath the terrible hail. Our colonel fell dead, our adjutant the same, and almost every officer we had with us fell dead or wounded, but still we pressed on until we were stopped by the *chevaux-de-frise*, and in front of that our poor fellows lay in piles.

We were there met with a perfect hell of fire, at about fifty yards from us, of grape shot, shell, canister and musketry, and could not return a shot. Our men could not advance and would not retire, but were trying to pull down the barrier or *chevaux-de-frise*. We might just as well have tried to pull down the moon. The "retire" was sounded all over the field, but the men stood sullen and would not heed it. Our men and those of other regiments were fast dropping; at last the remnant of the attacking column retired to the trenches amidst a storm of grape, which nearly swept away whole companies at a time.

The enemy mounted the parapets of the Redan, and delivered volley after volley into us. They hoisted a large black flag and defied us to come on. At length, our artillery got into play, and literally swept them down, so that they did not have it all their own way long. Our front trench was nearly 800 yards from the Redan. The cry of "Murder" could be heard on that field, for the cowardly enemy fired for hours upon our countrymen as they lay writhing in agony and blood. As some of our officers said, "This will never do, we will pay them for all this yet!" We would have forgiven all, had they not brutally shot down poor helpless wounded men.

On the left attack they were a little more. fortunate, led on by the gallant 18th Royal Irish and the 9th, the Norfolk, Regiment. These regiments let the enemy know what they might expect if we could only get at close quarters with them. Major-General Eyre addressed them in Irish, and said that he hoped their deeds that morning would make many a cabin in Old Ireland ring again. The men of that regiment were wrought up to a state of madness, and on they went, right into the town, but, as the other attacks had proved failures, they likewise were compelled to retire, and lost a great number of men the like of which could not easily be replaced.

The Royal Irish and the 9th were backed up by the 28th, 38th, and 44th Regiments, and as they carried all before them it was hard lines that they had to fight their way out of the town again. The Allies had been kept at bay for upwards of eight months—and out of all that vast army employed only two regiments managed to cut their way into Sebastopol on that terrible 18th June, and one of them was "the Holy Boys." Herein is another source of pride for Norfolk.

Major-General Eyre's address had a wonderful effect upon the 18th Royal Irish, and it was not lost upon the Norfolk regiment. The fighting in the cemetery was desperate. Not a shot did those two noble regiments fire, but with a ringing cheer they dashed at the enemy. No powder was wasted, but the Russians were fairly pitched out of their works. Their general's appeal had touched them to the quick, and these gallant regiments seemed to vie with each other in the rapidity of their movements, and in their deeds of valour, A few prisoners were taken. One huge grenadier, profusely bleeding, might have been seen dragging by the collar of his coat a monster of a Russian. Pat had fought and subdued his antagonist, and then remembered mercy, exclaiming, "Go it, lads; there are plenty more of them yonder. Hurrah for ould Ireland!"

The bayonet was used with tremendous effect by these regiments; but the other attacks had been driven back, or, in other words, mowed down with a fearful slaughter, and could not close in with the enemy. The French lay in piles in front of the Malakoff, and the ground beyond our then front trench was saturated with some of the best blood of Britain. There lay some hundreds of those who had led the way up the Heights of Alma, side by side with those who had taken a leading part in driving the Russians from the heights of Inkermann, who had fought with Vicars in the trenches, and, night after night and day after day, had kept the enemy at bay.

Our gallant Blue Jackets lay in heaps. They had volunteered to carry the scaling ladders for us, "The Stormers," and I must pay them a tribute of respect, for they stuck to us well under great difficulties, carrying heavy ladders, and died almost to a man rather than let the enemy see their backs. "All honour to the bravest of the brave." The columns of attack had not been driven back by the weight of numbers. Nay, they were mowed down with grape, canister, musketry, and broadside after broadside from the shipping; and, I am sorry to have to record it, the enemy seemed to take delight in shooting down poor helpless wounded men, who were trying to limp or drag their mangled bodies away from the devouring cross-fires.

For hours during that dreadful day they would not answer the flag of truce; but the black flag, or flag of defiance, was flying upon all their batteries, while some hundreds, yea, thousands of our poor fellows were lying with every description of wound, exposed to a burning sun—and here the reader should remember that the heat in the Crimea in summer is equal to that of India. There lay, I repeat, poor helpless men weltering in their blood, with an unnatural enemy actually firing upon them, and laughing at their calamity—such were the brutes that we had to fight against.

At length the white flag was seen to float upon the Redan, the Malakoff, and all the other batteries. The enemy placed a strong chain of sentries all along the front of their works—evidently picked men—and they had actually had a wash, and some of them a clean shave. All our men that had fallen in front of the *chevaux-de-frise* they brought and lay for us to take away. Reader, this was humiliating to the feelings of a Briton. They were, moreover, very insulting, and it would not have taken much, if our officers had not been firm, for our men (some of them at least) to have dashed their brutal heads half off with "one straight from the shoulder"; for they had no arms, except the sentries placed in front of our trenches. Our men were very quiet and sullen, but one could read "revenge" written on their countenances.

As soon as all the dead and wounded had been removed, the short truce terminated, the white flags on the different batteries were waved to and fro. and down they went, but were hardly out of sight when "bang" went the heavy guns at it again. And our sailors and artillerymen worked them as hard as they could load and fire, which soon made the frowning Redan, the Malakoff, and all the enemy's batteries very warm corners; for our huge 13-inch shell sent guns, platforms, and all that was anywhere near, flying into the air. So Mr. Russia found to his cost that we were not going to give the game up just yet.

Well, it must be confessed we had had what might be called a good sound drubbing, and I can affirm that our people are not good hands at putting up with much of that; officers and men wanted "to go at it again" and wipe out the stain or die—but we had to obey orders. We had been beaten, both French and English combined, and our men could hardly believe it. In returning to camp that morning, one could not get a civil answer from any of the men. If you told a man to do anything he would turn round and tell you to do it yourself. It was almost a miracle how any of the storming columns escaped.

My clothing was cut all to pieces, I had no fewer than nine shot holes through my trousers, coat, and cap, but, thank God, I was not touched. Out of my company, which went into action with 1 captain, 2 lieutenants, 4 sergeants, 4 corporals, 2 drummers, and 90 men, all that came out of it with a whole skin were 13 men besides myself; No. 3 Company returned to camp with 9 men out of 96. So I hope, reader, you will be able to see we stuck to them well before we gave in. We were burning to go at them again, but we had to pocket the defeat and wait our turn.

It did not matter to whom I spoke about that bloody repulse, all were nearly mad. The fault had to be thrown on some one. I must tell the truth—it was not the fault of the officers who led, it was not the fault of the men who formed that unlucky column of stormers. But, reader, we were sold that morning (I am sorry to have to record it) by traitors from our own ranks! Men (brutes, rather,) had deserted us because they had been justly punished for misconduct, and informed the enemy the exact hour and the precise signal for the advance. I knew one of these rascals, but for the sake of the gallant regiment to which he belonged I withhold his name.

I am happy to state, however, that he lived to reap a portion of his reward, for he was transported for life,—treatment too good for such a black-hearted villain, for he was the cause of some thousands of the bravest of the brave being launched into eternity. If we could have forced the *chevaux-de-frise*, the 9th and 18th would not have been the only regiments of the Allied Army to enter Sebastopol that morning, for we had some of the right sort of stuff with the Fusiliers. I do not believe a man of us thought one word about supports. It was simply "do or die" with that heroic column; but still the fact remains that a handful of men were sent to be slaughtered without supports. We had rated our enemy too cheaply; our commanders forgot that we could not get at them with the queen of weapons, but had to stand and be mowed down from behind good cover, and with a deep ditch between us!

Our camp presented a very mournful spectacle. Officers, non-commissioned officers, and men, were being carried home covered with wounds; some limping along, others besmeared with dirt, powder, and blood, doing their best to reach the camp, assisted by a comrade. A great number of "resurrectionists" turned up (men who did not return to camp with their companies, and were reported killed or missing). These had got so far in advance that they, poor fellows, could not get back until the flag of truce was up. So some got into pits, others into large holes made by shells, and there had to lie. It would have been madness for them to have attempted to reach our trenches across the open field amidst the withering fire that the enemy could have brought to bear upon them. We were only too glad to receive them back.

As it was, the poor old Fusiliers had suffered fearfully; we had paid dearly for leading the way. And although we had lost our brave colonel and adjutant, and almost all our officers had been hit more or less, still that indomitable pluck that will carry a Briton through fire and water was not all thrashed out of us. On all sides one heard such expressions as—"Well, we'll warm them up for this yet!"

The questions asked were "I say, have so-and-so come back?" "Have you seen ——?" "Has Sergeant come back?"

Men were running about the camp inquiring about particular friends, and as soon as they found me writing home, I was besieged. "Sergeant, will you write a line for me, please?" I think I wrote close upon twenty short notes for our men, some of whom were wounded slightly; others had nasty cuts and bruises, and wanted to conceal them, thinking that we should have another go-in before long. Our Allies, the French, seemed down-hearted, and very low-spirited. They cannot fight a losing battle; so long as they are victorious they do not appear to care much what they lose. As far as we were concerned, we knew well that we had lost a friend—our best friend—in our dear old colonel.[2] He was as brave as a lion, and his familiar cry was: "Come on men; follow me."

Not half-an-hour before he fell he was in prayer. He knew that he was going to lead the way, and that thousands must fall. But, reader, that gallant soldier was ready for life or death. He could have been seen walking up and down in the trench, addressing one after another. Some of his expressions were: "Men, when we advance, move your legs; remember, not a shot; all must be done with the bayonet." When the order was given to advance, we all rushed over the trench, the colonel shouting, "Fusiliers, follow me, and prove yourselves worthy of your title."

I was close to him. He had ordered a number of active non-commissioned officers to keep up with him; and, as we bounded across the plain, he waved his sword and shouted, "Fusiliers, follow me; come on!" Just before he fell he stopped to have a look around. At this time our poor fellows were falling one on the top of another; for the batteries in front, right and left, were like so many volcanoes pouring forth a never-ceasing stream of fire.

Truly it was an awful scene. It did not last much more than half-an-hour; and my readers may form some idea of the terrible fire we had to face, for our loss was as follows:—Killed, wounded, and missing, 7,988 French and British!

---
2. Colonel Lacy W. Yea.

Our men had been crushed beneath a terrific fire, but not subdued. We knew well that a day—a terrible day—of reckoning would come, and longed to be let loose at them. "Oh, if we could only get them well out into the open fields," said one old hand, "we'd make short work of them!" But, no chance of that. They had had several tastes of our bayonets, and wanted no more; so we had to set to work and hunt them out of one of the strongest fortifications in the world. Ultimately, the reader will find that we managed them.

The following was my letter home on this occasion:—

Camp before Sebastopol,
June 18th, 1855 (Waterloo Day.)

My Dear Parents,

How to express my feelings to the God of all mercies I do not know. I drop a line as quickly as possible, in order to catch the mail, to let you know that I am still safe and sound, as I know that long before this can reach home you will have heard of the slaughter we have sustained. Slaughter is hardly a name for it—massacre. We have been cut to pieces in an attempt upon the town. I have not time to say much, and am too low-spirited. About two o'clock this morning we attacked the Redan, the 7th Fusiliers leading the stormers.

Our dear old colonel was killed. He was one of the bravest of the brave, for where all were brave he would lead the way. Almost every officer of ours has been either killed or wounded. I am the only sergeant of my company returned to camp without being wounded. Oh, what a morning! but through the mercy of God I have been spared, although my poor comrades fell in heaps all around me, one on the top of the other. But truth will go the furthest, the enemy has beaten both French and English this morning.

Our poor fellows could not get at them, but were mowed down with grape, canister, and musketry, and broadside after broadside from their shipping. The sights all around are horrible, men continually being brought into camp with every description of wound. I heard one of our old hands say, a short time ago, although wounded and limping to hospital: 'This is only lent; we'll pay them off for it yet, and that before long.' The sole cry in the camp is—'Let's go at them again.' I hope you will excuse this short letter, as I must be off. I am for the trenches tonight.

Believe me, yours, &c., &c.,
T. Gowing,
Sergeant, Royal Fusiliers.

P.S.—I was robbed of all I had in this world while out fighting (except the small *Bible* you gave me—they would not have that).

We had not long to wait for our revenge, and revenge is sweet when in the field. We had received some good strong drafts—not recruits, but volunteers from various regiments at home—fine, able men, that filled up the gaps, or went a long way towards it. All stragglers were sent to their duty. Our chiefs had found out by some means that we were to be attacked about the 26th of June, by an overwhelming force; our batteries, trenches, and all our guns were to be taken from us; and we were to be put into the sea, or capitulate. Much easier said than done.

However, as we had to go into the sea, we took lessons in swimming—by way of taking plenty of ammunition with us. Although they had just thrashed us, we were not going to give up the game for one black eye. Sir G. Brown tendered his sword to defend the front trench with his division of ten regiments at his back. That noble old soldier addressed each brigade, in just a few suitable words, that a tried man like himself knew well how to deliver. As soon as we were formed up, the gallant old general was in the midst of us. He had not much bowing or scraping, but went at once to the point. "Well men, they," pointing in the direction of the town, "are going to take our trenches and guns from us tonight. I have offered my sword to defend the leading trench, will you support me?"

Suiting the action to the word, he drew his sword and waved it over his head. The answer that the brave old man got was a deafening shout, such a shout as that, a few hours after, struck terror into the boasting enemy; and we at once marched off to the post of honour. We had not gone far when another shout told us that we were not going alone.

The 1st brigade of the Light Division consisted of the 1st-7th Royal Fusiliers, 23rd Royal Welsh Fusiliers, 33rd Duke's own, 34th regiment, and 2nd battalion Rifle Brigade. Our comrades of the 2nd brigade consisted of the 19th, 90th, 77th, 88th and 97th regiments. The 2nd brigade came close behind us, backed up by the entire 2nd division, and a part of the Guards and Highlanders.

Into the front trench we went, and, as soon as it got dark enough, a good chain of sentries was thrown, out to give us timely warning of the enemy's approach. These men had to creep out on their hands and knees and lie flat on the ground, and as soon as they could see the enemy advancing, bound back to us and give the alarm; thus, all would be in readiness for them, although it was as dark as the grave. Everything was cut and dried, and they might come and try their hands at ducking us if they were game!

We had not very long to wait, for they were game to the backbone. They opened a terrible shell fire upon all our leading trenches, both French and English, and we lost many of our men, as we were rather thickly posted. About 11.30 p.m. our sentries came running in, with the news that the enemy was advancing in force. We let them come. Our batteries threw out a number of fire balls, which at once lit up the whole place as clear as daylight. We, in the leading trench, kept well down out of the way of our own guns.

The enemy came on through a perfect storm of shot, shell, grape, canister, and rockets; it must have mowed down their crowded ranks by wholesale, for they were coming on in massive columns, evidently for a fair trial of strength. All this time we in the trenches had not fired a shot. At a given signal our guns ceased, but the mortars still kept it up. Our two front ranks gave them a deadly point-blank volley, and at once stepped back, for we stood six deep in the trench waiting for them. The next two ranks then moved up and gave them another. They were not more than fifty paces from us. The front ranks of the column went down as grass before a scythe, and before the enemy had time to collect their wits they got another and another, which shook them to atoms.

To finish them off they got two or three more volleys, for the rear of the column was pressing the head of it on. The deadly fire was a little too much for them, and they broke, hesitating as to which way to go. While they stood bewildered, they got two or three more volleys, which literally tore them to pieces, and, to make things a little more uncomfortable for them, the words "*Faugh-Balah*" were shouted somewhere on our left—the gallant 88th got the credit of it. Translated into English this means, "Clear the road," or way, and, in less time than it takes me to write it, all hands sprung over the top of the trench and rushed at them with the bayonet.

We lost a number of men that we should not have lost had we acted solely on the defensive, for the enemy opened their heavy guns on friend and foe, in order to try and stop us. We chased them right up to the Redan, and then returned to our trenches. The next morning there was a flag of truce out, which was soon answered by our people. We could then have a good look at our handiwork of the previous night, and a ghastly sight it was, for hundreds of the enemy were cut to pieces by shot and shell.

I had seen the fields of the Alma, Balaclava, and Inkermann, and, in fact, everything of importance since the commencement of the campaign, but I had never seen anything to equal the sight that presented itself that morning; the enemy lay in columns as they had stood, or in places pile upon pile, four or five deep, in every conceivable position that mind could imagine.

The Minie balls had done some fearful work. Into that part of the trench on our right, manned by the Rifles, Guards, and Highlanders, the enemy had, in spite of the terrible fire, entered, but they were there met by the bayonet, and never went back to Holy Russia. The trench was in places completely choked, the dead lying heaped up level with the top.

Some of our nice boys joked the Guards and Highlanders next morning about leaving no work for the doctors, and some of those "feather-bed gentlemen" replied that they liked to do things well—they had been taught the first point. People may say what they like about our Guards, but they have proved themselves on many a hard-fought field very devils, particularly in a close fight.

Again I found opportunity to write to my parents, as follows:—

Camp before Sebastopol,
June 28th, 1855.

My Dear Parents,

Just a few lines to inform you that we have got out of debt. My letter of the 18th told you of the terrible thrashing that the enemy gave us that morning. Well, we have met them again, and paid them off for it; and I think we have proved that we can hit just as hard as they can. On, the 26th, about 11 p.m., they made a general attack all along our trenches—both French and English. We were ready for them, as they were for us on the 18th, and have paid them off in their own coin. It lasted about three-quarters-of-an-hour, and they have left close upon 4000 upon the field, dead and wounded; they boasted that they were going to put us into the sea; I for one, had a strong objection to this, as I cannot swim.

I never before saw our men fight so spitefully. Volley after volley was poured into their advancing hosts, and then, with a ringing cheer for old England, we closed upon them with that weapon they so much dread. Some of our men's bayonets were bent like reaping-hooks, which was a clear proof of the work we had been at. Although they beat us for once, we let them know that the Lion was on the war-path, and that he was well roused. I think our Allies got out of debt too, for they stuck to them well; we can always tell when they are winning, for they do not forget to shout.

Our men are as quiet as a lot of lambs until the bayonet comes into play, and then it's three British cheers, and sometimes three times three. The sights all over the field next morning, (the 27th), were horrible. We had a flag of truce out for about three hours, to allow the enemy to take away their dead and wounded, and during that time the greater portion of the troops that had been engaged returned to the camp. I got a slight scratch in the forehead, but nothing of any importance, so I have much to be thankful for. We did not lose many men, as we were under cover. We are creeping, bit by bit, up to the town; but the closer we get, the more bitter the fighting becomes.

We have now plenty to eat and drink; there is all sorts of life in the camp, and duty is not half so hard as it has been. We have still the unseen enemy—cholera—with us, but upon the whole we keep up our spirits remarkably well. Our men appear to long for the day when we shall be let loose at the town—bombarding does not seem to have much effect upon their works—it must be taken with the bayonet, and whenever the day of reckoning comes, it will be a heavy one. reinforcements keep joining us, both French and English, almost every day; and we have a splendid army, in spite of our heavy losses, ready at our commander's call to advance with the flag of old England, and plant it on the proud walls of this noble fortress, which has put all others in the shade.

Hardly a day passes but more guns and mortars are being mounted, and what the next bombardment will be I do not know. I will write as often as I can, but you must excuse some of my short notes; although I wear a red coat, I hope there is a warm heart beating beneath it. I must conclude with love to all, find double allowance for poor mother.

    Believe me ever, dear Parents,

Your affectionate son,
T. Gowing,
Sergeant, Royal Fusiliers.

Thus ended all the boasting of the Russians. The flag of truce was up for two hours, and then had to be renewed, for they had not all their dead and wounded removed. We acted with them as they did with us on the 18th. A chain of sentries was placed out about 60 yards in front of our trenches, and all that fell on the inner side of the chain were carried by our people and laid down for their friends to take away; their men were very sullen, and their officers sarcastic—inquiring as to when we were going to take the town.

Some of our officers told them we should awake them some of these fine mornings when they little suspected us; and our people joked them in return by asking when they were going to put us into the sea. A number of their officers could speak French, but few could speak English. The repulse that they had just sustained damped their spirits considerably; but the moment the white flag was out of sight, we were at it again.

I had nothing particular to record for a time except trench work, and as we had plenty of men our duty was not heavy. The enemy continued to torment us as much as possible; and as we were now creeping closer to the town, almost every night there was something going on, and daily we lost a number of men and officers.

Chapter 9

The Battle of Tchernaya

And now we had something else hanging on our hands; we had lost our brave commander-in-chief, The camp was startled on the morning of the 29th June, 1856, by the sorrowful tidings of the death of our much-beloved commander-in-chief, Lord Raglan. Men who had been accustomed to meet death looked at each other as if they had heard of the loss of some near relative. We did not know, until he was taken from us, how deeply we loved him. The army had lost a true friend—a friend to the combatant ranks. Our beloved country, and our much-beloved Sovereign, had lost a good, honest, faithful, and devout servant.

His courage knew no bounds, and it was backed up by true Christian piety. He was a perfect gentleman, and had proved himself a soldier of no mean sort on many a hard-fought field in Spain, Portugal, France, and the Netherlands, He had served his country faithfully for upwards of half a century; and now he had laid down his life in the performance of his duty to the flag he loved so well. He was lamented by all, both high and low. The enormous responsibility of that unparalleled siege, together with the disastrous failure on the morning of the 18th June, broke the dear old gentleman's heart. But he died as he had lived—a true soldier in a twofold sense, for he was not at all ashamed of his Great Captain. We mourned him as our commander who had repeatedly led us on to victory. We mourned him also as a Christian who had left a noble example behind him;—

All honour to the brave! he has gone to his everlasting home. All honour to him for his long and meritorious services. His old enemies, the French, against whom he had so often fought, now nobly stood forth to pay their respects and to do honour to one whose back they had never seen, and whom they never could subdue. The removal of the remains of our late lamented chief, Field-Marshal Lord Raglan, to Kazatch Bay, was a most imposing sight. The melancholy procession moved off about 3 p.m. on the 3rd July., All the way from the house in which his lordship had breathed his last was one continuous blaze of bright uniforms.

At the house was stationed a party of the Grenadier Guards, and the French Imperial Guards; our Guards, the *Zouaves*, field batteries, and horse artillery batteries, with regiments of the line, both French, English, and Piedmontese, lined the road; the artillery, stationed at intervals, firing minute guns. The body was escorted by the 12th Lancers, about four squadrons; a strong party of French Cuirassiers, about four squadrons; then a party of Piedmontese cavalry, about four squadrons; troops of French horse artillery; troops of British horse artillery; and a strong party of French *Chasseurs d'Afrique*. Then came the coffin, covered with a black pall and the Union Jack; General Pelissier, the commander-in-chief of the French army; Omar Pasha, the commander-in-chief of the Ottoman army; General Marmora, the commander-in-chief of the Sardinian army; and General Simpson, the commander-in-chief of our army, rode on either side of the body, which was carried upon one of our horse artillery gun-carriages.

Then came general officers of the British, the French, the Sardinian, and Turkish armies. Field batteries and horse artillery batteries were formed up all along the route, and fired minute guns as the solemn procession passed them. The united bands of various regiments were stationed at intervals, and played the "Dead March." Every regiment in the Allied Army was represented by officers, non-commissioned officers, and men. His remains were not permitted to rest in an enemy's country, but were carried with all honour down to the water's edge, and duly handed over to the fleets, to be escorted under the flags of England, France, Turkey, and Sardinia.

His loss to us as an army was great just at that critical moment. His name and memory were all that was left to animate us through the difficulties that were yet before us. The town was still firm, and the enemy's numerous batteries still bade us defiance. But, we knew that Sebastopol must fall; else what would they say of us in Old England? Why, that we were not worthy of our forefathers. Let the reader have patience and he will soon learn how the work was done. The news will set his ears tingling, but, alas! it has sunk deep into many a mother's broken heart.

July passed off pretty quietly, but there was something in the wind;

instead of returning to camp to rest, we all had to fall in at tattoo and march off to some part of the field, pile arms, and lie down. Our generals were not going to have another Inkermann job on their hands without being prepared for them.

The Russians could see that the town must fall. It was only a matter of another month or so. The French had a splendid position in the Mamelon, were daily strengthening it, creeping and sapping up to the Malakoff; while our people were advancing step by step. The closer we got to the town the dearer the ground became, the fighting became more bitter, and we lost more men and officers daily. Their marksmen were always busy. The enemy were determined to make one more effort on a grand scale in order to try and save the town, and we did not know the spot or the hour the storm would burst upon us, so it was best not to be caught napping. Our batteries were being strengthened, and more guns and mortars added every day; and an immense iron girdle was now around the town, or the south side of it.

The Battle of the Tchernaya.

On the morning of the 16th August, our camp was aroused by a tremendous firing to our right rear. The enemy had attacked us in the Valley of the Tchernaya, just to the right of Inkermann. We at once got under arms, the 2nd Brigade closing up, and there we remained. The firing got hotter and hotter; Prince Gortschakoff had now a vast host under his command, and he was making one more grand throw for victory. The fighting was very severe between the French and Sardinians on the one side, and Russians on the other. The Sardinians fought like men, and the *Zouaves*, as usual, like so many tigers, and the battle raged from morning until about 5 p.m.

The enemy never had the slightest chance of success. I went on to the field in the evening and had a good look round; I found that the fighting had been in earnest. On and at the Tractor Bridge the dead lay in heaps, while the arches over the river were completely choked or blocked up with Russian dead, the water running on either side of the bridge. The Russians, as usual, behaved in a most barbarous manner after the battle. They had been foiled at all points, and were compelled to retire. A party of French and Sardinians went to look up the wounded; the Russians could see plainly what the party was doing, yet they opened their heavy guns upon them! I came across a few French wounded *Zouaves*, and did all I could for them.

We were told not to go any further, or the enemy,, on the hill to our left, would open upon us. The words were hardly uttered, when "bang" came a round shot right in the midst of us, but luckily did no harm; it only knocked some of their own wounded to pieces. No condemnation could be too strong for such unfeeling wretches. Their loss had been close upon 10,000. Such was the terrible battle of the Tchernaya. We had but little to do with it; some of our artillery were engaged, and a portion of our cavalry were formed up ready for a dash at them, but were not let loose. Rumours were rife that the Russians would try their luck again at Inkermann, but they never did; they had already got a good sickening there.

The doomed city had now to take its chance, and I am approaching the last great scene of the campaign—the storming of the town that had kept the united armies and fleets of France, England, and Turkey at bay for nearly twelve months. The attention of the whole world was directed thither.

I wrote home at this time as follows

Camp before Sebastopol,
August 18th, 1855.

My Dear Parents,

Long before this can reach you, you will have learnt by the papers the results of the terrible battle of the 16th. In the Valley of the Tchernaya the enemy made a most determined attempt for victory, but the Allies met them at all points, and drove them back with terrific slaughter. I find that the Sardinians fought with desperation, well supported by the French, and backed up by some of our people.

The attacking force has been estimated at from 60,000 to 70,000 men of all arms, and 160 guns. The fight lasted all day, and the struggle in various parts of the field has been severe; in fact it has been, on the part of the Russian commander, a grand throw for victory, to try and raise the siege; but as an officer, who saw the whole, told me this morning, they from 9 a.m. had not the slightest chance, that their defeat was inevitable, and that a crushing one.

Our cavalry were formed up ready for them, under General Scarlett, but did not go at them; we were under arms all day, or nearly so, but did not advance. The enemy's loss has been fearful in killed, wounded, and prisoners. I saw some of them, they are fine-looking men, but very dirty; I hear the prisoners amount to about 3,600, exclusive of officers, that is, including wounded and unwounded. The field presents a horrible spectacle; a few of us went down to have a look at it, and it was not the enemy's fault that some of us did not stop there, for they pitched shot and threw shell right in the midst of us; we were doing all we could to relieve the poor wounded, both friend and foe.

The sights all over the field were sickening, and I hope never to see the like again; there lay the ghastly fruits of war, in some places heaps upon heaps; the sight at the Tractor Bridge I shall not forget as long as I live; we spent some two hours on the field, did all we could to relieve the poor wounded, then walked home to camp. I have got two Russian medals I found upon the dead. I found that our friends, the *Zouaves*, had in some parts of the field handled the enemy very roughly, they had crossed bayonets with them, and they lay locked in each other's arms dead.

I do not think Prince Gortschakoff, with all his boasting, will try his hand against us in the open field, for some time to come; the enemy have not got enough go in them, except they are half maddened with *rackie*, to face us manfully. What the enemy have lost we do not know exactly, but not much under 10,000 or 12,000, and the result has slightly damped their spirits. Our loss, that is, the French and Sardinians is acknowledged by them to be between 2,000 and 3,000 men, but I believe it must be much more, by the aspect of the field.

I believe you will now soon hear something that will set your ears tingling; this town cannot hold out much longer, and we are all ready at our commander's call to advance shoulder to shoulder with our gallant Allies, and plant our glorious old Standard by the side of the Red, White, and Blue, on the blood-stained walls of this famed fortress. Trusting this will find you all well, pray for me, and

  Believe me, my Dear Parents,
    Ever your affectionate son,
      T. Gowing,
        Sergeant, Royal Fusiliers.

P. S.—Thanks for the papers. I see that the eyes of the whole of Europe are upon us; we will give them something to talk about some of these fine mornings, but who will live to tell the tale, only One above knows. Try and keep up your spirits, all's well that ends well.—T.G.

Russian Attack in the Trenches.

On the evening of the 30th August, I went into the trenches with a party (and a good strong party it was) of our men—about 200, and a proportion of non-commissioned officers. We were under the command of the late Sir W. W. Turner, then Captain and Brevet-Major. The second in command was Captain Lord Richard Brown. We had, therefore, some capital officers with us, and men will go anywhere with officers upon whom they can rely. We had a good sprinkling of the right sort of stuff with us, *old soldiers*, or men that had been well tried upon field after field—from the Alma—and we had a few that had smelt powder on many a hard-contested field in India, such as Ferozeshah, Moodkee, Sobraon, and Goojerat—men that well knew how to do their duty, and were no strangers to a musket-ball whistling past their heads, who understood well a live shell in the air, and knew within a little where it was going to drop.

One feels much more comfortable with such men than with three times their number who have never smelt powder. The honour of our glorious little isle has been safe in the hands of such men upon many a field. Well, we marched off smoking, as comfortably as if we were going to a picnic or garden party, as we had often done before. The only thing that seemed to trouble some was, "Where's the grog party?" As for the enemy, we knew well that we should most likely make their acquaintance before morning. We found that we were told off, with detachments of the 19th, 23rd, 33rd, 34th, 88th, and 97th, to hold the fourth parallel. There was another trench in front of us, full of men from various regiments.

The firing was very heavy all night, or up to about 2 a.m., when all at once the word was given "Stand to! look out!" The enemy with an overwhelming force had attacked our front trench, and had either destroyed or routed our people out of it with the bayonet. I must say that the greater portion of the men in this front trench were recruits, men who had not learnt how to die, but who knew how to run. So much for placing the honour of our flag in the hands of a lot of boys, without mixing them with a good sprinkling of seasoned men. As soon as our poor frightened lads came rushing over the top of our trench our front was clear.

Then the 19th, 88th, and 97th, let out an unearthly yell of "*Faugh-à-balah*," and at them we went. Not a shot was fired, but the "piece of cold steel" came into play. The enemy fought well; but in the end, with a tremendous cheer for Old England, and another for Ould Ireland, they were fairly pitch-forked out of the trench; the open space between that and our front trench, or fifth parallel, being in places well covered with the dead and dying. Captain Vicars had now been dead upwards of five long months, which, under the trying scenes we had passed through, seemed a lifetime.

But the 97th had not forgotten that Christian hero, for, above all the din of war and the booming of heavy guns, they could be distinctly heard shouting, "Remember Vicars, boys;" and men could be heard responding with "Yea, boys; give it them." The enemy was chased back into the town, with a fearful slaughter, by comparatively a handful of Britons. Our loss was trifling, taking into consideration how we had punished the enemy. They went back much quicker than they had advanced, with their spirits slightly damped. Even before they reached the Russian works, their heavy guns opened with grape, thus killing and wounding a number of their own men; for the fire had to pass through their ranks before it reached us. We were not such fools as to stand still and let them mow us down; but, not being able to get at their guns, we got back as quickly as we could under cover.

Next morning we found the dead lying in ghastly piles—friend and foe mixed together—but our people were a long way in the minority, as the greater portion of the enemy had got the bayonet in the back. We had a flag of truce out to bury the dead, and after that the enemy's fire was terrible. We lost a number of men; but our sailors, manning our heavy guns, did not let them have it all their own way, and we had some rough music nearly all the day. We knew the town could not hold out much longer. It must have been something like a hell upon earth, each side trying which could pound the longest or hit the hardest. Everything around us indicated that the grand *finale* was fast approaching.

All our batteries now assumed an awful magnitude. New batteries, both for guns and mortars of the largest calibre, had sprung into existence all around the south side of the doomed city since the last bombardment, and everything now indicated that one of the bloodiest struggles that ever men undertook was about to ensue. We had been pummelling at each other for near twelve long months; but we all knew that many a fine fellow then in camp, in all the pride of manhood, would not, in all probability, see the first anniversary of the Alma.

We who had been present at the former bombardments knew well, by the preparations, that the coming struggle would eclipse them all;

and, with the number and size of the armaments opposed to each other, it would be the most terrible the world had ever seen since powder had been invented; for, in addition to all our vast batteries, our magnificent and united fleets were prepared to join in with us. Our men did not put themselves out in the least; they knew well the end must come.

No man out of camp could hardly credit the amount of life and activity that existed there. Some regiments even got up theatrical performances, and some of the actors, a few hours after, were pounding away at the enemy as hard as they could load and fire; and, as the reader may be certain, our Jack Tars were well to the fore wherever there was any sport going on.

CHAPTER 10

The Final Bombardment of Sebastopol

On the morning of the 5th September, 1855, the last bombardment opened with a terrific shock; close upon 1,600 guns and mortars were now blazing away at each other, the earth trembling the while—and so it continued all day. I went into the trenches on the night of the 6th—right into the front trench—and a warm corner it was. I remained there all night. Next morning we were ordered to remove to one of our rear trenches, where we had good cover, and, in spite of the tremendous firing, lay down and had a good sleep for two or three hours. We had a very narrow escape from a huge shell that came hopping right into the midst of us; we had just time to throw ourselves down, when it exploded, and sent our breakfast flying in all directions.

One of our officers inquired if anyone was hurt, and a nice boy of ours answered that he was, "for, by dad, he had nothing to eat." Reader, try and imagine, if you can, some hundreds of guns and mortars firing in salvoes. For a time the guns would stop, to allow them to get a little cool; then they would burst forth again, the thunder being enough to shake the very earth to its centre; and this lasted for hours. We were completely enveloped in flames, and covered with smoke, dust, and stones. An old adage says *Familiarity breeds contempt*.

That it is true I can bear witness, for a number of our men were in groups playing cards in the midst of the firing, our own shot flying close above their heads. Thus far I had witnessed five bombardments, but this was frightful. Some of our old hands said it was too good to last long. The Russian fire was very heavy; they had yet more guns in position than we, and made some of our batteries rather hot corners, while we came in for a fair share of shell, so that death was raining fast around.

But during all that terrible day I never heard a desponding voice. We knew well we were in for it, and speculation ran high as to whether we should attack that night, but some thought that the bombardment would continue for two or three days more. We remained under this awful fire all day, and just as we were on the tiptoe of expectation, looking out for our relief, an officer belonging to the staff, came up and got into talk with me in reference to our strength, and when I had told him I was directed to furnish 100 men to repair the Quarry Battery. I was left in temporary charge, as my officers had gone off on some duty.

Shortly after, I was directed to take the remainder of my party to the leading trench, and remain there for orders. I then began to smell a rat; something was in the wind, although everything was kept very quiet. In walking through the trenches one might notice a change in the men's faces. Savage they looked, but determined to do or die. We had now a great many very young men with us that had been sent out to fill up the gaps. They were brave enough for almost anything, but we had a job in front of us that was enough to shake the strongest nerves, and we wanted the men that had been sacrificed during the winter for want of management—they would have done it as neatly as they had turned the Russians back at the Alma and Inkermann.

The work that was about to be carried out was a heavy piece of business, and required at least 20,000 men who had been well tried. We had them, but they were not let loose; had they been let go, we should have had a star for Sebastopol, and should have had an equal share of the glory—that's if there is any in it—as we had up to then had, with our noble Allies.

Well, to the front trench I went with my men; it was about 200 yards from the Redan. I had not been there long, when an officer came up and wanted one officer, one sergeant, and thirty men, to go to the front as scouts or sentries; I told him my strength, I had no officer. He at once went and got sufficient men from the 31st Regiment, then came back and had a long chat with me until it got quite dark, which is what we were waiting for. He found out that I well knew the ground, and was no stranger to the work. I requested that the men we were going to take should be all picked men and not lads, as it was rather an important piece of business.

We had to creep on hands and knees nearly up to the Redan, and it required men with all their wits about them; so a number of the men were changed, and I would have staked my life that 10,000 such as I then got would have hoisted the glorious old Standard on the blood-stained walls of Sebastopol, and then stood beside it triumphant.

Well, to my story, which is an awkward one. We crept over the top of the trench in the dark, and cautiously advanced about eighty yards, then commenced throwing or planting sentinels at about five or six yards apart; we had done the job, the officer lay down beside me and gave me further orders, and then crept back to the trench, leaving me in command. My orders were not to attempt to hold my ground should the enemy attack me, but to retire and give the alarm.

After lying for some time we were attacked by an overwhelming force and retired. The enemy tried to cut us off and take us prisoners, but they found it was no easy matter.[1] But, to make things worse, during our absence from the trench it had been filled with men of various regiments; and, not knowing there was any one in front but the enemy, they opened a regular file fire, and we were in a pretty mess between two fires; our poor fellows dropped fast—some of them were shot dead, close to the trench, by our own people. We called as loudly as possible to cease firing, but with the noise they could not hear us.

On collecting my party afterwards in the trench, I had to take all their names, as most of them were strangers to me, and found that we had lost nineteen men and two corporals out of thirty. Yet it lasted only two or three minutes. The general officer inquired what regiment I belonged to, and, when I had told him, he expressed surprise, told me I had no business there, but ought to be in camp and at rest, as there was some sharp work cut out for the Fusiliers in the morning. That was the very first hint I got of the storming of the town.

The general officer directed me to go with an officer and another party, as I knew the ground, and show the officer where to place his men; I went again, posted all sentries and then returned to the trench, in doing which I stumbled across a poor fellow lying wounded and brought him in the best way I could. The men in the trench were this time told that there was a party in front; had that been done before the greater portion of my men would not have died, as they were nearly all shot by our own people.

These are some of the "blunders" of war. On returning to the trench the second time I reported myself to the general commanding,

---

1. It is well I had picked men with me, or all would have been taken prisoners or killed on the spot.

and he directed me to take my party home to camp at once. I reached the camp about 1.30 a.m., and afterwards found that, true enough, there was a warm job cut out for us.

We had led the way repeatedly—at the Alma, at the Quarries, and at the Redan on the murderous 18th June, and now we were told off to support the stormers, moving immediately behind them. I knew well that thousands must die—and a still small voice told me that I should fall. I know I tried to pray, begged the Lord to forgive my sins for His great name's sake, and asked for His protecting arm around me, and strength of mind and body to do my duty to my Queen and Country.

I then retired for a little rest, until about 5 a.m., when our men were up, and then no more sleep. I wrote a number of letters that morning for poor fellows—some of whom were laid low before midday, and others struck down maimed, some to rise no more, long before sunset.

The following, though it was never forwarded, was written at this time, in anticipation that I should fall:—

Camp before Sebastopol,
2 a.m. 8th September, 1855.

My Dear Parents,

I feel that I must drop you a few lines. I came off the trenches at one o'clock this morning, to find that this town, which has given us so much trouble, and has already cost more lives than all the inhabitants of Norwich and its surroundings put together, is to be stormed today; long before this reaches you, or before the ink that I now use is hardly dry, hundreds, perhaps thousands, will have been launched into eternity. I feel it is an awful moment. I have repeatedly, during the last twelve months, been surrounded by death, and since the Alma have not known, honestly speaking, what fear is, as far as the enemy is concerned.

But, dear parents, this is a solemn moment; thousands most fall—and we are told off to be in the thick of the fight. I feel confident that God's arm is not shortened, and into His protecting care I commit myself. I must be candid, there is a still small voice that tells me I shall fall, and if I do, I hope to meet you in a better world than this, where the nations shall learn war no more. I do not feel that I can say much, but let come what will, I am determined to try and do my duty for my Queen and Country.

I am glad in one sense that this hour has come; we have looked for it for months, and long before the sun sets that is now rising, Sebastopol must be in our hands. I will now say good bye, dear and best of mothers; goodbye, kind father; goodbye, affectionate brothers and sisters. This letter will not be sent unless I fall; I have given it open into the hands of one of our sergeants who is in hospital wounded, and if I fall he has kindly offered to put a postscript to it and forward it. May the God of all grace bless you, dear parents, and help you to bear the pending blow.

Believe me, ever
Your affectionate son,
T. Gowing,
Sergeant, Royal Fusiliers.

As I did not return to camp after the action, the comrade to whom I entrusted the letter added this postscript:—

P.S.—Dear Sir—I am truly sorry to have to conclude this kind letter: your noble son fell inside the Redan (Sebastopol is taken). Your son, from the day he joined the regiment, proved himself a credit to us, and a most determined soldier. I have every reason to believe that he is now where you would not wish to have him back from; a nobler death he could not have met with than that in the hour of victory. I know, Dear Sir, it is hard for you to lose such a noble boy, but I hope the Lord will give you strength to bear up under this trying blow.

I am, Dear Sir,
Your faithfully,
J. Holmes,
Sergeant, Royal Fusiliers.

I was brought into camp in time to prevent the foregoing being despatched, and after my recovery added the following, which will explain itself:—

Camp before Ruins of Sebastopol,
March, 1856.

My Dear Parents,

You see that I have, thank God, been spared to see what they had to say about me after I was supposed to be dead. It is true that I fell inside the Redan, and was totally unconscious for some time, but, thank God, though wounded heavily, am still where mercy is to be shown. I was carried home to camp and to the hospital just in time to save the above being posted, but I will keep it as long as I live, and if I live to come home will bring it with me, for truly I have had a merciful God watching over me, and am spared, I hope, for some good purpose, for this wonderful God of ours can see from the beginning to the end. He is the same unchanging God that the Patriarchs trusted in. There is talk of peace, and those who want to continue the war will, I hope, come out and show us the way, as General Windham did on the 8th September last; they would most likely soon give in. I am not one of those who would have peace at any price, but if I am allowed to express my opinion, I think our ends have been gained. The Russians have been considerably humbled. We have beaten them four times in four pitched battles, have rent one of the strongest fortresses in the world from them, and I think they have had enough of France and England. If I am spared to come home I will bring this with me, as its contents might be too much for poor mother to bear.

From your rough but affectionate son,
T. Gowing,
Sergeant, Royal Fusiliers.

CHAPTER 11

The Storming of the Town

We fell in at 9 a.m.; a dram of rum was issued to each man as he stood in the ranks; all hands had previously been served with two days' rations. There were in our ranks a great number of very young men, who had not much idea of the terrible work that lay before them; but there were others who knew only too well, having helped to unfurl the Standard of Old England, in conjunction with that of France, on the Heights of Alma, the 20th September, 1854; who had routed the enemy on the heights of Inkermann, and had had near twelve months' hard wrestling with the foe—and no mean foe either; men who had proved themselves on many a hard-fought field worthy the name of Britons, for neither the storms of autumn, nor the snows of winter, nor the heat of a July sun, neither the sword nor bayonet, nor the musketry fire could subdue them.

Although backed by a countless host, the Russians could not withstand "the astonishing infantry,"—which had not degenerated from their fore-fathers, who had stormed the bloody parapets of Badajoz, San-Sebastian, and Ciudad Rodrigo, and England might well be proud of them; and I can say it was a pleasure to look upon and attend to the wants of such cool, determined men.

We were about to face the enemy in deadly conflict once more. The defence of Sebastopol had raised the Russians in the estimation of the bravest of the brave, and their Sovereign and country had no reason to regret entrusting that defence to their hands.

Before I proceed to describe the assault, I would point out that Sebastopol had for the first time in military history, since powder had been invented, defied the united fire of some 900 guns of the largest calibre, exclusive of mortars, which had been directed on the devoted city from early morning of the 5th September. When the final bombardment opened, the very earth trembled beneath the terrible crash. It was grand, but awful. But after it the enemy's batteries looked as strong as ever. We might apparently have gone on bombarding until now.

The Redan and Malakoff appeared to be much stronger than when we first looked at them, although no fewer than 1,600,000 shot and shell had been hurled at them. I say again, the Russian nation might well be proud of the manner their army had defended that fortress. At last cold steel had to do what artillery had been baffled at. If my readers are at all acquainted with military history, they will know that large breaches have invariably been made by artillery fire in the enemy's fortifications before ever the "dogs of war" were let loose at them. But no breach was made in the fortifications of Sebastopol.

After remaining for a short time under arms, we marched off about 9.30 a.m. There was no pomp or martial music, no boasting; but all in that mighty throng moved with solemn tread to the places that had been assigned them; all, both old and young, seemed to be determined "to conquer or die." The older hands were very quiet, but they had that set look of determination about them that speaks volumes.

The bombardment was still raging on that terrible 8th September; every gun and mortar that our people and our noble Allies, the French, could bring to bear upon the enemy's works, was raining death and destruction upon them. The stormers had all got into their places—they consisted of about 1,000 men of the old Light and 2nd Division; the supports were formed up as closely as possible to them, and all appeared in readiness. History may well say the storming of a fortress is an awful task. There we stood, not a word being spoken; everyone seemed to be full of thought; many a courageous heart, that was destined to be still in death in one short hour, was now beating high.

It was about 11.15 a.m., and our heavy guns were firing in such a way as I had never before heard. The batteries fired in volleys or salvoes as hard as they could load and fire, the balls passing a few feet above our heads, while the air seemed full of shell. The enemy were not idle; for round shot, shell, grape, and musket-balls, were bounding and whizzing all about us, and earth and stones were rattling about our heads like hail. Our poor fellows fell fast, but still our sailors and artillerymen stuck to it manfully.

We knew well that this could not last long, but many a poor fellow's career was cut short long before we advanced to the attack. The reader will, perhaps, hardly credit that a number of the older hands—

The French attack on the Malakoff

both officers and men—were smoking, and taking not the slightest notice of the "dance of death." Some men were being carried past dead, and others limping to the rear with mangled limbs, while their life's blood was streaming fast away.

We lost, as I have said, a number of officers and men before we advanced. We looked at each other with amazement, for we were now (about 11.30 a.m.) under such a fire as was without parallel in the history of the world. Even Leipsic (where the Allies alone had 1400 field guns, and the French 1000) was eclipsed. Upwards of 100,000 dead and wounded lay upon that field, but the contest lasted three days and nights. The people at home were complaining because we did not take Sebastopol! A number of visitors—ladies and gentlemen from England—now saw that we were trying to do our duty. The appalling and incessant roar of the thunderbolts of war was deafening, and our enemies were bidding us defiance, or, in other words, inviting us to the combat; and I have not the slightest hesitation in saying that some of our visitors, who came out to find fault, or "pick holes in our coats," were horrified, and wished they had stayed at home. It was a warm reception for a number of lads that had just joined us; it really seemed a pity to send them out to meet such a fire.

As the hour of twelve drew near, all hands were on the alert; we knew well it was death for many of us. Several who had gone through the whole campaign shook hands, saying, "This is hot; goodbye, old boy." "Write to the old folks for me if I do not return," was the request made by many.

At about fifteen minutes before twelve a number of our guns were brought to bear upon the *chevaux-de-frise*, and sent it into a thousand pieces; so that it should not stop us, as it had done on the 18th June. Many of us cherished doubts as to the result, although we dared not express them. Our numbers looked very small to attack such a place as the Redan, and the greater portion of the attacking and supporting columns too young and inexperienced for such a fiery ordeal. But, as one old hand said, "We can only die!"

I know that I appealed to the Throne of Grace for strength of mind and body to do my duty to Queen and Country, and for the help of His protecting arm, which I knew well was not shortened.

Nothing is more trying than to have to stand under a dropping fire of shell, and not be able to return a shot. The enemy had the range of our trenches to a nicety, and could drop their shells into them just as they liked. We lost a number of men, before we advanced to the attack, by this vertical fire. But the grand struggle was now close at hand, when the Muscovites' greatest stronghold was to be torn from their grasp.

Capture of the Malakoff.

I was close to one of our generals, who stood watch in hand,[1] when, suddenly, at 12 o'clock, the French drums and bugles sounded the charge, and, with a shout of *Vive l'Empereur*, repeated over and over again by some 50,000 men—a shout that was enough to strike terror into the enemy—the French sprang forward, headed by the *Zouaves*, at the Malakoff, like a lot of cats. On they went like a swarm of bees, or rather, like the dashing of the waves of the sea against a rock. We in our old advanced works had a splendid view—it was grand but terrible; the deafening shouts of the advancing hosts told us they were carrying all before them. They were now completely enveloped in smoke and fire, but column after column kept advancing, pouring volley after volley into the breasts of the defenders. They, the French, meant to have it, let the butcher's bill be what it might. At about a quarter-past 12, up went the proud flag of France, with a shout that drowned for a time the roar of both cannon and musketry.

Capture of the Redan.

And now came our turn; we had waited for months for it, and at times almost longed for it. But it was a trying hour. As soon as the French flag was seen upon the Malakoff, our stormers sprang forward, led by Col. Windham; the old Light Division leading, consisting of 300 men of the 90th, about the same number of the 97th, and about 400 of the 2nd Batt. Rifle Brigade; and with various detachments of the 2nd and Light Division, and a number of Blue Jackets, carrying scaling ladders. Our men advanced splendidly, with a ringing British cheer, although the enemy poured a terrible fire of grape, canister, and musketry into them, which swept down whole companies at a time.

We, the supports, moved forward to back up our comrades, but anyone with "half an eye" could see that we had not the same cool, resolute men, as at Alma and Inkermann; though some of the older hands were determined to make the best of a bad job; and I am happy to record that the old Inkermann men took it very coolly; some of them lit their pipes, I did the same. A brave young officer of ours, a Mr. Colt, told me he would give all he was worth to be able to take it as comfortably as

---

1. The Generals' watches had been timed alike, and as the minute hand denoted twelve (midday) the French sprang forward.

some of our people did—it was his first time under fire—he was as pale as death and shaking from head to foot, yet he bravely faced the foe. The poor boy (for he was not much more) requested me not leave him; and he fell dead by my side, just outside the Redan.

Our people were now at it in front; we advanced as quickly as we could, until we came to the foremost trench, when we leaped the parapet, then made a rush at the bloodstained walls of the Redan— we had a clear run of over 200 yards, under a murderous fire of grape, canister, and musketry. However any one ever lived to pass that 200 yards seemed a miracle, for our poor fellows fell one on the top of the other; but nothing but death could stop us. The musket balls whistled by us more like hail than anything else I can describe, and the grape shot cut our poor fellows to pieces; for we had a front and two cross fires to meet. It seemed to me that we were rushing into the very jaws of death, but I for one reached the Redan without a scratch.

While standing on the brink of the ditch, I considered for a moment how best to get into it, for it appeared to be about twenty feet deep, with no end of our poor fellows at the bottom, dead and dying, with their bayonets sticking up; but the mystery solved itself, our men came rushing on with a cheer for Old England, and in we went, neck or nothing, scrambled up the other side the best way we could, and into the redoubt we went with a shout truly English. The fighting inside the works was desperate—butt and bayonet, foot and fist; the enemy's guns were at once spiked; some of the older hands did their best to get together sufficient men for one charge at the enemy, for we had often proved that they were no lovers of cold steel, but our poor fellows melted away almost as fast as they scaled those bloody parapets, from a cross-fire the enemy brought to bear upon us from the rear of that work. The moss of that field grew red with British blood.

The struggle at the Redan lasted about an hour-and-a-half, and the reader may form some idea of the fighting from our loss, which was as follows:—Killed and wounded of all ranks, 2,472, and 176 missing.[2] The mistake that our generals made was in not sending sufficient men. Twenty thousand men ought to have been let loose; we should not then have lost anything like the number we did, as very

---

2. A great number of these men were ready for anything, life or death. On the night of the 7th September they assembled in hundreds in front of their lines, and committed themselves into the hands of an all-wise God in prayer and praise, while others burst forth with the National Anthem. Such were the men who stormed Sebastopol. Hundreds of them never saw another sunset.

many officers and men were killed when retiring; but we had handled the enemy so roughly that they did not further attempt to molest us. The French officers and men were in ecstasies of admiration at the doings of our people at the Redan, and exclaimed, "English, you have covered yourselves with glory this day!"

And I now fearlessly assert that the handful of men who undertook that bloodstained work earned a rich wreath of laurels that day. Yet we were but a handful when compared with the vast hordes of the enemy.[3] But with all their strength they hesitated about coming to close quarters. Had we had even ten thousand men with us, the Russians would have gone into the harbour at the point of the bayonet, or else been made to lay down their arms. But no; men were sent up in driblets, to be slaughtered in detail! The few hundreds who did enter that bloodstained fortification fought with butt end and bayonet, and not many returned without securing some token in the shape of wounds more or less severe.

Still the few who did meet the enemy taught them to respect us, for they no more dared to follow us than they would a troop of lions. We had not been beaten, though we were crushed by cross-fires and heavy masses of men; yet all the time our trenches were crowded with men eager to be let loose at the enemy!

We had a Wolseley with us, it is true, but he was only in a subordinate position. We wanted such a man as he, or Sir Colin Campbell, or a Roberts, and we should have carried all before us. Then, in all probability, we should have had a star, but not without some hard work for it. As it was, we got no star, though we had for twelve long dreary months to be continually fighting—and the fighting was such as would almost make the much-vaunted heroes of Tel-el-Kebir blush: not that I wish to rob them of the honours that a grateful country has bestowed upon them.

The Fall of Sebastopol.

The night of the 8th September, 1855, is one long to be remembered. Our camp was startled by a series of terrible explosions, and we could not make out what was up, but at length discovered that the enemy were retiring under cover of the blowing up of their vast forts and magazines. Oh! what a night! It baffles all description. Many of our poor fellows were then lying on the ground, having been wound-

---

3. After our stormers had entered the Redan the enemy came at us in swarms, but were kept back by the bayonet.

ed in all sorts of ways, with the burning fortress all around them! The Redan was blown up, and a number of our men went up with it, or were buried alive! Reader, try and imagine the position of the wounded lying just outside the Redan.

The renowned Redan Massey was there weltering in his blood, together with a number of others, while hundreds of tons of powder was exploding within 300 yards of them! Those of the wounded who managed to reach the camp were well looked after; our doctors worked incessantly, they threw their whole heart and soul into it, and all appeared to do their best. Men were continually being brought home to camp with every description of wounds. I myself was carried thither, having received five wounds in different parts of the body, my left hand shattered, and two nasty wounds in the head. I was totally unconscious when taken out of the Redan, and for some hours afterwards.

At about 6 p.m., I found myself in our front trench, with a dead 33rd man lying across me; I got him off the best way I could, and then tried to get up, but found that I could not stand, for I had almost bled to death. Dr. Hale, V.C., did all he could for me; I then had to remain and take my chance or turn of being carried to camp, where I arrived about 7.30 p.m., when my wounds were dressed, and a good cup of beef tea revived me; there I had to remain for upwards of three months, but, with careful attendance, and a good, strong constitution, I was, by that time, ready for them again.[4]

THE TALE OF KILLED, WOUNDED, AND MISSING.

Our loss had been very heavy, but that of our noble Allies was fearful on that terrible 8th September. They acknowledged the following figures:—Killed, 5 generals, 24 field officers, 124 subalterns of various ranks, 2,898 non-commissioned officers and men; wounded, 10 generals, 26 field officers, 8 missing, 229 subaltern officers, 4,289 non-

---

4. It was an Irishman named Welsh who was instrumental in saving my life. It turned out that he had noticed me fall, and when he found that he had to retire from the Redan, he carried me up to the ditch and let me slip in, and then with assistance got me out of it, and carried me across that terrible 200 yards, being shot through both legs in doing so. Before he reached our leading trench, some other good Samaritan picked me up and ran away with me. Poor Welsh died in India, at Ferozepore, in 1865, and, as a mark of respect, I put a stone over his remains. He was a rough diamond, but every inch a soldier and a good loyal subject. I hope I may state now, without egotism, from the day I found out that Welsh had done me such service, I did all that lay in my power for him and for his poor mother.

commissioned officers and men, and upwards of 1000 missing; the total killed, wounded, and missing, or the finishing stroke of the butcher's bill, was, as regards the French, 8,613. Our loss in the different ranks was as follows:—Killed—officers 29, 1 missing; non-commissioned officers 42, 12 missing; privates 361, 168 missing. Wounded—officers, 144; non-commissioned officers, 154; privates, 1,918. A number of the missing were afterwards found to have been killed. Total killed, wounded, and missing, 2,839. Our loss, for the numbers engaged, was far greater than that of our Allies.

The enemy's loss was something awful. They acknowledged a loss, from the 5th to the 8th September inclusive, of upwards of 25,000 officers, non-commissioned officers and men! Thus the final effort for the capture of this town cost in round numbers between 35,000 and 40,000 men. Such are some of the so-called "glories," but I would rather say "horrors" of war.

The Spoil.

The extent of the spoil captured by the Allies was almost incredible, notwithstanding all that the Russians had expended or destroyed. The cannon of various sizes numbered 3,840, 128 of which were brass (a great number had been thrown into the harbour, in order to avoid their being taken); round shot, 407,314; shell, 101,755; canister cases, 24,080; gunpowder, 525,000 lb; ball cartridges, 670,000 rounds, and other articles too numerous to mention. The spoil was equally divided between our people and our gallant Allies.

This mighty contest was, for the time it occupied and for the means employed on both sides, without a parallel. The vast resources of the British Empire had been largely drawn upon before haughty Russia could be humbled. The forces employed, the greater portion of which were carried there and back by the fleets of Old England, were as follows:—210,000 French, 105,000 British, 40,000 Turks, 15,000 Piedmontese, with 1500 guns, and over 80,000 horses, to say nothing of the enormous quantity of war material and food required for that great host. This force had been confronted by far more than an equal number of Russians. The annals of war have nothing to compare with it, and all former campaigns sink into insignificance.

Four great battles had been fought and won by the Allies, followed by an arduous and unparalleled siege of eleven months' duration, terminating in a glorious victory, and the total destruction of 118 ships of war, the capture of a fortress defended by 6,000 pieces of cannon, and

INTERIOR OF THE REDAN AFTER ITS CAPTURE

the final defeat of an army of 150,000 men which defended it. Old England may well be proud of her army and her navy, which enable her to bid defiance to the world.

Inside Sebastopol

The horrors inside the town, where the enemy had established their hospitals, baffle all description. Some of our non-commissioned officers and men went into those places, and described the scenes as heart-rending and revolting in the extreme. Many of the buildings were full of dead and dying mutilated bodies, without anyone to give them even a drink of water! Poor fellows, they had well defended their country's cause, and were now left to die in agony, unattended, uncared for, packed as closely as they could be stowed away, saturated with blood, and with the crash of the exploding forts all around them; they had served their *loving friend* and master, the *Czar*, but too well; there they lay, in a state of nudity, literally rolling in their blood.

Many, when our men found them, were past all aid, others were out of their mind, driven mad by pain and the appalling sights in the midst of which they were. Our officers and men, both French and English, found their way there indiscriminately, and at once set to work to relieve them; medical aid was brought as quickly as possible to them, but hundreds had passed beyond all earthly assistance.

Such a Sunday! Our men were struck with wonderment and horror at the awful scenes—

These were the horrors of war! Though a soldier and fully embued with the spirit of patriotism, I would say with all my heart, "From war good Lord deliver us." The man who delights in war is a *madman*; I would put him in the thick of it for just one day, and he would then know a little what war to the knife means. Our men, I am happy to relate, did everything they could for those of the enemy in whom a spark of life was found. Yes, the very men who only a few hours before had done all they could to destroy life, were now to be found, in their right minds, doing all that lay in their power for their unfortunate foes as well as friends.

A soldier, it matters not what his rank, must not for one moment, when engaged, think what the consequences are or may be. It is his duty to destroy all he can belonging to the enemy; in fact, he is often worked up to such a pitch that he becomes a perfect fiend, or, as the Russians called us at the Alma, "red devils in petticoats." None but men who are mad could do in cold blood the deeds that were performed by some of our men.

It is an old saying that *if anything is to be done let it be done well,* and—I must again repeat it—our men now set to work with a will to do all that lay in their power to rescue from an untimely end as many as they could. The sights on all sides melted to tears many veterans who had resolutely stormed the heights of Alma, rode up the valley of death at Balaclava, and stood as conquerors on the field of Inkermann, which names will never be forgotten as long as language endures. Many bodies were fast decomposing, and had to be interred at once—one common grave answered for both friend and foe. The ditch in front of the Redan was utilised for all who fell anywhere near it; those that fell in our trenches were buried there, the parapets being in both cases thrown upon them; the stench was almost unbearable for weeks afterwards.

Some two or three hundred rough-looking coffins were found in the town—they were full, it was supposed, of officers, but the enemy had not had time to bury them. A steamer came over from the north side on Monday, the 10th September, 1855, under a flag of truce, and begged to be allowed to remove the wounded. The request was at once granted, for our doctors were only too glad to get rid of them, as they had plenty in their own camps to attend to: a very great number of these poor fellows had been suffering intense agony for forty-eight hours, when, without even a drink of water, they were removed out of our sight.

All our wounded found in the town were carried as quickly as possible to camp; and then the men set to work to get what they could for themselves out of the midst of the ruins—set to work plundering, if you choose to call it so. But it was dangerous work, and many of them lost their limbs, and some their lives, through their foolishness, by the fire from the enemy across the harbour. Some who were laden with all sorts of articles were stopped by the officers, who wanted to know what they were going to do with all that rubbish. The men would at once throw down their loads and salute the officers, who repeated the question, "What on earth do you want with all that rubbish, my men?"

"An sure your 'onor don't we mane to let furnished lodgings!" They were carrying chairs, tables, bed-cots, in fact, articles too numerous to mention; "Sure, your 'onor, we are not going to let the *Zouaves* have it all!"

A stalwart Irish grenadier, when being rebuked for pilfering, an-

A street in Sebastopol after the siege

swered, "Sure, an your 'onor, them nice gentlemen they call *Zouaves* have been after emptying the place clane out; troth if the divil would kindly go to sleep for only one minute them *Zouaves* would stale one of his horns, if it was only useful to keep his coffee in." Truly these gentlemen were capital hands at fishing up all that was likely to beuseful. Some of our Hibernian boys had got a good haul, and were making off as fast as possible, when a party of *Zouaves* stopped them and wanted to go halves; but Paddy was not half such a fool as he was taken for—he would not give up anything until he had found out which was the best man, so the load was thrown down, and the Frenchmen were very soon satisfied and only too glad to get out of the way.

It was a common saying in camp that there was nothing too hot or too heavy for the *Zouaves* to walk off with, and where there was room for a rat there was room for one of these nimble little gentlemen to get in. They proved themselves all during the fighting troublesome customers to the enemy; and now that the fight was over they distinguished themselves by pilfering everything they could lay hands upon; but they did not get all—our huts were made very comfortable by the wood that our men brought out of the town. Although the second winter was far colder than the first, we had means to resist the cold with, any amount of clothing and good shelter, with plenty to eat and drink. By degrees our wounded began to recover so as to be able to walk about the camp, and to return to their duty; and had the war continued, we should have had upwards of 100,000 men in our army alone, to march against the enemy, but, thank God, it was ordered otherwise.

The following will prove that the enemy suffered a terrible loss during that long siege, particularly in the last three months that the town held out. The *Invalide Russe* (one of their principal papers), published their loss as follows; but I have every reason to believe that it is far below the truth. The report stated that in our final efforts to take Sebastopol from them, they suffered heavily; during the fifth bombardment, which was in August, 1855, they acknowledged a daily loss of 1,500 men, exclusive of officers; and then at the Tchernaya there was a loss of close upon 10,000 men dead and wounded—that was on the 16th August, 1855. It added that whole brigades' disappeared, and the interior of the town was nothing but a slaughter house or a hell upon earth; then it went on to say that they lost 1,000 men daily until the last or final bombardment, and further, their loss was 18,000 men, exclusive of officers, from the 5th to the 8th of September! We know that they lost nearly double that number.

It is bad enough to be on the conqueror's side, but what must it be to be on the side of the vanquished? The conquerors have something to keep up their spirits, but the defeated lack every source of consolation.

We knew well that a grateful and kind-hearted people in old England were watching every move we made. Mr. Bull does not mind how deeply he dives into his pocket, so long as he can sit with his pipe and glass over a good fire, and shout "We have beaten them again, my boys": and we had given Mr. Bull something to talk about now that Sebastopol had been taken. The bells of old England we knew would clash for joy, in peal after peal, at the news of the fall of this town. But there is another side to the picture. Many a good, kind, fond mother lost her son, perhaps her only son; thousands were left fatherless; hundreds were left to mourn absent husbands; and many a heart-rending scene in many a formerly happy home was brought about by this terrible war.

While in hospital wounded, I caused the following to be sent to my parents:—

Camp before the Ruins of Sebastopol,
September 14th, 1855.

My Dear, Dear Parents,

Thank God I have been saved alive through the grand but bloody struggle. You will see this is not my writing. I may as well tell you at once that they have hit me again. You will, most likely, see my name in the papers as badly wounded, but you must not despair; I am at present very comfortable in hospital, with one of my comrades to look after me, who now writes this from my dictation. I must tell you they hit me on the head, in two places, and knocked my left hand about rather badly, but I live in hopes of getting over this, and I will warm them for it if ever I get a chance.

Well, to my story. To start with, I am happy to inform you that the town is taken at last, but it has been, as I always said it would be, a hard nut to crack. I told you in my last that I did not think we should be long before we were let loose at it; everything was kept very quiet; the last, our grand bombardment, opened on the morning of the 5th, and the roaring of the heavy guns was something deafening. I went into the trenches on the night of the 6th; had a rough little bit of work on the night of the 7th; it was then that I began to smell a rat that something was in the wind; some of our poor fellows who had gone through the whole campaign were, by a mistake, shot down by their own comrades; I was in charge of the party, thirty odd men, and lost two-thirds of them in two or three minutes, through the men in the front trench not being informed that we were out.

I did not find out what was before me until I reached the camp about 1 a.m. on the terrible 8th. I cannot now describe that awful day's work which ended in a glorious victory. I find our loss and that of the French has been frightful; it is reported that our united loss has been upwards of 12,000, killed, wounded, and missing. I do hope that this will be the last item in the butcher's bill. If we are to have any more fighting let's go at them in the open field, and then if our numbers are anywhere near theirs we will soon let you know who will take possession; they fight well behind earthworks, but they want a lot of Dutch courage into them to make them show up in the open field. I hope you will be contented with what I have said; I must not do anymore today; I must keep quiet.

Well, I've had a few hours' rest and I feel that I should like to bring this letter to a close; and will, if I am spared, give you a long account of that terrible fight that laid Sebastopol at our feet, and I am proud to say that a great number of Norfolk and Suffolk men have helped to plant our glorious old flag on the bloodstained walls of that far-famed town, Sebastopol. It was a Norfolk man that led us to the finishing stroke (Windham), and right well he did it—it was, 'Come on, boys, and I will show you the way!' The fighting, dear Parents, in the interior of the Redan was desperate; when I come to recall it, it seems almost too much for me.

I cannot express my gratitude to the King of Kings and Lord of Lords, who shielded my life,—I hope for some good purpose,—on those bloody parapets, when my poor comrades fell like Autumn leaves all around, to rise no more. It seemed utterly impossible that any could escape; and we had a great number of very young men with us who had come out with drafts to fill up the gaps. But they were too young for the trying work, many of them had not seen seventeen summers; plenty of them had not had two months' service. We wanted 20,000 tried veterans; but through some mismanagement they were kept back. I will write again as soon as I get a little more strength—so cheer up, dear parents.

Tell Tom he had better eat some more beef and dumplings before ever he thinks of soldiering; one in a family is quite enough to be shot at, at a time. Tell poor mother to cheer up, I will come home to Norwich some day, and give her as warm a greeting as the Frenchmen gave me at Malta. I must now conclude. Give my kind regards to all inquiring friends, and believe me, dear parents.

    Your affectionate son,
    T. Gowing,
    Sergeant, Royal Fusiliers.

P. S.—What a lot of nonsense they put in the papers—it's only filling up stuff, or, in plain language, boast. Men had far better not write at all, if they cannot confine themselves to the truth; for they only get laughed at, as the papers are read in the camp. Please send Illustrated.

    Yours, &c..
    T. G.

CHAPTER 12

After the Siege

THE CRIMEAN ARMY.

The following was the composition of the various divisions of the Crimean Army:—

Cavalry Division.

1st, 4th, and 5th Dragoon Guards, 1st, 2nd, and 6th Dragoons—Heavy Brigade.
6th Dragoon Guards, 4th and 13th Light Dragoons, 12th Lancers, 8th, 10th, and 11th Hussars, and 17th Lancers—Two Light Brigades.

First Division.

3rd Batt. Grenadier Guards, 1st Batt. Coldstream Guards, 1st Batt. Scots Fusiliers Guards—First Brigade.
9th, 13th, 31st, and 56th Foot—Second Brigade.

Highland Division.

42nd, 79th, 92nd, 93rd—First Brigade.
1st-2nd Batt. 1st Foot, 71st, 91st and 72nd—Second Brigade.

Second Division.

3rd, 30th, 55th, and 95th Foot—First Brigade.
41st, 47th, 49th, 62nd, and 82nd—Second Brigade.

Third Division.

4th, 14th, 39th, 50th, and 89th Foot—First Brigade.
18th, 28th, 38th, and 44th Foot—Second Brigade.

Fourth Division.

17th, 20th, 21st, 57th, and 63rd Foot—First Brigade.
46th, 48th, 68th, 1st Batt. Rifle Brigade—Second Brigade.

Light Division,

7th Royal Fusiliers, 23rd Royal Welsh Fusiliers, 33rd, 34th, and 2nd Batt. Rifle Brigade—First Brigade.
19th, 77th, 88th, 90th, and 97th Foot— Second Brigade.

Artillery,
Royal Horse Artillery, A. C. and I. Troops
Batteries A. B. E. F. G. H. I. Q. W. Y. and Z
Engineers.
Companies 1, 2, 3, 4, 7, 8, 9, 10, and 11,
Loss of English Horses in six months, during the winters of 1854 and 1855—Strength, 5048, Died, 2122.

The remainder of September and October, 1855, passed off pretty quietly. After the dead had been buried and the wounded removed to camp, our commanders were at liberty to turn their thoughts towards the enemy still on the north side of the harbour; the south side was well guarded by British troops and those of our allies (the French). There were as yet no signs of peace; we were still frowning at each other across the water. The enemy's fleets had all been sent to the bottom, but the booming of their heavy guns told us that although defeated the Muscovites were not yet subdued, and that if we wanted the north side we should have to fight for it. Our people were now making preparations for destroying the huge forts, barracks, and docks of Sebastopol. This had sometimes to be carried on under a heavy fire from the north side, but still the work did not cease.

Not a day passed without our losing a number of men and some good officers. By the end of October many of our wounded began to recover and to return to their duties; some, discharged from hospital convalescent, might be seen walking about the camps with their arms in splints, or with their heads bandaged, others limping about with the assistance of a stick or crutch—but all appeared in high spirits. That indomitable British pluck had been in no wise quenched, in spite of the wounds that had been received. Our men were burning to have another "shy" at the enemy on a grand scale, in order to wipe out the stain of the repulse at the Redan, although that was not all their fault. The first anniversary of the Alma was kept in camp in grand style, as far as our means would allow, and wine was sent to all the wounded Alma men then in hospital.

When we looked back, what an eventful twelve months that had been! Victory after victory had been added to our already long and glorious roll; but, alas! where were the noble sons of Britain who had gained them? Had all fallen? Had all been food for powder or succumbed to the deadly thrust of the bayonet? No! Hundreds, yea thousands, had been sacrificed by cruel hardships—little or no food, hardly sufficient clothing to cover their nakedness, in the trenches for twelve hours at a stretch, up to their ankles (or sometimes knees) in mud, half drowned, frozen to death, their limbs dropping off through frostbite! There is hardly one of those men now living (*at time of original publication*), who does not feel the effects of that terrible winter of 1854.

Thousands have since perished, through diseases contracted during that awful time; but the excitement, supported by an invincible spirit, kept them up then and for some time after. The first anniversary of Balaclava and Inkermann found me still in hospital, slowly recovering, able to walk about, but very shaky. Inkermann was another anniversary duly observed by the whole army. We had by this time got into capital huts, and had plenty of good clothing, in fact, more than we could stand under; and we had as much food as we required—thousands of tons of potted beef, mutton, and all kinds of vegetables, having been sent out by the kind-hearted people at home.

Indeed, it looked very much as though we were being fattened before being let loose at the enemy again. We could now almost bid defiance to a Russian winter. Each man's wardrobe consisted of the following:—A tunic, well lined with flannel; a shell-jacket, well lined; a fur coat, a rough sandbag coat, a summer coat, made of tweed; an overcoat, a waterproof coat that came below the knees, a forage cap and a fur cap, two pairs of cloth trousers, one sandbag ditto, one pair of waterproof leggings, two pairs of ankle boots, one pair of long ditto to go outside the trousers and come nearly up to the fork; three woollen jerseys, three linen shirts, two pairs of good flannel drawers, three ditto worsted stockings, and two cholera belts made of flannel.

It would have been rather a difficult matter to find out what regiment a man belonged to. The greater portion of these things had been sent us by our sympathising fellow countrymen and countrywomen; and we who received them were deeply grateful for the kindness shown. Had those gallant men who fought and conquered at the Alma, rode through and through the enemy on the plains of Balaclava, rolled their proud legions back time after time from the heights of Inkermann, and sent them headlong into Sebastopol in indescribable confusion—had they been supplied with one quarter of the clothing that we now had, we should have had them with us to help to storm the Redan, and a far different tale would have been told.

The Bells of Old England would have clashed again for victory, as at the Alma, Balaclava, and Inkermann. But, alas! the bones of the greater portion of those victorious Britons were rotting in the Valley of Death—

I must not leave this subject without just reminding the reader that the sick and wounded in the Crimea owed much to gentle English ladies, who bravely came out as nurses, but foremost amongst this devoted band was one whose name has since remained a synonym for kindly sympathy, tenderness, and grace—Miss Florence Nightingale.

Chapter 13

Sergeant Walsh's Crimea Experience

The following will, we trust, prove interesting to all classes of the community:—

On the memorable foggy morning of November 5th, 1854, I went on picquet with my company. No. 1 of the Royal Fusiliers, to relieve a company of the Royal Welsh, in the Whitehouse ravine. An officer of the 77th[1] commanded us, as we had not sufficient officers of our own, after our heavy loss at the Alma. We arrived at our post about the usual hour (a little before daylight), and relieved the Royal Welsh, who retired a short distance to wait for clear daylight before returning to camp—a practice observed when in presence of an enemy. Shortly afterwards our sentries came running in with the news that the enemy were advancing in great force.

Our officer at once disposed his picquet to the best advantage to resist them. They were soon upon us in overwhelming numbers, but were received with a fire that staggered them. The Royal Welsh at once rushed to our assistance; every rock and stone was hotly disputed, and the enemy received such a warm reception that they were compelled to fall back for a time. All ranks in the two Fusilier companies seemed to vie with each other in deeds of valour. This was only the first scene in that unequal contest that no native in our sea-girt isle need blush at, but remember with pride. The picquets on our right, composed of the Second Division, fought with desperation, hurling the Muscovites over the rocks in grand style.

It has been acknowledged by all ranks that the picquets thin

---

1. Lieutenant Bott.

morning nobly did their duty, and checked the massive Muscovite drunken columns until the main body of our army had time to get under arms. The cool intrepidity of a mere handful of men had saved the allied army; our principal magazine was just in our rear, and our orders were to hold this position to the last, and then retire to the five-gun battery; the massive columns of the enemy were gradually forcing back the picquet on our right, who retired in good order, disputing every inch of ground, but compelled to leave their poor wounded comrades behind, who were bayoneted to a man by the cruel enemy.

Our flank was now exposed, and the enemy got in rear of us, unobserved in the dense fog. As soon as we found that we were surrounded, we were ordered to make the best of our way towards the five-gun battery; a general rush was made in that direction, the enemy pouring volley after volley into us. A number of our poor fellows were shot dead or wounded. The wounded who were found afterwards were all bayoneted. I was in the act of loading when a number of them rushed at me with the bayonet. I at once fired, and one of the enemy fell. I was the next moment knocked down with the butt end and stunned.

When I came to, I found my arms tied behind me. They hurried me off under a strong escort. I had not proceeded far when I found they had another of the picquet, a corporal of the Royal Welsh. His arms were bound in like manner. We had not gone many yards when one of the cowardly brutes shot him dead. Every moment I expected the same treatment; but, thank God, my escort were more merciful (being Poles). I was taken to that part of the field where all the Russian staff were stationed. I was surprised when I arrived to see a number of my comrades of the Whitehouse ravine picquet; the officer (Captain Duff, Royal Welsh Fusiliers) and twenty of his men had been cut off, and taken, likewise seven of the Royal Fusiliers. I did not now feel so lonely; the officer who commanded our company was also taken, but his escort marched him towards Sebastopol. As soon as he got clear of the enemy's columns, he took out his revolver from an inside pocket of his overcoat, knocked the man down on his right senseless, shot the one on his left dead, and the third man at once surrendered himself his prisoner, whom he brought into our camp.

Most of the prisoners taken were shamefully treated, particularly the captain of the 23rd R.W. His uniform was torn off his back, and he was robbed of all articles of value, but recovered them by explaining in French to a general officer, and pointing out the men who had robbed him. The general gave them all a good thrashing, which quite amused us; but we soon found that this was a usual practice, the senior boxing the ear of the junior. During the whole of that dreadful day we were kept under fire from our own little army.

The attacking columns of the enemy were driven back with fearful slaughter. Liquor *vodkie* was freely used, until they were mad drunk. But, drunk or sober, our comrades hurled them back from the field time after time. Their princes and generals were mad with rage, to see their huge columns driven from the field, time after time, by a mere handful of men (they knew our strength); they were in such a rage we expected every moment they would turn upon us defenceless prisoners.

The attacking columns of the enemy numbered thirty thousand men, and their supports and reserves thirty thousand more. These columns were in such a state of disorder from the repeated vehement charges of the British that they had not the slightest chance of victory. They were nothing more nor less than a confused and enraged mob. Our men, and the French, who had come up to our assistance, continued pouring volley after volley into them, and some of our heavy siege guns were ploughing roads through them. Their loss at this stage of the battle was enormous. Their massive columns of supports and reserves were mowed down wholesale, until the dead lay in heaps.

When the retreat of this confused and enraged Muscovite mob commenced we expected every moment to be despatched by these well-thrashed drunken brutes. They carried as many of their wounded away as possible. Noticing the confusion all round, the captain of the 23rd passed the word for us to make a dash for our liberty, saying, "We can but die, my boys." We instantly got on the alert, but our good intentions were stopped. We were then doubly guarded, and hurried from the field. The retreat was in no formation, but a complete rabble, our huge Lancaster guns cutting lanes through them.

There was but one column we saw leave the field in anything like order. We were a little on their flank, when an officer of the leading company perceived us. He came over to us and addressed us in good English as follows, "Well, Englishmen, if you are prisoners, there is one consolation for you, you have given us a sound good thrashing today," and then rejoined his company. As soon as he left, our captain said, "Men, I believe that officer to be an English gentleman serving in the Russian army, and is delighted his countrymen have gained such a glorious victory."

The enemy captured no more prisoners, except a few wounded who escaped being bayoneted, and those were placed in carts with other wounded. I was one of those appointed to look after the poor wounded. My care was a Guardsman, shot under the left breast, passing out under the left shoulder blade; the poor fellow was bleeding inwardly, and I had to keep him in a sitting position. We were at this time in the centre of the retiring mass, when a wounded Russian drummer tried to get into the cart, and, in endeavouring to do so, placed his arm on the wounded knee of one of the men of the 47th whose kneecap had been shot away. He instantly struck the wounded Russian under the chin and sent him headlong amongst his retiring comrades. We then made sure that we should be all bayoneted; but no, all the pluck and *vodkie* was fairly thrashed out of them.

In crossing to the north side of Sebastopol on bridges of boats, the enemy suffered dreadfully. Our heavy siege guns mowed them down wholesale. How we escaped was a miracle. Our officer spoke to some of the Russian officers about our wounded, and one in particular he wished a doctor to see at once, *viz.*, the Guardsman. Our officer's request was quickly attended to; a doctor dressed the poor fellow's wound, passing a long piece of lint through the wound right through his body, causing the blood to flow outwards, not inwards. After the doctor had finished dressing the poor fellow, he said to our officer in French, "I thought the Russians were soldiers, but I never witnessed anything like this in the Russian army; I really believe an Englishman would bear to be cut to pieces and show no symptoms of pain." This poor fellow during the operation did not show the slightest symptom of pain.

Our wounded were sent into hospital in Sebastopol; not one of them left there alive, at least we never heard of them again. The whole of the night after the battle the handful of prisoners (thirty) were marched through their camp from regiment to regiment, and from one division to another, to exhibit to their troops what a great capture they had made. We had a little kindness showed us by these heathen Muscovites; they brought us some of their *vodkie*, but nothing to eat, which we wanted most. We had had nothing to eat up to the present. Next day we were placed in Fort Paul, and kept there three days. It was not till the third day, the 8th, that we received anything to eat. On the second day the two Grand Dukes visited us, and questioned us respecting our army, trying to pump all they could out of us. But the sucker was dry.

An old general said, "You think to deceive us, but we can tell even to the conversation that takes place in your tents." When they had done questioning us, the two Grand Dukes Constantine and St. Michael addressed us as follows, "We must admit that England is possessed of the finest infantry in Europe, but we do not care for your cavalry or artillery;" and informed us that we should next day commence our march to the place appointed for us while we were their prisoners, which place was about 1500 miles from Sebastopol; that we should find the people of the country very hospitable; also that we were classified,— the English first-class prisoners, French second, Turks third; and would receive allowance for support accordingly.

Before they left us we reported that we had had nothing to eat since taken. They said that we should have something at once, and gave instructions accordingly, but, nevertheless, we did not receive any till next day. We commenced this long and dreary march under great disadvantage, and with a Russian winter to contend against. We were very poorly clad, our clothing and boots nearly worn out, working in the trenches night and day, and our hardships were terrible to relate. We were allowed ten *kopeks* daily, which is equal to four-pence. Every article of food in Russia is very cheap, but they imposed on us, as we did not know the language, therefore we were nearly starved.

Our first halt was at Peracoff; here we remained a few days, and then proceeded to Simperopol. We had a few days halt here, and were joined by thirty Turks, taken at Balaclava. The whole of us here received one sheepskin coat and one pair of long boots, the only articles of clothing given to us whilst we were prisoners until the day of our exchange, when we received an overcoat and cap, similar to those worn by their infantry. We marched from Simperopol with a gang of convicts for Siberia. It was pitiful to see the way they were treated. They were classified according to crime. Some had the whole of their hair shaved off the front part of the head, the remainder left long; others the right half of the head shaved, some the left half shaved, and others the back part of the head. All wore irons on their legs, male and female. They were placed in two ranks at three paces apart.

A long chain was placed between them, one rank handcuffed by the right hand to this chain, the other rank by the left. Each of the prisoners had a certain number of lashes to receive annually during the term of imprisonment, of which they received a number daily before they marched. We witnessed this punishment. Every morning the culprit was placed face downwards on the ground, two soldiers held him or her whilst another administered the punishment with birch rods tied together. We often pitied them this long march, with the irons cutting to the very bone; the blood marking the prints in the snow.

These poor creatures, we were told, scarcely ever reach their destination. In every large town we picked up fresh convicts, whilst others were left behind to die. I often thanked God that I was born under the British flag. Every day's march was very nearly alike, except when entering large towns. Our guard sent word ahead to acquaint the inhabitants about the time of our arrival, and we were met at the entrance to the town by large crowds of people; some of whom spit at us and called us English dogs. I must say that the people who offered these insults to us were of the poor and ignorant class. The better class treated us with much civility, and visited us in prison after our arrival, and obtained permission from the Governor to take us out to dine with them. The gentry and middle class admired the English prisoners for their fine military bearing, and often compared us with their own slovenly soldiers.

We continued our march day after day, till we arrived at their University town, Kharcoff, a magnificent place with any number of colleges. We had a week's halt here, and were visited by many of our own country people and French people, all in good positions. Some of them were professors of languages in the colleges. We were out visiting daily; we likewise received a great many presents from our people, and from French and Russian gentry, in the shape of warm clothing, woollen and leather gloves, tea, and sugar, and a few roubles each. We had completed 500 miles, and during that long march seldom had a hot meal. This we mentioned to the Governor of Kharcoff prison. He asked us what our usual meals consisted of. We told him bread and butter.

"Well," he said, "You can have a change; have butter and bread today, and bread and butter tomorrow." This was all the pity we got from this gentleman. We received good news here. It got to the knowledge of our Government that we were badly off, and nearly starving with the small amount allowed us to live upon. Our Government requested the Emperor to raise our allowance to twenty *kopeks* daily—this is equal to eight-pence—and we were usually paid this allowance seven days in advance. We had now plenty of food, and picking up a little of their language, were able to make our purchases without being imposed upon; but the cold at night was something terrible.

We were allowed no covering of any sort, and nothing but our wet clothing to lie down in. Sometimes a little wet straw would be thrown in to keep us from the bare ground, after a long fatiguing march. Often the snow would be two or three feet deep. We left a number of men behind in towns where there would be a hospital, frost-bitten. Shortly after leaving Kharcoff, one day our march was thirty *versts* (a *verst* is three-quarters of a mile English).

On the morning before starting we were paid our seven days' allowance. We had completed half the distance, when an occurrence happened which was near the cause of us all visiting Siberia with our chain gang. There was what we call a halfway house here, and not another house within three *versts*. Our guard acquainted us of this, and told us we could have anything we wanted in the way of *vodkie*. We were delighted at this, for the snow at the time was over two feet deep, and hot grog was quite acceptable. The whole of the prisoners, Turks excepted, had refreshments, the guards receiving the same at our (the English) expense.

All went as merry as a marriage bell till the French did not want to stop any longer, but push on, and complete the journey. Our guard did not feel inclined to do 60, and we were of their opinion. The French would persist in marching, and made a start to go by themselves. The guard would not allow them till all marched together, and struck one of the French on the head with the butt end of his rifle, knocking him down. Although we were on good terms with the guard, we could not see our allies, the French, beaten; so at it we went, a regular hand to hand fight, the Turks remaining quietly looking on. The guard used their rifles and bayonets freely, we and the French our sticks. We disarmed our guard, and broke their rifles and bayonets, after giving them a good thrashing.

Both sides had their casualties: one Frenchman, three English, and seven Russians had to be taken to the next town in carts, and placed in hospital. One Russian was very badly wounded, his jaw-bone being broken. Had we been near a village not one of us would have told the tale. Another lucky thing for us was that the guard had sent on their ammunition with their knapsacks. The surrounding villagers had to be summoned to escort us to the next town, armed with every description of weapon they could lay their hands upon, such as pitchforks, reap-hooks, scythes, &c. (This was the result of indulging in *vodkie*.) The next day the affair was investigated by a Russian officer or magistrate. After hearing the guard's statement, he told us we should all be sent to Siberia; but we turned the tables on the guard.

One of the French asked the officer if he spoke French, and being answered in the affirmative, the Frenchman explained all truthfully as above quoted, and the guard came off second best. The magistrate, when in possession of the true facts, had the whole of the guard placed in irons, and sent back under escort whence they came.

We had then a fresh escort, commanded by an officer, but were deprived of our sticks for the remainder of the march, as they considered us dangerous even with that weapon. The weather was now getting more severe every day, which contributed a great deal to our hardships, having often to face a blinding, drifting snow all day, and then lie down in our frozen clothing. We still continued to receive great kindness from the better class of Russians. In due course we arrived in Veronidge, a distance of 1,500 miles from Sebastopol. We remained here until our exchange took place.

We were all located in a large house expressly taken for our quarters. A guard mounted daily over us, and we were allowed our liberty through the town, but had to be in our quarters at night. We had no work to do, and the gentlefolk of Veronidge vied with each other in having us at their homes to eat and sup with them. I must say that we were very comfortable here until bed time came. We had no bedding of any sort except a little straw, and our clothing was nothing but a bundle of rags. We were not very long here before we were supplied with a good suit of uniform by our countrymen, residents in Russia. The clothing was nearly a facsimile of our own.

Our men now looked quite smart with this new rig-out, and the inhabitants of the town seemed to admire us. We were not long before each of us had his sweetheart. After a time another party of English prisoners arrived, men who had recovered from sickness, who had been left behind on the road. Of course we must repair to a public-house to have a meeting glass. It was night time when four of us went in to enjoy ourselves, all peaceably inclined. We found the house full of Russian soldiers. We had only partaken of one glass when they insulted and struck us, but the white feather was not to be shown here anymore than on former occasions, no matter what their strength might be.

As soon as the Russians commenced the disturbance one of our men extinguished the lights: this added greatly to our advantage, as the enemy were numerous, and pitched into each other in the darkness. Our small party being equal to the occasion, one of them broke up a sleigh (a cart without wheels). I got possession of a portion of this and my comrades the remainder, which we used in good style, and soon cleared the house; upon our opponents gaining the street others quickly came to their assistance. One of them made a thrust at me with a sword. I warded it off my head, but received a wound in the right hand. The fellow who delivered the cut the next moment was biting the dust.

I was as unfortunate here as at Inkermann—was taken prisoner, and conveyed to the police-station, covered with blood from my own wound, as well as that of our adversaries. Next morning I looked much like a man just coming out of a slaughter-yard. I was taken before the magistrates just as I was, not being allowed to wash. The court was well filled with military officers.

I had not the slightest knowledge what the charge preferred against me was, being ignorant of their language. The magistrate believed every word of the witnesses against me, left his seat on the bench, came forward to me, and was in the act of slapping my face (a usual custom with their own prisoners), when I at once placed myself in position to resist it (a fighting attitude, English style).

This took the old gentleman by surprise, and set the whole court in roars of laughter, the military officers in particular. He retired a few paces, cursing and swearing at me, and again came forward to strike me. I again placed myself in defence; the laughter was greater than before. He never expected this from a prisoner. He had been used to despotic authority with his own people. He immediately sentenced me to seven days' imprisonment with black bread and water, and 500 lashes at the expiration of my imprisonment. I had done six days of it, when, fortunately for me, a general officer was sent from the Emperor Nicholas to visit the prisoners, and to ascertain if we were treated according to his instructions.

I was brought out of my cell to muster with the remainder, to show the number the authorities were issuing pay for. There is no trust to be placed in any Russian in authority; they rob each other from the highest to the lowest. This state of things is pretty well known, but through their despotic laws cannot be stopped. (The Emperor Nicholas once said to an English nobleman, he believed he was the only honest man in Russia.) The general asked us several questions as to the amount of pay we received, and if we received it regularly, and how we were treated by the authorities. I took a pace to my front and saluted him in English military style, which took his fancy, as the salute of the Russian soldier is to stand cap in hand when addressing an officer.

I asked him if he would allow me to have a word or two with him, which was at once granted. I explained what had occurred, and how I was treated by the very gentleman standing by his side, and also the sentence he passed upon me, that I had one day more to finish my confinement on black bread and water, when I should receive the corporal punishment of 500 lashes. The officer seemed delighted with my explanation, and the straightforward manner in which I told him everything. He at once placed his hand on my shoulder, and said, "You are a fine fellow, you are a good soldier; I remit the remainder of your punishment; you are released, join your comrades." I have not the slightest doubt that the 500 lashes would have killed me. This is one instance of the severity of their despotic laws.

One day on going to the bazaar, or market, with a comrade of my own regiment, we had to pass through a large square, and in this were mustered 15,000 men, new levies to join the army in the Crimea. Clergymen were present blessing their new colours, and also giving them their blessing previous to marching. One of the soldiers saluted my comrade with the compliments of the day, which he politely returned. Another of them deliberately spit in his face, calling him an "English dog,"

The words were hardly uttered by him when my comrade, a powerfully built man, knocked the fellow down like a bullock in their midst. We were instantly surrounded by numbers of them, and would soon have been made short work of only for the timely interference of an officer, who had witnessed the whole. This officer, with sword drawn, stepped in between us and them, and ordered them to stand back and clear the way for us to pass, saying at the same time to my comrade (malidates), "you are a fine fellow." Instances like this show plainly, no matter how British soldiers are situated, that indomitable pluck cannot be stamped out of them.

During our stay in Veronidge a police officer was appointed our paymaster. He was very irregular in issuing our pay or allowance. On one occasion he left us fourteen days in arrear. The consequence was we were in distress. We all marched in military order to his quarters and formed in line in front of his house. When he observed us he made his appearance at his front door, enquiring our business there, and came forward towards the right of the line. A tall, powerfully built Irishman, belonging to the 4th R. I. Dragoon Guards, stood on the extreme right, seemingly taking very little notice of what was going on, as we had appointed one to make our complaint. He walked straight up to this dragoon, and gave him a slap in the face.

The blow was no sooner delivered than the dragoon returned the compliment with a straight one from the shoulder. He fell as if he had a kick from a horse. In an instant a number of police rushed forward to arrest the dragoon, but we were equal to the occasion, and would not allow him to be arrested. This caused the affair to be officially reported and duly investigated, when it was proved the police officer was at fault. They cancelled his appointment, and severely reprimanded him; and also issued a *ukase* (a special order from the *Czar*) that no Russian officer was in future to attempt to strike an English soldier, as it was not a custom in the English army for officers to strike their men; and the Russian officer that struck an Englishman must put up with the consequence.

This order had the desired effect, for they never attempted it after this. The daily papers took it up, it ran thus, "the French are too polite to kick up a row, the Turks too frightened, but the English are neither one or the other. Whenever they think they are insulted or imposed upon, they resent it in grand style, no matter the odds against them." We were informed by an English gentleman of an occurrence that took place in St. Petersburg, with one of our officers, a prisoner of war, who was in company with a Russian gentleman of rank, walking in the streets, when he was met by a Russian noble, who grossly insulted him, and spit in his face. It was at once resented in true English style; our officer's friend made it known to the *Czar,* who had this brave noble summoned before him.

The *Czar* said, "I am informed you very much dislike the English, that you have already given proof of the same, by insulting an English officer and gentleman. I require such people as you; you shall have a good opportunity of giving vent to your dislike, you will be deprived of rank, all your property confiscated, and join immediately our army at Sebastopol, as a private soldier." This is another instance of their despotic laws. We might well say, "O! England with all thy faults I love thee still."

After a few months stay at Veronidge, we were visited a second time by an officer of rank from St. Petersburg. He informed us that our exchange had been arranged, and that we should start next day for Odessa. The names of all the prisoners were called over, and those cowardly ruffians called deserters, separated from the men lawfully taken in action. Addressing the latter, he said, "I am commissioned by our Government to inform you, that any who wish to remain can do so; all who remain in our country will receive two years' pay at the same rate as you receive now, a piece of ground will be given you, and house rent free for your lives; should you marry and have children they will be all free subjects of Russia."

After coaxing us a little time, he said, "Step to the front all who wish to remain in Russia." I am proud to say not a man embraced the offer. He next addressed the deserters, informing them that they were at liberty to return to their own people. At the same time he reminded them of the severity of the English martial law against deserters. "It is death, as no doubt you are aware. When peace is settled, you will be sent to some country where your own language is spoken; you will not be allowed to remain in Russia; you are traitors to your own country, and no ornament to ours."

Two of the deserters stepped to the front, and expressed a wish to return to their own army. He again reminded them of the consequence. One man said he did not care, that he would sooner be blown away from the guns of his own army than stay a day longer in their d——d country. The other man was of the same opinion. These two men returned with us, and strange to say neither of them were deserters, but out of their lines skirmishing for grog, lost their way and got nabbed by the enemy's outposts, but through some mistake of the Russians were returned as deserters. The punishment awarded them was, on rejoining, to forfeit their pay and service whilst in the hands of the Russians.

We did not march this time, but were conveyed in cars covering from ninety to one hundred miles *per diem*, changing horses every twenty-five miles. We were not long before we arrived at Odessa; there were ninety of us all told, but only fifty fighting men, the remainder being camp followers. But the crafty Muscovite returned them all as English soldiers and exchanged as such. We had to remain a few days in Odessa for a ship to receive us. One morning whilst there, the combined fleets of England and France assembled before the town, and a small steamer with a flag of truce put off from the fleet. She was met by one from Odessa also bearing a truce; this was to give notice to the authorities that the Allied fleets would open fire on the town next morning.

When this information was announced to the inhabitants, I never shall forget the confusion that followed, old and young, rich and poor, male and female, carrying their movable property inland, out of the range of fire. The whole town was lighted up with torch lights, to enable the soldiers and press-gang to erect barricades in the streets. The authorities at Odessa at once wired to Kinburn for assistance. A strong force was at once put in motion from that garrison, which was three days' march from the threatened town. Next morning not a ship of war was to be seen; all disappeared during the night. The force from Kinburn had just got half way when the bombarding of that town could be distinctly heard.

This was a capital game of war-chess by the Allied fleets. They had no intention of bombarding Odessa from the first, British and French capital being largely invested there, but it had the desired effect of weakening the Kinburn garrison. After bombarding the forts in grand style for a couple of hours, troops were lauded and the garrison surrendered. Next day the Agamemnon came to Odessa for us in all the majesty of war, when we were duly handed over, and right royally did these Trafalgar Lambs and Nile Chickens treat us. She at once steamed off to Kemish Bay and landed us, where we were directed to find our respective regiments, and once more faced the enemy till the conclusion of the war. I need hardly say we got a warm reception from all ranks on rejoining from those who had escaped the carnage of war during our absence from the front.

James Walsh,
Sergeant, 7th Royal Fusiliers.

CHAPTER 14

Lieut. Hope and the 7th Fusiliers

But I must proceed. We were, as I have said, now very comfortable. Sir W. Codrington, the former commander of the First Brigade of the Light Division, was appointed our commander-in-chief in the beginning of November, 1855. Sir William had no sooner assumed the command than a terrible catastrophe occurred, that for a time threatened to destroy the whole of the old Light Division. About 3.30 p.m. on the 14th November, our camp was startled by a terrible explosion close to the Fusiliers' Hospital. We could not conceive what was up, but all at once, shot, shell, grape, canister, &c., were sent flying in all directions.

One of the principal magazines in the French artillery park, just in rear of us, had exploded. Some hundreds of guns that had been captured from the enemy—some loaded with shot, some with shell, some with grape, and pointed in all directions—had been fired by the heat or the concussion, sending death and destruction all around for upwards of a mile.

Wounded men were killed as they lay, and others wounded again. Some 500 shell were up in the air at one time, and about 60,000 ball cartridges were flying about the camp like hail. Huts were smashed to pieces and tents blown into the air. A number of poor fellows were so shattered that we could not tell who they were, or what regiment they belonged to.

Our Allies suffered heavily. Their loss was 19 officers, and nearly 400 non-commissioned officers and men killed and wounded. Our loss, in a few seconds, was 5 officers and 116 non-commissioned officers and men.

It was truly a horrible scene—men going about with baskets or *skeps*, picking up the remains of their comrades who had been blown to atoms. But, even in the midst of all this, men could be found ready to face almost certain death. A large windmill close by had been converted into a powder magazine by our people. Close upon 200 tons of powder and other explosives were lodged in it; the roof, doors, and windows were blown in, and the contents thus exposed, with tons of powder going off, and hundreds of rockets flying in all directions. The peril was imminent. Had one spark dropped into the mill, or had one of the fiery rockets fallen or burnt into it, another explosion would have ensued, and all within a radius of at least half a mile must have been destroyed.

In the midst of the excitement, General Straubenzee exclaimed: "If the mill goes up, all is lost." Then, he called, in a voice of thunder, for volunteers from the 7th Royal Fusiliers, for an enterprise more hazardous than a forlorn hope—to climb the walls of the powder mill, and to cover it with tarpaulins and wet blankets. "It must be done, or all is lost!"

Lieutenant Hope, and 25 men of the Fusiliers, immediately stepped to the front, and the gallant Lieutenant led his Fusiliers up to the top of the mill and covered it; while another party, consisting of men of the 34th regiment, the 2nd Battalion Rifle Brigade, and artillerymen, courageously volunteered to block up the doors and windows with sandbags.

Lieutenant Hope was presented with the Victoria Cross for his conduct,—and he deserved it. But surely every man of that noble band ought to have had something, if not the Cross! Had the mill gone up, our hospital, huts, and marquees, would have been destroyed, with every wounded and unwounded man in or near them, as we were only about 300 yards from the scene. As it was, we lost several men in killed and wounded, and would probably have lost many more, but for the fact that the greater portion were out on fatigue some three miles away.

One man who has within the last few years made himself famous was dangerously wounded that day—Lieutenant F. C. Roberts, now Lieutenant General Sir F. C. Roberts, V.C. Thank God, I escaped once more, although it seemed as if all would have been destroyed. Our camping ground was covered with fragments of shell, and musket balls lay about in thousands. The hut that I should most likely have been in, had I not been in hospital, was blown to pieces with shell, the only man in it being dangerously wounded.

Once more I wrote home as follows:—

Camp before the Ruins of Sebastopol,
26th December, 1855.

My Dear Parents,

Just a few lines from this cold, bleak corner once more. I am happy to inform you that, thanks to the good people at home, we had a good day yesterday; Christmas was kept up in camp in grand style, with plenty of good beef and pudding, and a good fire or two in our huts; the day passed off very comfortably, the only drawback being that both the geese intended for my subdivision of the company, were walked off with by some hungry Frenchman—the *Zouaves* got the credit of it. I for one hope they did them good, as we had plenty to eat without them.

It's bitterly cold, but we have all got plenty of warm clothing and waterproofs, and can almost bid defiance even to a Crimean winter. If last year we had only had half what we now have, many an aching heart at home would be rejoicing, for men whose bones are now rotting in the valley of Death, would most likely have been with us.

Our men look well and cheerful. We have got all sorts of things out of the town, and are making ourselves quite at home; the enemy treat us now and again to a long ranger, just to let us know, I suppose, that we did not kill them all on the 8th September. I have done no duty yet, am still convalescent, my arm is in a sling and so is my head, but I am happy to inform you that I am getting on capitally, I must not walk about much, as it's so slippery. There is any amount of life in the camp, and plenty of books to read; a great number of the men who have been wounded keep returning to their duty, and I do believe in the spring we shall march to the north side the Russians to bleed, that is, if they do not get out of the way.

Our men are kept well in exercise, marching out two or three times a week, from ten to fifteen miles at a time; it would amuse you or anyone else, to see our men returning to camp with icicles, some of them six or seven inches long, hanging to their beards and moustaches, but yet we have capital health. I have had two or three attempts at this letter. I hope you will be able to make out this scrawl. My hand, I am sorry to inform you, is very painful just now; the wounds in my head are rapidly healing. I hope you will not forget me at the Throne of Grace. I must now conclude.

Believe me ever, Dear Parents,
Your affectionate Son,
T. Gowing,
Sergeant, Royal Fusiliers.

A Few Facts.

The following facts may be of interest. According to the statement of one in high position just after the war was over, Russia lost half-a-million of men by sword, sickness, and fatigue, in forced marches through the inhospitable regions they had to traverse. The expense of the war that England had to bear, up to February, 1856, exceeded sixty millions sterling; the British had to convey nearly the whole of the French and Sardinian Armies to and fro, and nearly 400,000 tons of military stores. Without our transports our Allies would have been powerless—and yet our own men were dying like rotten sheep for the want of a few tents! The Turks might well say afterwards that our Government looked to others and forgot their own! It was not the fault of the Government, but there was a great deal too much red tape.

If men were dying by wholesale, and the requisition for stores or necessaries was not properly made out, or in accordance with some intricate form that some old maid had been driven nearly mad in trying to bring out during the forty years' peace, the articles, it mattered not what they were, could not be had; "the return was incorrectly filled up," the men that would go anywhere and do anything might die! The cold was so bitter that one could hardly feel the pen, but the return must be correct or no stores would be sent!

Thousands of tons of food, clothing, blankets, and everything that could be thought of by a kind-hearted people at home, were, as I have stated in an earlier chapter, lying rotting at Balaclava, and could not be brought up to the front, for the want of a few hundred mines, that could be procured in Asia Minor and elsewhere for about £5 each. But I will leave this painful subject, as the deeper we go into it, the more offensive it becomes.

After the Peace.

After peace negotiations had been settled, the Russians, our late enemies, came into our camp in droves, and we entertained them as friends, regaling them with the best that our stores could produce. The exchange of prisoners had taken place, and some of our men who had been in Russian hands for upwards of twelve months, proved themselves very useful as interpreters. Our old enemies made themselves quite at home, walking about, arm in arm, with the very men they had so often confronted in deadly combat.

The French and the Russians, however, did not get on well together; and whenever they were under the influence of drink this was manifest, for they often exchanged blows, and our people had to rush in and separate them. On two or three occasions a party of Russian sergeants, numbering from twelve to twenty, dined with us, and seemed delighted to think we were once more friends. We were repeatedly invited over to their camp to spend a day with them, and our non-commissioned officers and men went in numbers, and were hospitably entertained. On one occasion a wag of a sergeant of ours got up a party of some twenty-five non-commissioned officers (all picked men) from various regiments of the Light Division—not a man under six feet. We obtained permission from our respective commanding officers, met at the place of rendezvous, and away we started.

We quietly walked into Sebastopol, crossed the harbour, and were welcomed by a party, who had on more than one occasion dined in our mess. We were taken first to Fort Constantine, and shown all over that noble structure, and from thence to other fortifications. All ranks seemed to vie with each other in showing us attention. The whole of our party had on their breasts the Crimean medal with three clasps, *viz.* Alma, Inkermann, and Sebastopol, which seemed to afford much attraction to all ranks, and, as far as we could see, the higher in rank the more courteous they were towards us. We all dined together, on the best the camp could afford. The greatest drawback was that we had not a sufficient number of interpreters.

After we had dined there was a little speech-making, and many kind things were said, one half of which we did not understand. Our leader proposed the health of their Emperor, which was received with applause, and drunk with three times three, all standing uncovered. After a short time the chief of our hosts proposed the health of Her Most Gracious Majesty, which was drunk with tremendous applause. As we were about to resume our seats, some four or five French sergeants walked in, which seemed to have a very happy effect. After any amount of embracing and kissing, they were requested to take their seats, and make themselves at home.

The health of the Emperor Napoleon was now proposed, and responded to in flowing glasses, with cheers that could be heard for a mile. Some two or three Russian officers entered, one of them a very venerable-looking gentleman. He shook hands all round, and embraced one of our party, expressing a hope that we should never again meet as foes, and that those who made the quarrels might do the fighting. A number of our party at once surrounded the old gentleman. He eyed us from head to foot and inquired what division we belonged to; and when it was explained to him that we all belonged to the Light Division, it seemed to tickle him, for he wanted to know, if we were specimens of the Light, what the Heavies were like—several of our party being considerably over six feet, and stout in proportion.

The old gentleman then proposed the health of the Light Division, which was responded to, and drunk with tremendous cheering. After a time he inquired about the regiment that rode grey horses,[1] and what they were, "for," said he, with his eyes flashing, "they are noble fellows, and I should like to embrace one of them." He took but little notice of the French. After embracing some eight or ten of our party (the writer being one of them) he took his leave. He had not been gone more than half-an-hour, when two men brought up a case of brandy from the old general (for that was his rank), with a note requesting that we would drink the Emperor's health, and his also, if we thought him worthy—a request that was, I need not say, at once complied with.

Before we parted we found it required no small amount of generalship to keep ourselves sober; for, had we drunk one quarter of what they wanted us to do, we should not have slept with the Light Division that night. As it was, however, we parted with our friends on the best of terms, perfectly sober, they coming down to the water's edge with us; and after much embracing we jumped into our boats, bidding them farewell, and asking them to come and see us whenever they pleased.

Shortly after this we had a review in our camp on a grand scale before Prince Gortschakoff. With French, English, Sardinians, and Turks, we mustered nearly 300,000 men. It took us from morning till late at night to march past. It was a grand sight. As far as the Light Division was concerned we were nearly up to our full strength—not made up with boys, but with men who had been frequently wounded, but had recovered, and returned to their duty—and went by the Prince with trailed arms, at a swinging pace, to the tune of "Ninety-five—I'm Ninety-five." This was one of the greatest military sights that has been beheld during the present century. (*At the time of first publication.*)

---

1. The Scots Greys.

The Russian Priest's Wife.

In Russia it is a common mode of expression to say: "As happy as a priest's wife." The reason why she is so happy is because her husband's position depends upon her. If she dies, he is deposed and becomes a layman, and his property is taken away from him and distributed, half to his children and half to the Government. This dreadful contingency makes the Russian priest careful to get a healthy wife if he can, and to take extraordinary good care of her after he has secured her. He waits upon her in the most abject way. She must never get her feet wet, and she is petted and put in hot blankets if she has so much as a cold in the head. It is the greatest possible good fortune for a girl to marry a priest—infinitely better than to be the wife of a noble.

Chapter 15

Embarked For Home

Well, we at last broke up camp, and embarked for dear old England, leaving those cold, bleak, inhospitable regions behind. The first night on board ship, homeward bound—what a night for reflection! A flood of thoughts came across my mind regarding the different fields I had fought on, and the many hairbreadth escapes I had had. I thought of the Alma, and my Christian comrade who lay buried beside the river; I thought of the wild charge of our handful of cavalry at Balaclava, of our desperate fight at Inkermann, of our terrible work in the trenches—night after night, day after day, up to our ankles in mud, half frozen, half dead, as hungry as hunters, with nothing to eat, but yet having to fight like a lot of them.

And after all I had gone through—death in a thousand shapes, both in the field and camp, for upwards of twelve long months staring me in the face—truly I had much for meditation, verily I had much to be thankful for. Thousands had fallen all around me, heap upon heap, and pile upon pile; and yet I had been spared. I thought of poor Captain Vicars, and what a noble fellow he was—he fell in almost his first fight; and yet a merciful God had thought fit to throw His protecting arm of love around me.

What a night of reflection! I found myself on board a noble ship—homeward bound. I knew well that a grateful country was waiting to receive us, and that we should most likely have a warm reception, to say nothing of the affectionate greetings from those who were near and dear to us by the ties of nature. I will pass over the voyage home as quickly as possible, for it was a very pleasant one; every morning brought us nearer to that dear old isle that many of us had shed our blood for.

At last we arrived in Portsmouth Harbour, on the 26th July, 1856.

We at once landed and marched to the Railway Station, or rather we eventually found ourselves there safe, for how we got there it would be difficult to say—one would have thought that the good people had gone mad. They had witnessed hundreds come home from the seat of war, maimed in a most frightful manner, mere wrecks of humanity. They had now got hold of the men that they had read so much of. In their excitement they lifted us right out of the ranks, and carried us on their shoulders through the streets, which were packed by thousands of people, who were determined to give us a cordial welcome.

They wanted to kill us with kindness, for as soon as they got hold of us, it was brandy in front of us, rum to the right of us, whiskey to the left of us, gin in rear of us, and a cross-fire of all kinds of ales and lemonades—to say nothing of the pretty girls, and we got many a broad-side from them. It did not matter much which way one went, all appeared determined to give the men who had stormed the Heights of Alma, defended against such odds the Heights of Inkermann, routed the hordes of Muscovites from the Plains of Balaclava, and twice stormed the bloody parapets of the Redan—a hearty reception, and well they did it! We did not want to tell them what hardships we had to endure in the trenches; we did not want to tell them how often we had faced the foe—they knew it all.

Many a loving wife embraced her fond but rough-looking husband. The dear children did not in many cases know their long-bearded fathers. Mothers that had come for miles fell fainting into the arms of their soldierly but affectionate sons: many brothers and sisters, too, had come great distances to meet and welcome long absent brethren,—all helped to swell that mighty throng that were only too happy to welcome home the conquering sons of Albion. As for sweethearts, I will leave my young readers to guess all about that, for the "pretty little dears" were as warm-hearted and had as long tongues in 1856 as they have now; but we could not get on well without them. The whole nation appeared to have made up its mind to do honour to the Crimean Army.

Hundreds, yea, thousands had previously come home maimed, and many had since found rest in the quiet grave, but all were looked after by the nation at large. Her Most Gracious Majesty shewed a kind motherly feeling, shedding many a tear as she looked at her maimed soldiers. This evidence of Her Majesty's sympathy was most touching, and as a rough loyal old soldier from the Emerald Isle called out at Aldershot, after the Queen had said a few kind words to the troops, and thanked us for doing our duty, "Where is the man who would not fight for such a Queen?" I would re-echo that cry and add "Where is the Briton who would not do or die to uphold our glorious old flag?"

One of the most touching scenes, that melted many to tears, was witnessed on the 18th of May, 1856, when Her Most Gracious Majesty, accompanied by the late Prince Consort, the then young Prince of Wales, the Duke of Cambridge, and a host of others, assembled to witness the presentation of the Crimean Medals to a number of officers, non-commissioned officers and men that had faced the foe on many hard-fought fields. Her Majesty betrayed much emotion, her whole frame indicating the deep throbbing of her heart. When each maimed warrior was brought into the presence of Her Majesty, the whole mighty assembly gave utterance to their feelings, but not in cheers; it was as if an audible throb broke from the heart of Queen and people at once; the people felt that they had a Sovereign worth battling and bleeding for.

Three officers were wheeled up in chairs, Sir Thomas Troubridge, of the 7th Royal Fusiliers, was the first; he had lost both his feet at Inkermann; that kind motherly heart could not stand that, it was too much for her, and she burst into tears. The other two were both of the Light Division, Captain Soyer of the Royal Welsh Fusiliers, and Captain Cuming of the 19th Foot. During this scene Her Majesty must have been amused by Jack's dumbfounded expression and bearing—he appeared to be out of his latitude, but there was no mistaking his proud look after receiving the distinction. A number of officers and men had to move slowly along by the aid of a stick, or the assistance of a comrade; others could only approach Her Majesty on crutches. Queen and people were deeply affected.

And now, before closing this narrative, as far as the Crimean campaign is concerned, I wish just to relate a few amusing incidents that came under my own observation, and in which I was an actor.

ANECDOTES.

Paddy isn't half such a fool as he is often taken to be. During the Crimean campaign, a genuine son of the Emerald Isle was brought before his Commanding officer for stealing his comrade's ration of liquor. Being (as most of his countrymen are) witty, he was not at a loss for a defence when brought before the green baize covered table, and the charge was read out to him. His commanding officer asked him what he had to say for himself.

"Well, sur, I'd be sorry indade, sur, to be called a thief. The quartermaster sergeant put the liquor into the same bottle that mine was in, and shure enough I was obliged to drink his, to get at my own. Och! shure sur, I'd scorn the action; a thief I never was." This ingenious defence got him over it, with a fool's pardon.

Another, a man of my company, was continually setting himself into trouble. He had proved himself, from the commencement of the campaign, a valiant soldier. About a month before Sebastopol fell, I gave him some money with which to go and purchase some soap; at the same time Pat asked for the loan of a couple of shillings. He did not turn up any more that day. Next morning he was a prisoner in the guard tent. We all knew that he was on his last legs; but as he was a general favourite with the company, the men pitied him. Some were of opinion that his wit would not forsake him when brought before the commanding officer, and he told the man who brought his breakfast to him that morning that he would get over it with flying colours. In due course he was brought before the tribunal and the charge read out—"Absent from camp, from 10 a.m. on the 15th August, until 5 a.m. 16th August."

"Well, Welsh, you have heard the charge. What have you got to say for yourself?"

The old rogue pulled a long face, and then commenced: "Shure, yer honour, the whole regiment, you know, was very fond of our poor old Colonel Yea, that was kilt on the 18th of June, and shure, yer honour, I wouldn't tell ye a word of a lie, but I wint and sat on the poor old jintleman's grave, and I sobbed and sobbed, till I thought my heart would break, for sur, he was a sodjur every inch of him; and shure, I fell asleep and slept till morning, and then got up and walked to the guard tent."

"Now Welsh, are you telling the truth? for you know I promised you a Court Martial, if ever you came before me again for absence."

With both hands uplifted, he exclaimed—"Och! shure yer honour, never a word of a lie in it."

Some of the young officers came to the rescue, and stated that they had frequently seen men standing and sitting around the colonel's grave; and thus he got over it without punishment.

Private Patrick Lee was a "Manchester Irishman," that is to say, his parents were both from the "land of praties and butter-milk," but he himself was born at Manchester. He was a powerful athletic fellow, and knew well how to use his hands, feet, or stick. Some six months after Sebastopol had fallen, I was sergeant in charge of the Quarter Guard. Pat had, contrary to orders, gone into the French camp to look up some cognac, for he was fond of "his drops." It appears that he had paid for two bottles of liquor, but could neither get the liquor nor his money returned. But Paddy was not such a fool as to put up with that without knowing the reason why, so he quickly took the change out of the Frenchman by knocking him head-over-heels, and with the unearthly row the delinquent Frenchman made, he soon brought others to the rescue.

In less time than it takes me to write it, Pat had some half-dozen Frenchmen sprawling on the ground like a lot of "nine-pins." They had each received one straight from the shoulder. Pat then armed himself with a good cudgel which he had picked up, as by this time he was surrounded by enough "frog-eaters" to eat him. They appeared determined either to kill him or take him prisoner, but he fought his way through them all, and like a deer bounded into our camp and gave himself up a prisoner to me. He was covered with blood, and appeared much exhausted.

Next morning he was brought before the commanding officer on the charge of trying to obtain liquor in the French camp. Some fifteen or sixteen Frenchmen, with their arms in slings, and their heads bandaged, appeared to testify to Paddy's rough usage; and a French officer stated that some of his men had been so fearfully kicked and knocked about, that they were unable to appear against him. The man was sentenced to be severely punished, and the Frenchmen left our camp apparently satisfied. But when Pat came out of the tent from the presence of his commanding officer, he gave the Frenchmen such a horrible look that one needn't ask how men appear when they are frightened.

After the Frenchmen had cleared our camp, the prisoner was recalled and asked why he had disgraced himself and his regiment in such a manner, when he told the whole story in true Irish brogue—"that the blackguards robbed him, and then set to to bate him, but he floored them all as fast as they came up to him. They wanted to take him prisoner. He found it was getting rather hot, so he gave them all leg bail, and ne'er a one, nor the whole French army, could catch him."

The colonel then told the prisoner that, had he allowed himself to be taken prisoner by the French, he would have tried him by Court

Martial, but as it was he mitigated his punishment.

COMMISSARIAT MULES.

One day in March, 1855, I was one of the sergeants, with a party of men, that had been sent to Balaclava to bring up supplies, in the way of biscuit and pork, or salt junk (salt beef). We had a young officer with us, well mounted, who had but little compassion for poor fellows who were doing their best, trudging through the mud up to their ankles, with a heavy load upon their backs. The party were not going fast enough to suit the whim of our young and inexperienced commander, who called out to the writer, "Take this man's name, sergeant, and make a prisoner of him when we get home. The unfortunate man was doing his best to keep up, and he gave our young officer such a contemptuous look as I shall not forget as long as I live. Throwing his load of biscuit down in the mud, he exclaimed, "Man indade! soger indade!—I am only a poor broken-down commissariat mule." Here a light-hearted fellow burst out with—

There's a good time coming, boys!

The poor fellow was made a prisoner of at once, for Insubordination; but when I explained the case to our gallant, noble-hearted colonel, he took quite a different new of the matter, forgave the man, and presented him with a pair of good warm socks and a pair of new boots; for the poor fellow had nothing but uppers, and no soles on his old ones; and, in order to teach our smart young officer how to respect men who were trying to do their duty, sentenced him to three extra fatigues to Balaclava, and to walk it the same as any other man.

On another occasion, I had to take charge of a party of men (about forty), march them to Balaclava, to bring up blankets. In due course, after trudging through the mud for nine miles, I presented my requisition to the deputy-assistant quartermaster-general, who informed me that it was not signed by the quarter-master-general of the division, and that I should not have an article until it was duly signed. I informed him that the men were dying daily for the want of blankets. He ordered me to be silent, and, with language that is not parliamentary, he informed me he did not care—(a correct return, or no stores)—shouting like a half-mad man: "Here, take this document back, and when it is correctly signed you can then have the blankets."

I informed him that I had a party of forty men with me, and that if he gave me the blankets, the return should be sent back, correctly signed. But, no! He had not the feelings of humanity in him. I was ordered out like a dog. I at once handed my men over to another sergeant of ours, that was stationed at Balaclava to look after the interests of the regiment, and, with a little coaxing, managed to borrow a good strong mule; and away I went back to camp, as fast as the poor brute could move, straight to the colonel's tent.

The first salute I got, from one that had the feelings of humanity, and who had frequently proved himself as brave as a lion (Col. L. W. Yea), was: "What's up, Gowing?" I at once explained all, handing the document to him. As quick as thought he called to his servant: "Brock, get this sergeant something to eat and drink." Mounting his old cob, that had carried him through the fields of the Alma (where he was bravely followed by his grenadiers, whilst shot and shell flew like hail about their ears), Little Inkermann, and throughout that memorable foggy morn at Inkermann, away he went, and in less than fifteen minutes was back again. Bushing into the tent, he exclaimed: "Well, sergeant, what are you going to do now?"

"Go back, sir, and get the blankets, if you have got the signature of the quarter-master-general."

"Here you are, then." I was up and out of camp before he had time to say more. I found my mule had a lot of pluck in him, so I gave him his head and let him go. We looked a pair of beauties when I pulled up at our young swell's hut, and presented the signature. I at once got my stores of priceless blankets, and marched back. I found that a number of my men had been taking water well diluted during my absence. A wild youth from the Green Isle said that that was the best fatigue he had had since he left ould Ireland—handing me a bottle to whet my eye with.

I found that most of my party had something besides blankets to keep out the cold; but we got home all right, without any trouble. In less than a month after, I had the pleasure of meeting our gallant deputy-assistant quartermaster-general in the trenches, up to his knees in mud and water, like the remainder. He had been sent to his duty. I thought at once of his treatment of me and my party. He appeared such a shiftless creature, shrivelled up with cold, that I felt compelled to offer him my tin pot of hot coffee, to revive him a little. He, poor lad, recognised me, and apologised for his treatment, which I knew well arose from want of experience and thought.

Heavy Odds.

The true Briton generally comes out in his proper colours when under difficulty. During the Crimean campaign, a man joined us who had some little experience in the prize ring. There was nothing particular to note about him, further than that he was a fine specimen of humanity, about five feet eleven inches, and forty-six in. round the chest; he was strong as Hercules, and knew it. But he was as meek as a lamb unless well roused, and it took not a little to accomplish that. Only once during that trying campaign was he ever known to stand upon his dignity, and that was with a big bully, whom he settled in less than five minutes. Whilst the fighting lasted, our gallant allies, the French, got on well with us.

It was nothing strange to hear them applauding us with *Bon Anglais, Bon Anglais*. They were loud in their expressions of admiration at our conduct at Balaclava, and after Inkermann their exultation was beyond all bounds. They looked at our men in wonderment; they knew well we were but a handful against a host; and with thrilling shouts of *Vive l'Empereur* and *Bon Anglais*, they threw their arms around many a grim face covered with powder, blood, and mud, and impressed kiss after kiss in token of admiration.

But what a lot of faces some people carry under one hat; and we proved before we parted with our excitable little neighbours that we could not stake horses well together. After the fall of that far-famed town, Sebastopol, we had but little to do but drink each other's health, which often ended in a row; and it was nothing strange to see one of our men defending himself against half-a-dozen half drunken Frenchmen, and proving the victor. If they started to kick, some of our Lancashire lads would soon give them a lesson in "pausing" and "purring." So things went on week after week.

A YORKSHIRE BITE.

Some six months after the fall of Sebastopol, when peace negotiations were being carried on, some four or five non-commissioned officers (I being one of them) had been out for a walk on a Sunday afternoon. Returning home to camp up one of the ravines that had been the scene of the desperate strife at Inkermann, we met a party of some fifteen half-drunken Frenchmen coming down the hill. It was an awkward place for a row. The road was narrow; on one side was a solid rock, and the other a nasty slope of some thirty or forty feet, like an ugly railway embankment. As soon as the French caught sight of us they commenced to shout *"Anglais non bon; non bon Anglais"*— "English, you are no good; you are no good."

One of our party was the gallant bruiser, to whom I have before alluded. He was what is called a well-scienced man, and of tremendous strength—"Yorkshire bite," we had nicknamed him, as he hailed from Leeds. He immediately took command of us, directing us to sit down under the rocks. "Now lads, set thee doon," said he. "If these fellows interfere with us, you set still, and leave this little lot to me, and if I cannot settle them, my name is not Jacky Frith."

They were rapidly approaching us, still shouting like madmen, "*Anglais non bon; non bon*," and cursing us with all the most filthy oaths they could muster, which we all understood, having been mixed up with them for two years. Well, we all sat still under the embankment, with the exception of our Yorkshire sprig. A monster of a French artilleryman was the first to come up—and the first to go down. He deliberately spat in our hero's face, shouting disdainfully "*Anglais non bon*." The Yorkshireman's arm at once came into play,[1] with a blow that lifted him clean off his feet and sent him rolling from top to the bottom of the cudd. Another, or two, went at him, and he sent them to look after their comrade. Others rushed at him, but he proved himself more than a match for the lot.

As far as we could see, one blow was quite enough. We all sat looking at the fun, almost bursting our sides with laughter, until the last had disappeared down the cudd. Our hero then put his hands into his pockets, and, looking over the cudd, shouted out that the English were *bon* enough for them on the field of Waterloo, and were so now; and turning round to us with "Come on, boys, let's go home," left the French to get out the best way they could. Next day there was a parade for all hands, in order to pick out the men who had so disgraced themselves and the regiment, as our friends had stated that they had been overpowered by numbers, and that those who had attacked them belonged to the Fusiliers. I must say they all looked in a most pitiable plight; some with their heads bandaged, some with black eyes; others with their arms in slings, and some limping with the assistance of a stick. They were accompanied by a French general officer (I think MacMahon).

After a minute inspection up and down the ranks, not a man could be picked out, but they still persisted that the party that had given them such an unmerciful beating belonged to us. The colonel then formed square, with this nice little party in the centre. He then ad-

---

1. Foreigners have no more idea than a child how to use their hands; they will scratch and kick, but if you give them a good go-along, they will not face up again.

dressed us, expressing a hope that those who had disgraced themselves would step to the front. Four out of the five who had constituted our party at once complied. We were made prisoners, and the colonel proceeded to question us; but when it was made known to him that *we* had been attacked and grossly insulted, and that one man, who was not then on parade, had settled the whole, without any assistance from us, the regiment was at once dismissed, and our gallant pioneer corporal sent for.

As soon as our friends caught sight of him, there was no need to ask if they recognized him, for they at once commenced to jabber like a lot of magpies. When Gen. MacMahon had satisfied himself that we had been the injured party, and that this solitary man had settled the lot, and further stated that he was ready for as many more, provided they came singly, the general laughed heartily, and applauded the man's conduct, requesting the colonel not to punish any of us. We were at once released, and the case dismissed.

CHAPTER 16

The Commencement of the Mutiny in 1857

This India—the brightest gem in Her Most Gracious Majesty's crown, was shaken to its foundation in 1857. It was held by a few desperate Britons, who could well lay claim to the motto of Napoleon's old guard: *They might die, but not surrender.*

The Mutiny had been predicted by a far-seeing man—Sir Charles Napier—years before the Bengal army showed their teeth, for Sir Charles wrote to the Government of India when he was commander-in-chief, telling them that some of these mornings the much-pampered *Sepoys* would find out their strength, and that they would upset the King, the King would upset the magazine, and the magazine would be ignited, and blow up both King and country. Sir Charles was not liked by the directors of the East India Company, and was sent home, but his every word came true. He told them how to avoid it, but they laughed at him. Had that grand old soldier's advice been taken, England would not have had to mourn over the horrible tragedies of 1857-8-9, when her supremacy hung in the balance, and for a time it was doubtful whether we should not have to reconquer the whole of India.

I will now try and trace the Mutiny from its commencement, and describe some of the most revolting scenes as far as it is prudent to mention them; but there were many sights that no pen can or would dare to describe. The blood runs cold to think of poor helpless creatures—delicately nurtured ladies and children—in the hands of such bloodthirsty fiends; but stern vengeance was inflicted before we had done with them.

Our commanders were now called upon to undertake a most trying military operation, *viz.*, to wage war against a fanatic enemy, formidable in numbers and resources, with an inadequate force at their disposal. The following table will show the strength of our several armies in India, at the commencement of the Mutiny:—

		Total.
Bengal Army	Europeans 22,698	
	Natives 118,663	141,361
Madras Army	Europeans 10,194	
	Natives 49,737	59,931
Bombay Army	Europeans 5,109	
	Natives 31,061	36,710

India therefore contained, in January, 1857, in the Company's service:—

European Troops	38,001
Natives, exclusive of Irregulars	200,001
Grand Total	238,002

It was the Bengal Native army that had been trained by us with so much care, that now put their masters at defiance, and carried torture and death throughout the land. It was just 100 years since the first regiment of the Bengal army was raised by Lord Clive in 1757, and from that date it had been gradually increasing until, in May, 1857, it numbered no fewer than 350,000[1] well-armed and well-drilled men, officered by some of the best blood of Britain. Some of the foremost of our generals had fought in its ranks—Clive, Lake, Beard, Wellington, Hastings, Hardinge, Gough, Evans, Brown, Campbell, Havelock, Outram, Hudson, and others, had frequently led that deluded army on to victory.

With such men the Bengal army had carved out a name for themselves and an empire for old England, but in 1857, through mismanagement, this army was, with a few bright exceptions, in a state of insubordination or open mutiny. From beginning to end the officers had had unbounded confidence in their men. In many cases they doubted the faithfulness of other regiments, but looked upon their own as thoroughly reliable, and blindly kept with them until they were shot down by the very men whom they had for years commanded or

---

1. Including irregulars.

patted on the back and treated as children. The fact is, our people had played with the cat until she found out she could use her claws.

But the Government was determined to grapple with the mutineers; and, during the fifteen months ending April, 1858, 47,000 men from England were landed in India to uphold the supremacy of our rule. All that was wanted was a few men with clear heads, honest, upright, and fearless. And we had them. The right man was soon put into the right place—Sir Colin Campbell, afterwards Lord Clyde. This grand old hero quickly collected around him men with heads as clear and hearts as fearless as his own, to lead the troops on from victory to victory, until the last spark of rebellion was well stamped out, and the murderers and would-be murderers were cringing at our feet.

Many of the natives were under the impression that nearly the whole of the British army had been destroyed by the Russians in front of Sebastopol, and that we had no more to send out. But they were speedily undeceived, for, as I have said, no fewer than 47,000 British troops were landed in India within little more than a year after the first evidence of the outbreak.

The First Mutineer.

The spirit of insubordination first showed itself in the 34th Native Regiment, at Barrackpoor, and the first victim was the Sergeant-Major "Hewson." The adjutant went at once to the rescue of his sergeant-major, but his horse was shot, and before he could get disengaged from his charger he was cut down; the wounded sergeant-major rushed to the assistance of his officer, but was felled to the earth like a bullock with the butt end of a rifle. A strong guard was looking on all the time, but would not interfere. A *sepoy*, named Mungul Pandy, was the first mutineer. He was hung.

In the early part of January, 1857, placards were posted in various places, calling upon all the faithful and true believers to rise against the English infidels, and drive them from India, or destroy them root and branch, and proclaiming a holy war against us (all those who fell in such a war would be venerated as martyrs). The 34th Native Regiment, as I before remarked, appear to have been the ringleaders in this bloody revolt. The 19th Natives were *en route* to Barrackpoor, which is about sixteen miles from Calcutta, and had arrived within eight miles, when a deputation from the 34th met them, with the proposition that they should unite, set fire to all the bungalows, surprise and massacre all Europeans, old and young, rich and poor, secure the guns, and then march into, sack, and destroy Calcutta.

The 19th were hardly ripe enough for that, but they kept all knowledge of the proposal to themselves. The Government could not believe that the army would rise, but thought the disturbance only began and ended in the plot of a few bad characters; they were, however, suddenly awakened to a sense of danger.

On the 10th of May, 1857, the Mutiny burst forth in all its fury at Meerut. It was Sunday, and the cowardly brutes waited until the European troops were in church before moving. There were two splendid regiments there, besides artillery, and if they had only been let loose, not a man of the three regiments that started the Mutiny would have lived to tell the tale. The troops in the cantonment consisted of the following:—6th Dragoon Guards, 60th Rifles, and two batteries of Bengal artillery (all Europeans); Natives, 11th and 20th Infantry, and 3rd Cavalry.

Every man, woman, and child (Europeans) that fell in their way was murdered. And, as an eyewitness of some of these scenes, I can say that every horror, making war hideous, attended this dreadful outbreak. The cry of murder from poor defenceless women and children echoed throughout the land. Death in all modes was rampant—from the sword, bayonet, water, flames, and starvation. The barbarity of these fiends has never been equalled. The number who perished during that unparalleled revolt will never be known.

The reader will ask, "What were our men doing?" Their hands were tied. They had an "old woman" in command, and he was fearful that if he let the cavalry and artillery loose some of the "bungalows" might get burnt. There was the whole station in a blaze, and yet not a sword was drawn to save a single life until the mutineers had thought fit to move off to Delhi!

One of the officer's wives might well exclaim, "Oh, agony! what a night! Every house in sight was blazing; shots were fired at me; some of our men at last dashed into our compound (garden). I saw the cavalry uniform. 'Come, come,' I shouted, 'and save me;' 'Fear nothing,' shouted the first man, 'No one shall injure you.' Oh how I thanked them. If our artillery and dragoons had been let loose, the mutineers would never have reached Delhi."

The three regiments of rebels at once marched off to Delhi—37 miles, and the cavalry reached it next day at 8 a.m. The three regiments of Native Infantry at Delhi—38th, 54th, and 74th—received the 3rd Cavalry with open arms, and allowed their officers to be cut or shot down by them without attempting to defend them.

The Scenes at Delhi.

In describing the revolting scenes at Delhi, I will quote the words of those who had the misfortune to be there. The officers of all the regiments, *viz.*, 38th, 54th, and 74th, and the artillery, had the greatest confidence in their men, and at once marched them to attack the mutineers just arrived from Meerut. But, poor deluded men, they were soon let into the terrible secret; their own men turned their arms upon them and at once shot them, or allowed the Meerut contingent to ride up to them and cut them down, exclaiming, "*Feringhee! Ko! Maro, Maro!*"—kill the Englishmen; kill, kill. Then the carnage commenced. What a scene!

The mutineers united to exterminate all that they could lay their hands upon, without distinction of age or sex—all that those bloodythirsty wretches could reach were launched into eternity, for no other crime than that they had a white face. No pen can describe the awful deeds of these cowardly villains. Poor defenceless creatures were cut and hacked to pieces, after being stripped and subjected to brutality ten times worse than death. Poor women were hunted up by these fiends, and, when found, were dragged from their hiding-places and tortured. I will just give a few instances to show how they were treated.

After some of these poor creatures had been subjected to worse than death, they were tied to trees in a state of nudity, old and young, their children were then tortured before them, by being cut limb from limb, one joint at a time, and the flesh was crammed down the parents' throats; wives, and in many cases young maidens, were ravished before the eyes of husbands and fathers; they were then mutilated in a manner too horrible to relate, and burnt to death in one common pile. Others, pretty, very pretty girls, were seized, stripped naked, tied to a cart, and taken into the midst of these brutes to be violated; while many died under the brutal treatment they received.

Can the reader wonder, after reading these details—which give only a very faint idea of the horrors that attended this mutiny—that our men retaliated? They would not have been human had they not, at the bare recital of such deeds, been wrought up to a state bordering on madness. British soldiers could not stand this. They crossed their bayonets and swore to give no quarter, but that they would have a life for every hair that had been dishonoured by these scoundrels! And they kept their word.

The Greased Cartridges.

I will now leave the rebels at Delhi for a time, and proceed to Umballah to notice the steps taken by the commander-in-chief. It was here that the much-talked-of "cartridge difficulty" came to a head, but it is not my province to enter into any lengthened explanation as to the origin of the allegation as to greased cartridges having been issued—the matter having been much discussed at the time both at home and in India. However, the dissatisfaction of the Native troops now exhibited symptoms of increasing strength, so that at length the European officers suggested the expediency of discontinuing the issue of cartridges.

With this view the commander-in-chief coincided, and he issued a general order withdrawing the cartridges, and ordering ammunition to be made up by each regiment for its own use. But though many of the natives professed to be satisfied by this step, it soon became evident that the excitement was by no means allayed. Incendiary fires broke out in all directions, and a vast amount of government and native property was destroyed. About the middle of May (the date of the outbreak at Meerut) many of the native troops seized their arms, as if expecting a simultaneous movement on the part of their comrades elsewhere, and an outbreak appeared imminent, but the judicious interference and counsel of some of the native officers availed to calm them, though the conduct of the native troops was still far from satisfactory to the Europeans near.

The commander-in-chief had gone to Simla for the season, and as soon as the news reached there of the deeds of the Mutineers at Delhi, all the available troops were ordered to march at once on Umballah. It was now, as I have said, about the middle of May, and the heat was something fearful. But the supremacy of Old England hung in the balance, and heat or no heat these noble regiments marched forward to measure their strength against bloodthirsty villains, and they went from victory to victory. The cowardly brutes could murder poor defenceless women and innocent children, out they soon found out, to their cost, that our arm was not shortened, and before four months were over the cringing fiends had paid with their lives for the unspeakably atrocious murders perpetrated. The horrible scenes enacted were enough to make one's blood run cold, and I dare not attempt to recount them.

The Avenging Army.

But the avenging army was now on the track, and although it was only a small one, every man composing it was worth his weight in gold to the Government. The head of the Mutiny must be crushed before it had time to collect its forces. The 60th Rifles, 6th Carabineers, and Major Tombs' battery of Horse Artillery from Meerut, had the honour of first opening the ball. The old 60th gave it them in right good style; and the gentlemen from Delhi got a taste of the *Carabineers*, but, not having an appetite for any more of such treatment, bolted into the city, leaving all their guns behind them. This force was afterwards joined by one from Umballah, and then marched upon the doomed city, which they were not strong enough to attack, so they pitched their camp on the parade ground, telling the mutineers plainly that a day of retribution was at hand, that every English bayonet was destined to exact revenge—yea, a fearful revenge—for their murdered countrymen and countrywomen, and the poor helpless children.

The whole country was now up in arms, and that vast empire that had taken us 100 years to build up, was shaken to its foundations. But it was held with a tenacious grasp by men whose heads had been screwed on right, backed by those who had been worked up to a state of madness or desperation by the fiend-like deeds of the brutes whom previously we had drilled, fought side by side with, and pampered,, while they had looked upon our kindness as a sign of weakness. The revolt was spreading with rapidity. Cantonments all over the country were in flames.

In the meantime, horrible accounts kept coming in from all parts of Bengal. Jhansie was lost; the men, women, and children, had all been massacred. They made a noble stand in a little fort, as long as they had any food; but at last had to give in for the want of provisions. They evacuated the fort under a faithful promise that their lives should be spared; but as soon as the rebels had got their arms from them, they set to and tied them to trees, subjecting both male and female, old and young, to treatment too horrible to mention—deeds such as have no equal except at Cawnpore.

I am sorry to have to record that the "*Ranee*," Queen of Jhansie, was at the head of this rising, and this fiend in the form of woman is believed to have stood by and given the order to slaughter our poor defenceless women and children, after they had suffered worse than death itself. Nowgong and Saugor were gone, and all that could not escape were shot down. Some of the officers managed to escape with their lives by riding night and day to Agra.

Nana Sahib at Cawnpore.

All eyes were now directed to Cawnpore and Lucknow. Sir H. Wheeler was at the former place with the 1st Light Cavalry, 53rd and 56th, two batteries of artillery, some Oude Irregular Cavalry, and some 500 or 600 of Nana Sahib's troops—this gentleman being supposed, up to the present, to be loyal to our Government. All the reliable forces that Gen. Sir H. Wheeler had consisted of a number of officers who had made their way as Fugitives from other stations and the officers of the above-named regiments, together with detachments from the following regiments that had been pushed up country: a few of the Madras Fusiliers, about 60 men of the 84th, and a company of the 32nd from Lucknow. His whole force consisted of about 250 fighting men, including officers, with whom he had to protect no fewer than 620 defenceless women and children.

Had it not been for these poor creatures he would have cut his way through to Allahabad. Being compelled to retire to his intrenchments, he defended himself against a host, although cut off from all communications. The rebels first thought of marching off to Delhi, to join with those who were trying to exterminate the *Feringhees*. But the wily Nana Sahib persuaded them to return to Cawnpore first, and to destroy all the English in that place—old and young, rich and poor, all had to die. In order to induce them to do so, he promised double pay if they would only fight for him. They at once marched back and summoned the General to surrender or die.

The *Nana* at once attacked the intrenchments, but was driven back with terrible slaughter. They then brought up heavy guns and opened a destructive fire upon them. Numbers of the poor women and children were killed, but our men peppered them pretty well. They came on repeatedly to try and take the works, but the rifle, so much despised by them, threw death and destruction in their ranks. The heat was something fearful, and as our poor women had no shelter from the scorching rays of the sun, a number of them were stricken down by it to rise no more. They were the most fortunate of the whole. Many were cut to pieces with shot and shell.

One poor woman sat nursing her twin boys, but a few months' old, when a round shot from the enemy took off both her arms, and killed her two dear little ones. The agony of that poor mother, no pen can describe. At times the air was full of shells bursting in all directions, but still this noble little garrison held out, and repeatedly drove their assailants back. Our people did not forget the bayonet, and all those rebels who were more daring than the rest got it with a vengeance; they soon began to get tired of it, and wanted to be off to Delhi.

All who fell into Nana Sahib's hands met with a horrible death. He was told by more than one lady that their countrymen would avenge all this useless slaughter, for none ever before were known to kill women and children. But this brute was beneath all feeling. On the 12th of June, some 126 fugitives from Futteghur—men, women, and children—were dragged before this monster, and were ordered to be cruelly murdered in cold blood. Day after day rolled on, and Gen. Wheeler nobly held out, although the host around him was being daily augmented, and all were panting for the blood of the *Feringhees*.

Almost every day poor fugitives from other stations, not knowing that Cawnpore was in the hands of the rebels, came rushing into the very jaws of death; the men were at once shot down, while the poor women were reserved for a fate worse than death at the hands of a mob, who were now in a state of madness on account of the noble stand that a mere handful of men were making. Some of the poor defenceless women begged hard for the lives of their little ones; but the order had gone forth that every man, women, and child of European blood had to die, and every device that could be thought of to work upon the poor deluded natives to deceive and animate them to the most fiend-like deeds, was carried out.

But this treacherous murderer of women and children soon began to find out his mistake. He had a mere handful of men in front of him, but even these he could not subdue. He moved about Cawnpore in great pomp, having now under his command a strong force of disloyal troops that had been well drilled by us, and often led on to victory.[2] And these poor deluded creatures believed that our *raj* (or reign) in India was over, and all that they had to do was to destroy us, root and branch, and "all the yellow-faced, narrow-minded people would be sent to hell,"

But the heroic defence that Gen. Wheeler was making in an old open intrenchment, exposed to a burning sun in June, nearly drove this black-hearted coward mad.

This little band of heroes held out until the 26th of June, repuls-

---

2. They consisted of six regiments of cavalry, 14 regiments of infantry, a number of batteries of artillery, all drilled troops, and a great mob of followers, all well-armed out of our magazines.

The scene of the massacre at Cawnpore (morning of 17th July, 1857)

ing with great slaughter all attempts to defeat them by force of arms, when, having nothing to eat or drink, Gen. Wheeler accepted the *Nana's* terms of peace, and laid down his arms, having received a faithful promise that not a hair of their heads should be touched, but that the general and his officers, all his men, the women and children, should be sent on to Allahabad in boats, and they were all taken down to the boats, but here a crime was committed that stands unparalleled in the annals of Indian history. The party arrived at the water's edge, and embarked in large country boats, each sufficient to carry forty or fifty people. Then a wholesale butchery commenced.

As they put off, masked guns opened upon them with grape, canister, shot and shell, together with volley after volley of musketry. Some of the boats took fire, and many of the women jumped into the water, in order to avoid being burnt to death; then the *Sowars* (Cavalry soldiers) waded in and cut the poor things down! There were fifteen boat loads, consisting mostly of helpless wounded men, women, and children. About 115 women and children escaped this massacre, to be tortured for a few days more, and then to receive treatment worse than death.

THE MASSACRES.

The few men who escaped, including General Wheeler, were dragged ashore and thrown into prison. Some of the women could not, and would not, be separated from their husbands, exclaiming "If my husband is to die, I will die with him." That fiend *Nana* ordered his soldiers to separate them, but it could not be done except by killing them. The minister or chaplain requested permission of *Nana* to pray with them. It was granted; his bonds were partially loosened, and, as soon as he had ended, the whole were shot down, those who gave signs of any life remaining being cut and hacked to pieces with swords. After this the women and children were taken to Nana Sahib's house, which was afterwards the scene of a fearful massacre.

They were kept here until the defeat of Nana Sahib's troops by the army under Sir Henry Havelock, and subsequent investigation revealed the horrible fact that, immediately upon the result of the action becoming known to Nana Sahib, the whole of the women and children detained by him., with such other Europeans as could be found secreted within the city, and several Bengalese residents who had become obnoxious to the Mohammedans by their connection with the Europeans, were put to death under circumstances of re-

GENERAL SIR HENRY HAVELOCK. K.C.B.
(THE CHRISTIAN SOLDIER.)

volting barbarity. The courtyard of the building in which the women and children had been confined appeared to have been the principal scene of slaughter; and, when entered by our men, it was covered, to the height of two inches, with blood, and with the tattered remains of female apparel. The walls, too, were covered with splashes of blood, and on one of the pillars the victims of the fell deed had written in letters of blood—"Avenge us, fellow-countrymen." But there was no need for this exhortation. Our men were already fully aroused, and were determined to exact the utmost vengeance. Of upwards of 200 innocent and helpless women and children that had been confined in the Subada Kothee, not one remained alive at the close of that day!

The following description of the scene which met the horrified gaze of our soldiers, when they entered the city, I take the liberty of transcribing:—"Accustomed as those stern men had been to scenes of blood and the devastating ravages of war, the sack of towns, and the carnage of the battlefield, the spectacle that now met their gaze unmanned the strongest in the ranks. Before them lay a paved court, strewn with the wrecks of women's clothing and children's dresses, torn and cut into ragged and bloody fragments, as if hacked from the persons of the living wearers! Gory and dishevelled tresses of human hair lay trampled among the blood that had yet scarcely congealed upon the pavement!

Exclamations of horror subsided into deathlike stillness, as the men rushed across that slippery court into the building before them. Traces of brutal violence, of savage and ferocious murder, told in each apartment the fearful history of the preceding night; but not one living being was there to disclose the awful secret yet to be revealed, or indicate the spot in which the survivors (if any there were) of an evident massacre had taken refuge. At length the fearful truth was realised; a huge well in the rear of the building had been used by the murderers as a fitting receptacle in which to hide their martyred victims from human eyes; and here, yet reeking with blood, stripped of clothing, dishonoured, mutilated, and massacred, lay the bodies of 208 females and children of all ages—the dying and the dead festering together in that hideous well!

There lay the hapless mother and her innocent babe; the young wife and the aged matron; girlhood in its teens, and infancy in its helplessness—all—all had fallen beneath the dishonoured *tulwars* of the Mahratta destroyer, and his fierce and cowardly accomplices in prime. Upon the walls and pillars of the rooms in which this astound-

THE WELL AT CAWNPORE
SACRED TO THE PERPETUAL MEMORY OF A GREAT
COMPAMY OF CHRISTIAN PEOPLE. (208), CHIEFLY
WOMEN AND CHILDREN, WHO NEAR THIS SPOT
WERE CRUELLY MASSACRED BY THE FOLLOWERS,
AND BY ORDERS, OF THE REBEL NANA OF BA-
HADOOR, AND CAST (THE DYING WITH THE DEAD)
INTO THE WELL BELOW,
ON THE 15TH JULY, 1857

ing act of pitiless barbarity had been perpetrated were the marks of bullets, and of cuts made by sword-strokes—not high up as if men had fought with men, but low down, and about the corners, where the poor crouching victims had been cut to pieces! On those walls, in some places nearly obliterated by the blood that yet clung congealed in all directions, were discovered short scraps of pencil writing, and scratches upon the plaster. In one apartment was a row of women's shoes and boots, with *bleeding amputated feet* in them! On the opposite side of the room, the devilish ingenuity of the mocking fiends was shown in a row of children's shoes, filled in a similar way!"

One deed of heroism that has been recorded deserves mention here. A daughter of General Wheeler's was taken off by a *sowar* and put into his house along with his wife, near the church. This girl remained till nightfall; and when he came home drunk and fell asleep, she took a sword and cut off his head, his mother's head, two children's heads, and his wife's head, and then walked out into the air; and when she saw other *sowars*, she said, 'Go inside and see how nicely I have rubbed the *rissalder's* feet.' They went inside, and found them all dead. She then jumped into a well and was killed.

The Recapture of Delhi

A noble band, in spite of the terrible heat, had marched down from the hills, where they had been located to screen them from the intenser sun of the burning plains, and Mr, Pandy soon found out his mistake. This little force—but a mere handful of men—confronted them twice just outside the city of Delhi, and gave them such a thrashing as they little expected, which caused them to bolt into the city to get behind its ramparts. At this time (May, 1857), the population of Delhi (without the mutineers, who flocked there in thousands) amounted to 200,000. The British empire trembled on that ridge in front of Delhi in the early part of June, 1857.

The supremacy of Britain was held in the hands of 3,000 grim-faced men, who had made up their minds that if India was to be torn from our grasp, *they* would not live to tell the tale. All honour to them! Night after night, day after day, week after week, and month after month, they fought to uphold the honour of Old England; yea, I say, they fought, as it were, with their shrouds around them, against a host of murderers who were thirsting for their blood. It is but right that this small force of heroes should be enumerated, for they were the first to grapple with the enemy, so confident of victory and exulting in their strength.

They consisted of the 6th Dragoons or Carabineers, two squadrons of the 9th Lancers, six companies of the 60th Rifles (the 75th), 1st Bengal Fusiliers (the present 101st Fusiliers), six companies of the 2nd Bombay Fusiliers (the present 102nd Fusiliers), the Sirmoor Battalion Ghoorkas—noble little fellows; and about 30 guns of various batteries of Bengal artillery. This little band was afterwards augmented by the 8th, 52nd, 61st, and 104th Fusiliers, and a number of loyal native troops from the Punjaub.

THE DELHI FIELD FORCE.

The last man and gun had been sent by Sir John Lawrence from the Punjaub. Not a sword or bayonet had as yet reached them from England, although thousands were on the way. It was not the first time, however, that our highest martial interests had been safely left in the hands of a Norfolk man. Britons will for ages to come be justly proud of the name of Wilson—the name of a respected Norfolk family. The whole force that Sir Archdale Wilson had now under his command amounted to 8748. It was do or die. If Delhi was not taken, and that at once, the whole of India would have to be reconquered. The Punjaub was tottering; and, unless we could prove to Sikhs, Ghoorkas, Punjaubees, and Afghans, that we were the descendants of their conquerors, they would turn their arms against us. Thus it was time for Britons to "strike home."

The enemy was gaining strength and confidence every day, whilst our ranks were being rapidly thinned by cholera, sunstroke, and the continual attacks of the mutineers. But on the morning of the 14th September, 1857, the storming columns of attack were formed up, and our batteries thundered forth the summons to the murderers of defenceless women, whilst the sword of justice was just about to plunge itself into their cowardly hearts. After a short address from their noble leader the columns dashed forward—all being left to the bayonet, as it had often been before—and in our men went, shoulder to shoulder. The enemy was ready, and fought like demons, for they knew well that they were fighting with halters around their necks.

But the bloodthirsty brutes could not withstand British pluck. In some cases, when they found that they had to confront our men, they fought with desperation; in other cases they threw down their arms, and had the audacity to beg for mercy! A thrust of the bayonet was the immediate and only answer. But as a rule the enemy fought with desperation from house to house, and had to be hunted out of their hiding-places with cold steel. For seven days and nights this unequal contest lasted—a handful of men against a host,—but on the 20th our proud old flag was once more floating over the whole of Delhi—this guilty city was again in our hands. But what a scene presented itself! We had lost some of the best blood of Britain. Poor Nicholson was no more, and out of our small force we had lost, from the 14th to the 20th, 64 officers and 1680 non-commissioned officers and men.

The head of the rebellion, though not severed, had now received its death wound. Stern justice had overtaken many of the fiends. Gallows were erected at every station, and were daily claiming some of those much-pampered gentlemen, who had boasted that they would destroy us root and branch. A terrible day of reckoning had dawned; reinforcements in thousands, by the end of 1857, were landing in almost all the ports of India; and Mr. Pandy soon found to his cost that the Russians had not destroyed the whole of the British army.

The first Crimean Infantry regiment that had the honour of grappling with the murderers was one of the noble regiments that had led the stormers at Sebastopol (the 90th). But they were soon supported by others. The enemy appeared to be struck with wonderment as to where all the men were coming from. The people generally had not thrown in their lot with the mutineers; but they, too, were filled with surprise and awe.

Disarming Regiments at Peshawur.

Retribution was fast setting in, and summary judgment had overtaken them in a number of places. At Ferozepore and Peshawur an example that struck terror into their inmost soul was made of some of the would-be murderers. The 37th and 45th Native Infantry, with the 10th Native Cavalry, were stationed at the former place, with our 61st regiment, the latter being very weak. The three regiments fought the 61st for the magazine, but got a good drubbing. They were confronted, and, with the assistance of a battery of artillery, were disarmed. The ringleaders were then selected, tried by court-martial, and sentenced to death, which sentence was carried out at once—some of them being hung, others being blown from the guns; while their countrymen were marched up, disarmed, and compelled to witness the awful scene.

At Peshawur there was a strong force kept, it being situated just at the mouth of the Khyber Pass. The lawless hill-tribes are ever ready to pounce upon and destroy any unfortunate *Feringhee* who happens to

The following return will be of interest. It shows the strength, with the number of the killed and wounded of the Delhi field force up to the final capture of the city by Sir Archdale Wilson, Bart., K.C.B. 20th September, 1857:—

CORPS.	Strength Sep. 14, '57	KILLED.			WOUNDED.			Grand Total
		Offrs.	Men.	Total.	Offrs.	Men.	Total.	
STAFF.	36	4	..	4	9	..	9	13
Artillery (including Natives) ..*	1350	5	69	74	24	245	269	343
Engineers ditto ..*	722	5	38	43	20	66	86	129
6th Dragoons or Carabineers ..*	223	1	18	19	2	49	51	70
9th Lancers ..†	391	1	36	37	3	94	97	134
4th Irregulars (disarmed) ..†	178	..	..	..	..	3	3	3
1st Punjaub Cavalry ‡	147	..	4	4	2	27	29	33
2nd " " ‡	114	..	2	2	1	14	15	17
5th " " ‡	107	..	7	7	1	16	17	24
Hodson's Horse ‡	462	1	20	21	4	87	91	112
8th King's Foot ‡	322	3	24	27	7	129	136	163
52nd Light Infantry ‡	502	2	36	38	5	79	84	122
60th Rifles ..‡	590	4	109	113	10	186	196	309
61st Foot ..‡	402	2	30	32	7	120	127	159
75th " ..†	459	5	79	84	14	194	208	292
1st Bengal Fusiliers (European) ..†	427	3	95	98	11	210	221	319
2nd Bombay ditto †	470	4	79	83	6	156	162	245
Sirmoor Battalion Ghoorkas ..*	612	1	118	119	4	237	241	360
Kumaon ditto ..†	560	1	90	91	5	183	188	279
Guides Cavalry and Infantry ..‡	585	7	88	95	16	235	251	346
4th Sikh Infantry ‡	414	3	48	51	10	116	126	177
1st Punjaub ditto ‡	664	6	78	84	11	189	200	284
2nd " .. ‡	650	2	51	53	6	113	119	172
4th " .. ‡	641	1	19	20	4	86	90	110
1st. Belooch Batt. †	422	1	17	18	4	75	79	97
Pioneers (unarmed) †	320	1	36	37	2	142	144	181
Grand Total	11770	63	1191	1254	188	3051	3239	4493

* Regiments that first confronted the rebels at Ghazee-oo-deen-Nuggur, and again at Badulee-Ke-Serai, under command of Brigadier Wilson. Two batteries of Artillery and a portion of Engineers were with the column.
† Regiments that joined them from Umballah, just after the last fight, under Sir H. Barnard, K.C.B., who then assumed command of the army.
‡ Regiments that joined the field force on the heights of Delhi, at various periods during the siege.

fall in their way, and it was well to guard against any mischance here. In the month of May, 1857, things had come to such a pass that the natives refused to supply our people stationed in the cantonment with the necessaries of life (or, in other terms, we were boycotted), and it was discovered by our authorities that every man, woman, and child, of English extract, was sentenced to die on the 23rd of May.

The native force in cantonments consisted of the 21st, 24th, 27th, 51st, and 64th Bengal N. Infantry, with the 5th Light Cavalry, and six batteries of artillery—most of the guns being manned by natives. Five other regiments were stationed in forts close by, with swarms of Mohammedan fanatics who were thirsting for the blood of the hated, but dreaded, *Feringhees*. It was known that the chiefs of the hill-tribes were in communication with our pretended friends, the mutineers, for they believed that all was ripe.

The other regiments were to have come in to help to exterminate every Christian in and around the station. In the ranks were found a few who, in the midst of the general wreck, were faithful—faithful unto death—and came out as bright and shining lights, although of the same creed and caste as the bloodthirsty mutineers. These few were as true as steel, and loyal to the backbone; some of them divulged the whole plan, and thus our people were ready for the rebels. To confront this force we had two regiments of infantry, and two batteries of Bengal Horse Artillery, manned by Europeans. The infantry consisted of the 87th Royal Irish Fusiliers (or *Faugh Balahs*), and the 27th (or Enniskillen Fusiliers). Our people were not going to wait to receive the first blow, but boldly went at them. The cantonments of Peshawur are very much scattered

An order was issued that all regiments—both European and native—were to parade on their respective private parade grounds at a certain time, for the general's inspection. The 27th and 87th paraded accordingly, with their rifles loaded with ball. One regiment took the right and the other the left, and confronted the regiments of would-be murderers. An order was then read to them that they had proved themselves traitors, and were no longer fit to be entrusted with arms. The European officers with the colours, and the native Christians that were in their ranks, were then ordered to fall out and join our people.

The mutineers were next ordered to pile arms and take off their accoutrements; and, being marched away from their arms, our people at once advanced and took possession. Thus their teeth were drawn.

They were all disarmed in the same manner, with the exception of two regiments. The 51st were confronted by the 87th, and refused to give up their arms.

The 87th at once went at them, and destroyed them to a man—it was all done in about twenty minutes. The bodies were then cast into a well. The 50th Native Infantry[3] would not yield, but boldly offered to fight it out. They at once got a volley into them, and the bayonet did the rest. Some of them escaped for a few days, having fled into the hills; but a reward of ten *rupees* (£1) per head was offered, and we soon had them all. Thus the whole of the native force in the valley of Peshawur was disarmed in one day.

An Execution Parade.

Sir Sidney Cotton was determined to make an example of some of these would-be murderers, and for the information of the reader I here attempt to describe on execution parade.

It was truly an imposing scene: all the troops in garrison, both European and native, armed and disarmed, loyal and disloyal, were drawn up on parade, and formed up carefully in three sides of a square, but so arranged that any attempt on the part of the disloyal to rescue the doomed ringleaders from the hands of justice would be met with a terrible slaughter. The guns that were intended to be used to execute the traitors were drawn up, with their muzzles pointing towards the blank side of the square; thus:—

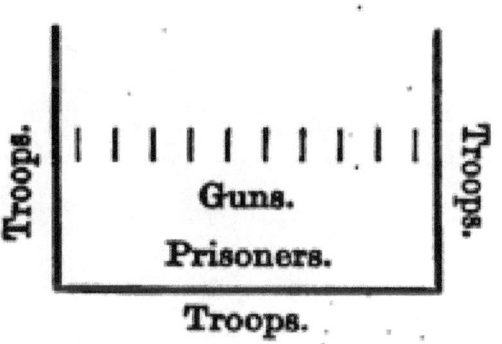

---

3. Which was stationed at Fort Murdan.

BLOWING THE MUTINEERS FROM THE GUNS

The prisoners, under a strong European guard, after marching around the inside of the square, were formed up in rear of the guns; their crimes and sentences were read aloud to them, and at the head of each regiment; the first batch of ten or twelve were then marched up to the guns and their arms and legs tied—their arms being fastened to the wheels of the gun, and their backs placed against the muzzle, so that they could not move—and at a word or signal from an artillery officer the whole were launched into eternity. A horrid sight it was: a complete shower of human fragments—heads, arms, legs, and all parts of the body, being hurled into the air—and when the smoke cleared away there they lay, Hindoos and Mussulmen all mixed together. Ten or twelve more were then marched up to the guns, and in about two minutes the same horrible scene was repeated; and so it continued until all who had been sentenced met their doom.

It makes one's blood run cold to recall the scene, but the horrible atrocities committed by these fiends left no room for pity in our hearts. A look of grim satisfaction could be traced on the gunners' faces after each salvo. But far different was the effect upon the native portion of the spectators; their black faces grew ghastly pale at each salvo— as they gazed breathlessly upon the awful spectacle, they trembled from head to foot like aspen leaves, while some of them turned all kinds of unnatural hues. This is the only death that a native dreads. If he is hung, or shot by musketry, he can have the funeral rites required by his religion; but by such a death as this he knows well that he will be blown to a thousand pieces, and that as Mussulmen and Hindoos are all mixed together there is no chance of his ever reaching Paradise. It likewise had a wonderful effect upon the Peshawur natives and the hill tribes that were looking on at a short distance; they became very civil.

All kinds of things were brought and offered for sale to the *Sahiblogs* or *Gora-logs* (gentlemen, lords). Everything that these cringing cowards could do was done in order to regain our good opinion; for they suddenly found out that the *Feringhee ray* (English reign) was not all over. We had turned the tables upon them. The news flew across the mountains, and the Afghans flocked in thousands to offer themselves to fight for us if the *Sahib* would only go with them. They ranged themselves by the side of Hodson, Probyn, and Watson, and did good service throughout the Mutiny, and afterwards in China, and have proved themselves, under good guidance, first-rate soldiers.

The following will prove what can be done by determined pluck:—

Meean-Meer was occupied, in the early part of May, 1857, by three strong regiments of Native Infantry, *viz.*, the 16th Grenadiers, the 26th and 40th, and the 8th Light Cavalry. A part of our 81st was stationed there; they had two strong detachments out, one of three companies at the Fort of Lahore, and one or two companies at Umritsa. In 1856 they had suffered heavily from cholera, and could barely muster 300 men under arms. There were two batteries of artillery in the station, and General Corbett, backed by Sir John Lawrence, was determined to disarm the whole native force, or die in the attempt.

It had been decided that all Europeans in and around the station had to die on the evening of the 14th May. A ball had been announced to come off on the night of the 13th, and all the *elite* among the European residents, both military and civil, attended. All was kept quiet, but our people were on the alert. On the morning of the 14th, a grand field-day was to take place, and every man out of hospital was to attend. In accordance with orders, all ammunition was taken from the men and deposited in a place of safety, and twenty rounds of blank cartridge issued to all hands, except the 300 of H.M. 81st, and the two batteries of European artillery, who were served with plenty of ball ammunition, and the artillery with plenty of grape, and when the native regiments arrived on parade they found the 81st formed in line, with artillery at intervals, and as many artillerymen as possible, mounted to act as cavalry, formed up on either flank.

The guns were loaded to the muzzles with grape, and the port fires lit. All was in readiness. There were about 490, all told, against near 4,000, for the natives were up to their full strength. The 16th Grenadiers were the finest set of fellows I ever looked at, and had the reputation of being the best fighting regiment in the East India Company; but the determined front that was shown them by that thin red line was too much for them. The order was read by the brigade-major. They stood panic-stricken as the word "Ready" rang out from the general. It was too much for them; their black hearts quailed. In accordance with orders they piled their arms and took off their accoutrements.

The cavalry next dismounted and took off their swords and laid them down. They were then ordered to retire, and our thin red line at once advanced and took possession, threw the arms into carts, and sent them off to the fort of Lahore. Our people could then go home to breakfast, for they had earned it. Not a drop of blood had been shed, although the crime committed by the mutineers was of the deepest dye. The letters they had written to their comrades at Delhi had been opened at the post-office, and it was quite clear that they had intended to murder every European, sack the treasury and the fort, and walk off' with the booty. One can fancy the dismay of their friends in the fort, for on that very day they were to have been relieved by a wing of a native regiment from the cantonments; but to their utter dismay a strong party of Europeans were marched in, the wing that was inside was ordered to parade at once, and, being confronted, they were challenged to give up their arms or take the consequences.

As the word "Ready" sounded along the line our people got their arms and at once kicked them out of the fort and encamped them under the guns, that would have made short work of them if they had not kept a civil tongue in their heads. Had the gentlemen at Meerut been confronted in like manner, the Mutiny might have been avoided, and hundreds of precious lives would have been spared. But then our officers in the Punjaub knew their work, and were not going to be caught napping; if they had to die they were going to die as soldiers—sword in hand—and show the enemy a determined front to the last. It was this evident resolution that made the mutineers quail before them.

Gallantry of the Lincolnshire Regiment.

Through all the annals of war there is nothing to surpass "Intrepidity so superb" as that which gave occasion to the 10th Lincolnshire Regiment, at Benares, for conduct that was exceptionally gallant. At the breaking out of the Mutiny, the 10th Loyal Boys were stationed with the 37th Native Infantry, a Sikh regiment, and an Irregular Cavalry Regiment, with one battery of European artillery belonging to the Company's service, commanded by Captain (now General) Olpherts V.C. The 37th broke out into open mutiny and were ordered to give up their arms, but instead of obeying the order they fired into the 10th, killing and wounding several men.

Our men immediately advanced against them, with the Sikhs and cavalry behind them as a support; when all at once our pretended friends made up their minds to throw in their lot with the 37th, depending upon their numbers. The Sikhs then opened fire upon the poor old 10th, and the cavalry got ready to charge them. It is under such circumstances that the British soldier comes out in his true colours. Then was seen the boldness and bravery of the sons of Britain, whom nothing could daunt or dismay. They instantly grappled with the black-hearted villains. The front rank went at the 37th and routed them; the rear rank turned about, and with a headlong charge routed the Sikhs and cavalry from the field, Captain Olpherts mowing them down with grape from his guns, which they had not the heart to charge at and take.

I am happy, however, to record that in the midst of all there was a "silver line" running through the darkness, for some of the Sikhs and cavalry boldly came out from the midst of their treacherous comrades and proved their fidelity by ranging themselves under our banner and fighting against their own deluded countrymen. Lincolnshire is justly proud of the 10th, for no regiment was ever before placed in such a desperate situation, or ever came out of an encounter with such glory. All honour to the old 10th! The honour of England was in their keeping in this instance, as much as it was in ours (the 7th Royal Fusiliers), on the heights of Alma, and both regiments knew well how to hold it. It was with them death or victory!

CHAPTER 17

Lucknow & Beyond

By the fall of Delhi, and the capture of the great Mogul King and his black-hearted murdering villains of sons, the Mutiny received its death blow. Still there were thousands and tens of thousands of the Mutineers who had not as yet been confronted by stern justice. The rebels had been routed from their stronghold, and, if they had not been so divided in their counsels, would have caused us much more trouble than they did; all they wanted was someone with power to organize them. It has been estimated that some 25,000,000 of natives were thrown into a state of agitation between Calcutta and Allahabad, so the task before Sir Colin Campbell was no light one.

After the fall of Delhi, movable columns were formed and sent in pursuit of the enemy, and no end of little battles or skirmishes were fought. Knowing well that they were fighting with halters round their necks, so to speak, the mutineers fought as only madmen will fight, but to little purpose, for the steady determined rush of the thin red line was too much for them. Our people made good use of the rifles the rebels had so much despised, and all that stood in the way were made short work of; the remainder would bolt, as our cousins across the Atlantic say, "like a well-greased flash of lightning," and it was no use poking about in the dark after them.

We had, however, one very disagreeable lesson at Arrah towards the end of July, 1857. A mixed force of about 450 Europeans and Sikhs was sent to relieve that place, and, making a forced march in the dark, fell into an ambuscade, and lost 290 men in a very short time. The news flew fast, and our loss was magnified fifty-fold, but their boasting lies did not live long. Major Eyre was soon upon their track, and, routing them, relieved the little garrison of Sikhs that had held out so nobly. The enemy now began to lose all heart, and, but for the inroads that cholera, dysentery, fever, sunstroke, and apoplexy were making in our ranks, the Mutiny would have been crushed before a single Crimean regiment got up country; for our men were worked up to a state of frenzy, and burned to avenge the blood of our outraged countrywomen.

Not a day passed but news of more butcheries kept reaching their ears. The enemy attempted a surprise at Agra. Our troops had just come in from a long fatiguing march, when they had the audacity to attack our camp, but got such a mauling from our mud-crushers and artillery that they soon bolted. Our cavalry got at them; and the 9th Lancers and Horse Artillery chased them for miles, regardless of the terrible heat, destroying some 600 of them. It had a wonderful effect upon the "*budmashes*" (bad men, low characters) of Agra, who kept very quiet; for a native had not to open his mouth very wide in 1857-8 before he had a ball put into it, or was strung up to the nearest tree, and then tried afterwards. Had we stood upon ceremony, India was gone. As it was, we hovered between life and death, and consequently sharp remedies were required.

THE RELIEF OF LUCKNOW.

Thus far the enemy had been settled; and Sir Colin Campbell, who was now commander-in-chief of the army in India, was determined not to give them breathing time. Troops were pushed up country as fast as they landed. Lucknow had been relieved to a certain extent by that Christian hero, Havelock, but it was still hemmed-in by overwhelming numbers of the enemy. The whole of Oude had joined the Mutineers, and the Delhi gentlemen were making their way thither as fast as their legs could carry them. But Major-General Sir James Outram had quite sufficient men with him to make the enemy keep at a respectful distance from him. Sir Colin was determined to make Lucknow a hot corner, and to relieve it if possible.

Accordingly, a compact little force was collected at Cawnpore in November, 1857, consisting of the following regiments: 8th, 42nd, 63rd, 75th, 93rd, 2nd and 4th Punjaub Infantry, 9th Lancers, 1st, 2nd, and 5th Punjaub Cavalry; Naval Brigade under Captain Peel, and Artillery, Horse and Field Batteries. The total force, including those already there, amounted to about 18,500—all ranks. The enemy, confident in their strength, were determined to face us. A strong force was sent on ahead to the Alum Bagh, with provisions for Sir J. Outram's people.

Our men had to fight their way to the Residency; but the Enfield rifle, that had been so much despised by the rebels, mowed them down by wholesale. They then took refuge behind stone walls; between 2,000 and 3,000 of them got into a place called the *Secunder-Bagh* (King's Garden). This place was surrounded by high and very thick walls, and a heavy fire was kept up upon our people from it. The artillery were brought up, but the light field guns could make no impression—the shot rebounded from the walls as if they had been of India rubber. Sir Colin could not stand this.

The heavy 68-pounders were then brought up, maimed by sailors, under command of that noble Crimean hero, Captain Peel, R.N. They brought their guns into action as though they had been laying their frigate, *The Shannon*, alongside an enemy. The massive walls soon crumbled beneath their ponderous fire, and a breach was made. Sir Colin said a few words to the 93rd Highlanders that were to storm it, and then they were ordered forward. It was a race between the 4th Sikhs and the Highlanders. The gallant Sikhs got the start, but Scotia proved a little too nimble for them.

The first man who entered the breach was the sergeant-major of the 93rd, This brave fellow bounded through like a deer, and met a soldier's death before he had touched the ground; but hundreds were close behind him. The fighting inside was desperate, but the mutineers were cringing cowards. Some of them threw down their weapons, and on bended knees, with hands upraised in supplication, begged for mercy; but the only answer they got was "Cawnpore" hissed in their faces, followed by about twelve or fifteen inches of cold steel!

Retribution had overtaken them, and death held fearful sway in that beautiful garden; for the slain lay in heaps in terrible confusion, mixed with roses and other sweet-smelling flowers as if in derision. Upwards of 2,000 of the rebels were counted next morning, nearly all of whom had died by the bayonet. We, too, had suffered heavily, for some of the mutineers fought like madmen, when they found there was no back door open.

The enemy defended the "*Shah-Nujeef*" (a large tomb) with desperation. But again the 93rd Highlanders and Sikhs were let loose, and with a wild shout it was carried by the queen of weapons. There again the enemy lay in ghastly piles in and around that charnel-house. They made another determined stand at a place called the Mess House—a large native building in the shape of a castle, with a deep ditch around it. After bombarding it for several hours, our people went at it, the Highlanders again leading, side by side with the 53rd and our friends the Sikhs, who would not be second to any.

The Residency was now close at hand; our men having cut their way through a host to relieve their unfortunate countrymen and countrywomen. The commanders met and arranged their plans; and, under a terrible fire of shot, shell, and rockets, which Sir Colin opened upon the enemy to attract their attention in an opposite direction, withdrew the noble little garrison that had fought so well, night and day, for near five long months. Sir Colin laid his plans so well, and they were carried out so accurately, that not a hair of one of the unfortunate women or children was touched.

They were, so to speak, taken from the jaws of the tiger without his knowing it, and conveyed to a place of safety. In delivering the imprisoned half-starved garrison, we had lost 45 officers and near 500 men. Our men, as I have often said, are at all times ready to enter upon the most hazardous enterprises to uphold the honour of our flag. In this case ladies' and children's lives were in jeopardy; and what won't a brave man do or dare to rescue those who are dear to him? Sir Colin was determined to leave Lucknow for a time, and Sir James Outram was selected to remain behind in a strong position with 3,500 troops, and plenty of food for several months.

General Windham Overmatched.

We now shaped our way back to Cawnpore; but before our force could reach it, news came that the hero of the Redan, General Windham, was more than overmatched by strong bodies of the enemy. He had with him a little over 2,000 upon whom he could rely; whilst a force of upwards of 25,000 of the Gwalior contingent, and others who had thrown in their lot with the rebels, came down upon him. It is not for me to criticize this brave soldier s actions or generalship. He had on former fields proved his metal, and was acknowledged to be the bravest of the brave; for no man could have led a storming party with greater coolness or more dash, than General Windham led the stormers at the Great Redan, on the 8th September, 1855.

The enemy at Cawnpore gained a partial victory; but the "hero of a hundred fights"—Sir Colin Campbell—was close at hand, with men who never stop to count numbers. After placing the women and children in safety. Sir Colin's eagle eye soon detected the enemy's weak point and at them he went. The fiend Nana Sahib commanded the enemy, who, although flushed with victory, were driven in headlong confusion from the field. They were completely routed, leaving all their guns (between thirty and forty) in our hands. For months (December, 1857, January, February, and part of March, 1868), small columns, from 2,500 to 6,000 strong, were hunting the enemy down all over Bengal. Grim justice was staring the rebels in the face. Our people did not trouble to seek for a suitable gallows, so long as there was a tree close by. To have shown the rebels any kindness would have been looked upon as weakness, but when once it was found that we had crushed the movement, then we could, and did, show mercy to thousands of these poor deluded wretches.

LUCKNOW AGAIN INVESTED

Meanwhile the rebels had been collecting in great numbers in and around Lucknow, and Sir James Outram had all he could do to hold his own against the repeated attacks of their overwhelming hordes. Lucknow contained at this time (March, 1858), a vast host in arms against us. Its population exceeded 300,000, thousands of whom were in arms, and determined to fight it out to the bitter end. The Insurgents had collected in numbers—computed at from 35,000 to 60,000 men; and some 50,000 or 60,000 of the Oude people had joined them; while every corner had been extensively fortified, there being upwards of 100 guns in position, beside field guns.

Thus Sir Colin Campbell had no light task before him. But this gallant old hero knew well how to play his cards. Alter rolling up the enemy in all parts of the country with movable columns, he suddenly collected at Cawnpore and its vicinity some of the best regiments in our service—men who had been well proved on many a field— and with these forces he was determined to rout the boasting enemy out of their stronghold. The following were the regiments that composed his army:—The 2nd or Scots Greys; 7th Hussars, 9th Lancers, Hodson's Horse, Sikh Cavalry, some fifty guns, and the 8th, 10th, 20th, 23rd, 34th, 38th, 42nd, 53rd, 75th, 79th, 82nd, 84th, 93rd, 97th, 101st, and 102nd regiments, two battalions of the Rifle Brigade, a good strong brigade of the Blue Jackets, and some 25,000 Natives, including Ghoorkas—men who were loyal to the backbone, and had often vied with our people for the post of honour.

The forces in front of Sir Colin, under Sir James Outram at the Alum-Bagh, consisted of the 5th Fusiliers, 64th, 78th, 90th, and a number of loyal natives, and all helped to co-operate in the final attack. The enemy fought with desperation from behind their stone walls; but Jack's 68-pounders soon brought the bricks, stones, and mortar, about their ears, and they were then pitched or ejected out of the forts and batteries with the queen of weapons; whilst our nimble little friends, the Ghoorkas, did not forget to use their favourite deadly weapon—the knife.

For days the rebels cling with the tenacity of despair to every post until it was made completely untenable. Meanwhile our cavalry were not idle, for as fast as the mutineers came out of their hiding places they fell beneath swords wielded by English arms, or succumbed to the deadly thrusts of our troopers' spears or lances. But before they entirely evacuated the city, the principal places where they had taken refuge had to be stormed. In some large buildings which had been converted into forts, the enemy had made up their minds to die, and here they fought as only fanatics or madmen will fight or die. Jung Bahador's Ghoorkas taught the mutineers, the murderers of defenceless women and children, some very salutary lessons, which, however, they never lived to talk about; and the Sikhs vied with them in destroying all that came in their way. There were no prisoners or wounded; this was a war of retribution, and all who opposed us—whether mutineers or those who sided with them—met a traitor's death.

One of the noblest soldiers that ever fought under our flag (Captain Hodson) fell in the taking of the Kaiser Bagh. This officer was he who captured the King of Delhi and his sons. He had been in at least fifty different fights—all through the Punjaub campaign—and the Sutlej campaign against the Sikhs. At the breaking out of the Mutiny, he obtained permission from the Government to raise a strong regiment of Afghans, with whom he marched down to Delhi, and there did good service, for those men would go anywhere with their beloved chief, and when he fell they cried like children who had lost a fond father.

The rebels were at last dislodged from their strongholds, but a small body of them still held the Moosa Bagh, about four miles from Lucknow, whence Sir Colin was determined to oust or destroy them. Accordingly two strong Infantry brigades, with about 1500 Cavalry, and some 30 guns went at them, and they were dislodged in masterly style. It was at this place that a strong body of the enemy, dressed in clean white robes and armed with shields and sharp swords, sallied forth, headed by their *doroger*, (priest or head man), an enormous fellow. They had all received a blessing, and were prepared to die. They had plenty of *bhang* (country liquor) poured down their throats to give them courage, and they fought with an utter contempt of death, cutting down our gunners at the guns.

The 7th Hussars were at once brought up and sent at them, but a number were unhorsed and killed. The Highlanders then went at them, and destroyed them to a man. The enemy now broke up and dispersed. Some 20,000 of them made their way to Fyzabad, and other places.

FORMATION OF FLYING COLUMNS.

Columns were next formed under various officers, namely Hope Grant, Brigadiers Russell, Horsford, Kelley, Harcourt, Rawcroft, and others. But to go into details of the different fights that took place throughout Central India, with these columns and those under Sir R. Napier (now Lord Napier), Sir H. Rose (now Lord Strathearn), Colonel Whitelock, and others, would require a larger book than I intend to write. Our loss in following up the enemy from sunstrokes and apoplexy was fearful, although as much marching was done at night as possible. There was the enemy, and our commanders would admit of no excuse or delay; they must be got at, and the command was continually—"Forward! Men, the honour of our flag is at stake."

Our guns would sometimes stick so fast in mud, that they could not be extricated by horses. At times as many as twenty horses would be attached to one gun, and the longer it remained the deeper it sank. Then that massive animal, the elephant, would be brought into requisition, while the horses all stood on one side. One of these noble creatures of the forest would put his head and trunk to the gun, whilst another would pull at the traces, and walk off with it without any apparent exertion. We must have left a number of our heavy guns behind had it not been for these sagacious animals.

THE END OF THE REBELLION.

The enemy's heart for fighting had been broken, or, in other words, the conceit about fighting had been all thrashed out of them by the end of 1858; and in marching after them we lost far more men from the effects of the sun than from actual conflict. They could run well, but fighting was out of the question,, and consequently we had to run them down. They were intercepted at all points, and in trying to escape one column, they were almost sure to fall in with another. As soon as the proclamation of pardon was issued to all who had not been guilty of murdering defenceless women and children, men came in by hundreds, yea, thousands, and laid down their arms at our feet, supplicating for mercy, which was not refused. One *rupee* (or two shillings) was given to each, with passes to their respective homes, ' together with the caution that if they were found in arms against us any more they should die.

Our faithful adherence to the proclamation had a wonderful effect upon the native mind. It was painful to behold some of these poor deluded wretches; they could not understand how it was we could forgive them. They said that when we were weak in numbers we destroyed all that came in our way; but now, when the whole of Bengal was bristling with European bayonets, the *Sahibs* were merciful. Many poor fellows were really to be pitied; for several of the regiments had not hurt one of their officers, but had protected them and their wives and children from danger.

Yet they had gone over to the enemy—they said it was fate. They now found out that it was the will of a strong Government whom they had defied, that they should lose their pensions, which hundreds had been entitled to; for plenty of them had seen some of the roughest fighting against the Sikhs that ever India had witnessed. Master Pandy had played a doubtful game for heavy stakes, and had lost all.

A great proportion of the troops, both horse and foot, that went out to India in 1857-8, never fired a shot, though they were on the spot had their services been required. A large force had been sent on to the Punjaub, to strike its warlike inhabitants with awe. Nothing was left to chance.

The native troops were confronted at all points, and the poor deluded *sepoys* could not make out where all the men were coming from. They had been given to understand, as I have already stated, that the whole of the British army had been destroyed in front of Sebastopol, and when we landed, with so many medals on our breasts, they began to inquire where we had been fighting.

Being informed that we had just fought the Russians, they looked with amazement, for their priests had told them that we were all killed. All the native troops in Bengal, and in a part of the Bombay and Madras presidencies, were disarmed; and there was not much ceremony about it. We marched up to them; an order was read; the European officers and natives were then ordered to fall out; and the remainder commanded to pile arms and to take off their accoutrements, Thus their teeth were drawn to prevent mischief, and they were then made to do duty, with a ramrod only as a weapon.

CHAPTER 18

With the Royal Fusiliers in the Punjaub and Elsewhere

The 7th Royal Fusiliers soon marched up country (leaving all their women and children behind), right up into the Panjaub, and pleased enough the 81st at Meean-Meer were to see us. From Mooltan we pushed on rapidly in bullock carts, covering 50 miles a day. A strong force of the enemy were at Meean-Meer (four regiments of infantry and one of cavalry), and we were directed to take charge of them. A gallows was erected just in front of our lines and hardly a day passed but it claimed its victims—sometimes four or five, morning and evening.

The murderers, or would-be murderers, were quickly launched into eternity; they had not a nine feet drop, and the hangman was never complained of for being clumsy. Some of them abused us as long as they could speak. When Mr. Jack Ketch had all ready, he would jump off a long form, about two feet high, and knock down the odd leg (for it was a three legged one). Their comrades were compelled to witness the execution, while a company of our troops were under arms to see that the law was carried out.

One night during the summer of 1858, our people were performing in the play house or theatre, when in rushed an officer, covered with dust, and placed a dispatch in the hands of General Windham who was in command. The general opened and read it; there was a little whispering going on between the general and our then Colonel Alsworth. The performance was permitted to go on until the act was over, when the adjutant (Mr. Malon), called out in a loud voice: "All men of the right wing go home and prepare for active or field service."

The shout that followed shook the house. The old Fusiliers were ready to face any number of men whether black or white. The Russians had quailed before them, and woe be to the mutineers who should attempt to oppose them. They were off long before daylight with the band in front playing "For England's Home and Glory," and had a long hot march before them. The wing was about 800 strong, for we stood near 1,600 bayonets at the time. A wing of the 7th Dragoon Guards, a battery of Horse Artillery, and a regiment of Ghoorkas accompanied us.

A strong force of natives had shown disaffection at a place called Dera Ishmal Khan; but the force that General Windham sent struck terror into them, and they begged for mercy. All the ringleaders were tried, and shot or hanged; the remainder were at once dismissed, so that there was no further bloodshed. This column lost a number of men on the march from heat, from apoplexy and cholera, but still they pressed on.

The mutineers were in camp opposite our barracks. Heavy guns loaded with grape almost up to the muzzle were pointed at them. All was ready at a moment's notice; for some of our men, trained as gunners, were always at, or close to the guns, and any attempt at an outbreak could be checked at once. Thus, the reader will observe, one wing of the fusiliers had to keep five regiments in subjection. The other wing of the 7th Dragoons, and also two batteries of artillery, were about a mile from us. One night, about tattoo; an alarm was given. Shots were fired into the enemy's camp, and we all stood to arms and faced them.

The cavalry and artillery came to our assistance at a break-neck pace; but after remaining under arms for some time, it turned out that some of our recruits acting as sentries, had noticed some of the mutineers moving about their camp, and had at once fired at and wounded some of them. They were not allowed out of their tents after tattoo, and it had just sounded. It was well that the heavy guns did not go off, as they would have rushed out of their camp in order to escape, and would have been all cut or shot down.

At the end of 1858 we were still at Meean-Meer. It is one of the hottest and most unhealthy places in India, and we there lost a number of non-commissioned officer and men from apoplexy and fever. In the beginning of 1869 we marched up country on to Jhelum and Rawul Pindee. The neck of the Mutiny was now broken, and the country began to settle down. Rawul Pindee is one of the loveliest places that I had as yet seen; it is just at the foot of the snow-capped

Himalayas, which rise majestically in the distance. We remained there for one summer, and were then sent off to Peshawur, then the extreme frontier station.

Here we had a rough lot to deal with, for we found ourselves in the midst of thieves and murderers. These gents go about at night, armed with daggers, almost in a state of nudity, with their bodies well greased from head to foot, so that if anyone got hold of them they would slip out of his grasp like an eel, and he might look out for the dagger, for he was bound to have it. Our people, therefore, often fired first, and then challenged "Who comes there?" I must say these fellows proved themselves the most expert thieves I have ever met, for nothing was too hot or too heavy for them. If they could creep up to a sentinel, it was all over with him; he would be stabbed to the heart, and then the assassin would walk off with his rifle and accoutrements.

At other times they would creep or crawl into the barracks, and walk off with rifles, accoutrements, men's clothing, or anything that they could lay their hands upon, such as the company's copper-cooking utensils, &c., and if anyone stood in the way, he was at once murdered. Some hundreds of medals were, in 1860, stolen off the coats of the 93rd Highlanders, whilst they were on parade in undress uniform. The only way to catch these gents was to shoot them; and our people, the Highlanders, and Rifles, pretty well thinned them.

Peshawur is one of the prettiest stations we have on the plains, but it is also one of the most deadly; it is excessively hot in summer, and very cold in winter. It is almost surrounded with snow-capped hills; and one can there see snow all the year round, yet, in the summer, the heat is enough to roast one. Regiments were sometimes brought so low with continual fever that companies 120 strong could not furnish three men for duty—all being down with the fever and ague. We were right glad to get out of it.

In 1862 we marched to Ferozepore, on the banks of the Sutlej. We found this place very hot, and often experienced what it is noted for—"sandstorms." Reader, if ever you witness a good sandstorm, you will be ready to think it's all up with you. It comes rolling along like huge mountains, the wind blowing a perfect hurricane, until you are completely enveloped; a few drops of rain will often follow, succeeded by a perfect calm.

The following are a few of my letters from India from 1857 to 1876. I trust that they will prove of more than passing interest. Some of them will be found amusing, whilst others will be found heartrending, and will sink deep into more than one parent's heart, and set them thinking, "Where is my boy tonight?" Many of them were written under great difficulty, not with the thermometer below freezing point, but in the midst of heat that was almost enough to give one a slow bake, with the thermometer indicating in the sun 140° of heat, and in the shade 120°, with the sweat rolling off one like rain: in some stations with the hot winds, 30° can be added. But I felt it my duty and a privilege to write as often as I could to those that are near and dear to me. The following are all that can be found:—

Kurrachee, 28th Nov., 1857.

My Dear Parents,

Thank God, we have landed safe and sound once more on *terra firma*, after a long and tedious sail across the ocean. We had what is called a splendid voyage until we got near the Cape of Good Hope, when a storm that threatened our entire destruction overtook us. It was truly awful, with the appalling claps of thunder (the loudest I have ever heard), and the flashes of lightning were dreadful; while a heavy sea broke completely over us, carrying all before it. I was on watch on deck. It was about three o'clock a.m. on the 19th of October. Half the watch were ordered below and the hatches fastened down, when, with a crash, down came the foremast.

The shrieks of the women and children below were piteous, while the cries of the poor fellows gone overboard with the fallen mast were dreadful. The watch, I am happy to say, were calm and did all they could to help the sailors; but alas! the poor fellows that had gone overboard, we could not save. The sea was rolling mountains high, and no boat could live one minute in it. It was as dark as the grave, save when the flashes of lightning revealed our misery.

Then another terrible sea caught us, dashed us on our beam-ends, swept away all our boats, with the bulwarks on the port side, and the two remaining masts were snapped asunder as if they had been twigs. To all human appearance the Headquarters of the Royal Fusiliers (about 350 strong) were doomed to a watery grave, when the good ship (the *Owen Glandore*) righted herself. We looked in a terrible plight. A portion of the mainmast was left, with the mainsail all in ribbons. Seventeen poor fellows were washed overboard to meet a watery grave. Ropes were thrown to them, but it was all in vain. The captain was an old salt veteran of some fifty years; and with his trumpet gave his orders as calmly as possible.

All was right with such a man, in life or in death. The sea was now breaking completely over us, and we had to hold on the best way we could. About five a.m. she gave a terrible dive, as we thought; it was a huge wave passing completely over us. The timbers of the noble ship cracked, and she shook from stem to stern; the captain, lashed to the poop, still calm. I think I see that manly face uplifted, as he exclaimed with a loud voice: "Thank God! she still floats." He then shouted to our Colonel Aldsworth, "If the mainsail goes, all is lost; you are in greater danger now than ever you were in front of Sebastopol." We (the watch) could but look at that calm face, but not a word was uttered. Death was all around us, but as true Britons it was no use murmuring; all was quiet, all were calm.

We were truly, dear parents, looking death in the face, for there were no back-doors. But just then, when skill had done its best, and when to all human appearance we were about to be launched into eternity, to meet a watery grave, a still inaudible voice said: "Peace be still." The wind ceased, and the storm was all over; but the sea was still rolling heavily, and we were but a helpless tub in the midst of the raging billows of the fathomless ocean. Gradually, however, the ocean became a heavy swell, and in a few hours as calm as a fishpond.

We had had a most miraculous escape, and our brave old captain requested the colonel to have prayers at once, and thank Him fervently who said to the raging billows: "Peace be still." All hands were at once set to work, and all who could use a needle were set to sail-making. Jurymasts were brought up out of the hold, and in a few days, without putting into port, we began to look quite smart again, and went on our way rejoicing, to help to revenge our murdered countrymen, women and children. The captain complimented our colonel upon having such a cool body of men.

We find this country in a terrible state, but I see no fear but what we shall be a match for them before it is over. I have not time to say more at present; will drop a few lines, if possible, next mail, and give you all the news I can. I am happy to say I am quite well, and we must make the best of a bad job. It will not do to give in at trifles. We are to have an execution parade

this afternoon; there are twelve of these beauties to be blown from, the mouth of the cannon. We have had one such parade before. 'Tis a horrible sight—legs, arms, and all parts of the body flying about, and coming to mother earth with a thud. The sight is so sickening that I do not care to dwell upon it. Give my respects to all old friends, and
Believe me.
 My dear Parents,
  Your affectionate Son,
   T. Gowing,
  Sergeant Royal Fusiliers.

      Kurrachee, East India, 4th Dec, 1857.
My Dear Dear Parents,
Once more, a line from what some people call a glorious land, but to give it its proper name just now, it is a hell upon earth. The fiend-like deeds that are being perpetrated daily out here are beyond description, and should these brutes get the better of our troops, every European here will have to die a terrible death, and we shall have to commence with another "Plassy." But I see no fear. Mark me, we shall beat these murderers of women and children, but it will not do to stop to count them. Thousands of men who fought and conquered at the Alma, Balaclava, Inkermann, and twice stormed the bloody parapets of the Redan, are not men to be easily subdued.

I see our Government has put the right man into the right place as our commander and leader. Sir Colin Campbell is not a man likely to be "taken short," but is a regular go-ahead, fire-eating old cock. He is, moreover, no novice, has been trained in a rough school under Wellington, Gough, and Napier. It was he that put the finishing touch on the Russians at the Alma and commanded the thin red line at Balaclava, thus nobly sustaining the prestige of the flag that has waved triumphant out here since Plassey (1767), and which may now with safety be entrusted to his keeping.

We had no idea when we left Portsmouth that we were bound for such a hell-hole as this, or I do not think we should have brought our women and children with us. I find we are to move up country shortly; we are waiting for reinforcements; the women and children and all extra baggage to be left behind.

That looks like business. Our Government is not going to play with these gents; and, as true Britons, if we are to die, we shall meet death sword in hand.

Our men are roused to a pitch almost of frantic madness to get at the cowardly brutes. Cawnpore and Jensie will be wiped out with a terrible retribution. Britons have the feelings of humanity, but one's blood runs cold to read and to hear daily of the dastard base deeds (of the rebels), to poor defenceless women and children, for no other crime than that they have white faces. I dare prophecy that the enemy will find out we are the true offspring of their conquerors at Plassey, Seringapatam, Ferozeshah, Moodkee, Sobraon, Goojerat, and scores of other fields where they have had to bow in humble submission to our all-conquering thin red line.

As for myself, I see no fear. I shall not die till my time comes, and the same powerful Hand that has protected me thus far, is able to do it out here. Our line—the ever-memorable thin victorious line—is already advancing, and it will not halt until our proud old flag is again waved in supremacy over all the fortresses, cities, and fertile plains of India, and these cringing brutes begging for mercy (what they are now strangers to). I will, if I am spared, take notes, and write as often as I can. You must try and keep your spirits up. I am as happy as a bug in a rug. I never go half-way to meet troubles, and I believe the best way to get over all difficulties in this world is to face them.

I have a few pounds that I have no use for; please accept them as a mark of love from your wild boy. Poor mother will find a use for them. I enclose a draft on Gurney's Bank. We have a number of Norwich men in the Fusiliers, most of them finelooking men; they joined us as volunteers from other regiments just before we left home

It is now the depth of winter, but we find it quite warm enough during the day. I intend to adhere strictly to temperance, hot or cold. I could stand the cold in the Crimea without drink stronger than coffee; and as we crossed the equator twice on our voyage out here, I think I know a little already of what excessive heat is, and I did without it then. Our doctors all agree that the temperate man out here has the best of it. He is more prepared to resist the different diseases that prevail among Europeans, such as fevers, rheumatism, disorder of the liver, and even cholera; that I can testify from my experience in Turkey and the Crimea.

I find the inhabitants out here are a mixed up lot, but if one can once master the Hindoostanee language, he can make himself understood all over the vast plains, from Calcutta to Peshawar. As soon as things are a little bit quiet, I shall go in for Hindoostanee. Tell poor mother to keep her pecker up. I do not believe this "row" out here will last long, as troops are landing in all directions; and if they could not subdue a handful of men that were in the country when it started last May, what may they expect now that the Crimean veterans are thrown into the scale against them.

It will be a war of extermination. I do not think our men will wait to quarter the foe; if we can only close with them, it will be one deadly thrust with that never-failing weapon, the bayonet, and all debts will be paid: retribution must eventually overtake such bloodthirsty wretches. But I most bring this to a close. Give my kind regards to all old friends, trusting this will find yon as it leaves me, in the enjoyment of that priceless blessing, good health.

  And believe me,
    My dear Parents, as ever,
      Your affectionate Son,
       T. Gowing,
       Sergeant Royal Fusiliers.

P.S.—I find our old friends of the Light Division the 2nd Rifles, the 23rd Fusiliers, the 88th Connaught Bangers, the 90th and 97th have already had a "shy" at the foe, and thus helped to revenge poor defenceless creatures. Our turn will come yet; it will then be "*the d—l take the hindermost.*" Please address as above; it will follow me if I am above the soil. Keep your spirits up, mother dear.
  T. G.

        Camp, Meean-Meer (Punjaub),
        5th April, 1858.

My Dear and ever Dear Parents,

From my former letters from Kurrachee and Mooltan, and by the newspapers, you will see how near the verge of ruin this large appendage to our empire has been brought; in fact, it has been shaken to its foundations, by (what shall I say), mismanagement. And these much puffed-up *sepoys* (native soldiers) have been spoilt; and, depending upon their strength and our weakness (for kindness has evidently been looked upon as weakness), they have risen up to crush us.

The determined stands that our handful of men have made on the heights around Delhi and other places where the honour of our glorious old flag has been at stake, has been sublime, and rendered them worthy to rank beside the heroes of Albuera, Salamanca, Vittoria, Waterloo, Alma, Inkermann, the Nile,, and Trafalgar; and whilst Old England, side by side the brave sons of Ireland, can produce such men to stand beside and guard her flag, she has nothing to fear; and the *sepoys* out here will find, I dare prophecy, before twelve months have rolled over, that we are the true descendants of these conquerors.

If they could not subdue a mere handful of men, what may they expect now that the veterans of Alma and Inkermann are thrown into the scale against them. A terrible day of vengeance has dawned; the sword of justice will be plunged into the hearts of the murderers of defenceless women and children. The lion in the Briton is roused, the blood of the innocent cry for vengeance. But remember, it's only the native army that has risen against us; the inhabitants generally are on the side of law and order. And, I will be bound, our troops will take tea with the traitors before we have done with them, and bring them on their knees begging for mercy (to which they are strangers).

Now for a little news. In my letter from Kurrachee I told you that we expected to re-embark and go round to Calcutta; but instead of that, our Government, with the reinforcements that were arriving almost daily, were determined to grapple with the mutineers, North, East, West, and South, at the same time; so strong reinforcements have been pushed on into the Punjaub to strike its war-like inhabitants with awe. And the Royal Fusiliers—second to none—about 1800 bayonets; the 94th, 1200 strong; the 7th Dragoon Guards (or Black Horse), about 800 sabres, and three batteries of Horse and Field Artillery, with 24 guns, moved up country. The natives received us in every camp with joy and gladness.

It was very pleasant when we left Kurrachee in December last; we had a march of about 120 miles to the banks of the river

Indus—it's a noble stream. We found the road or track very sandy—we sank near to our ankles in sand at every stride—which made it hard work to get along. But the honour of our flag was at stake, and I think I may say, without egotism, that it was safe in our hands. We had native guides to take us across the desert, as in many places there was no trace of a road. The inhabitants-brought all sorts of eatables in the way of fish, vegetables, eggs, fowls, and fruit into our camp.

The accounts that appear in the country papers daily are enough to make one's blood boil. The murdering, bloodthirsty villains will all meet their doom yet. I told you a little of how we treated them in Kurrachee and Mooltan, and should we ever cross the path of these murdering traitors, I will be bound to say that our fellows will give it them right and left.

We found flat-bottom boats awaiting us on the Indus, and at once marched on board. Each steamer had a flat-bottomed boat to tow up; with each pair they could stow away about 400 men, with kits and arms. As soon as all were on board, off we started. Our destination, as far as we then knew, was Mooltan. We found we had to face a very strong current, with a native at the head of the boat constantly sounding.

It was very amusing to hear him shouting continually, from morning till night: "No bottom, no bottom." "Stop her; back her." "*Teen put*" (3 feet). "*Chay put*" (6 feet). "No bottom" "*Sanadoo put*" (2½ feet). "Stop her!" Often we would stick fast on a sandbank, when all the crew, and perhaps some 50 of our men, would jump into the water and shove her back. At other times we would have to land half our men at a time, with long ropes to pull the steamer and flat along, or we should have lost ground. Sometimes it was rough work, with so many creeks to cross up to our middles, and sometimes our necks, in mud and water.

The first to cross would be a native boatman to make the rope fast; then it did not matter much how deep it was. You would be astonished how quickly our men got over. We have a very witty Irishman in my Company, and he often kept us all alive, One morning, as we were about to get over one of these nice creeks, he shouted out: "Here go, boys, for ould Ireland's home and glory," as he dashed into it. As you know, I do not drink, and so our witty friend often gets my go of rum.

We found the river abounded with gigantic, amphibious reptiles—crocodiles. We had a little sport daily, shooting them; also huge snakes in abundance. So it was not safe even in the creeks to have a bathe. We lost one man overboard; the poor fellow was snapped up by a crocodile before a boat could reach him. We lost another man by the bite of a snake; both these men had gone through the whole of the Crimean campaign. In due course we arrived safely at Mooltan—1300 miles from Kurrachee.

Here we remained for a few days and had a good look at the citadel from whence the valuable Koh-i-noor—worth about £2,000,000 sterling—was taken by Lord Gough, and presented to Her Most Gracious Majesty in 1848. We then pushed on here by bullock carts through a vast desert, the road all the way being strewn with straw. We had to take turns at riding, one company being sent on daily until we had all left Mooltan. We had five days of this sort of travelling.

On the evening of the fifth day our first company—about 130 strong—marched in here. The 81st were delighted to see us. They were very weak, having suffered heavily last year with cholera. They had been holding on by the skin of their teeth, for there are about 4000 mutineers here, and the 81st were only about 300 strong at headquarters, having two strong detachments out. Those of our men who were with the leading companies, came out to meet us with all sorts of news.

We all landed here safely by the end of February, except sick, lame, and lazy, and women and children who were left behind at Kurrachee, as we expected to take the field. Our men were almost mad with rage when the order came in for us to remain at Meean Meer; the old Fusiliers wanted to measure their strength with these bloodthirsty wretches at Lucknow. But we found, after sending out two or three strong detachments, that we had a handful here, prisoners being brought in daily from the surrounding country, tried, and executed at once.

The execution parades are ghastly sights to witness, but the horrible, fiend-like deeds that they have perpetrated leave but little room in our hearts for pity. We execute, more or less, every day. The blowing away from the mouth of the cannon is a sickening sight, and I do not care to dwell upon it. Since we came here I have been appointed drill-sergeant of the regiment. It carries one shilling *per diem* extra; but I am at it from 4 a.m. until 7 p.m., but rest during the day time. You, I think, will notice the date of this. I know poor mother will remember it. I am just 24 years in this troublesome world. I enclose a small draft for poor mother's acceptance; it is the first three months' extra pay, and a little with it to make it up to a "fiver."

Mind, this is for mother's use, and no one else is to interfere with it. If we are ordered into the field I will drop a line if possible, but not a little newspaper. I see no fear; I shall not die till my time comes; I do not believe the man is born yet that is to shoot me, or surely I never should have escaped so often as I did in the Crimea. When I look back to the fields of the Alma, the two Inkermanns, the night of the 22nd of March, the 7th and 18th of June (1855), the dash at the rifle pits, and no end of other combats, including the storming of Sebastopol, I cannot but think that I am being spared by an All-wise God for some special purpose; that, to all appearance. He has built a hedge around about me, and has permitted the deadly weapons to go thus far and no farther, to show me in days to come the finger of His love.

Again, dear parents, look over my letter wherein I describe that terrible 19th of October, off the Cape of Good Hope, when to all human appearance the ship *Owen Glandore* was lost, and all on board consigned to a watery grave. You note that we lost all our boats, masts and sail, and were nothing but a helpless tab floating with a freight of 390 human beings, expecting every moment to be launched into eternity. But just as our gallant captain said all was lost, an inaudible voice said: "Peace be still," when the wind ceased, and all, except 17 men that had been washed overboard, were saved. I find by the country papers that summary punishment is being fast dealt out to these wretches all over the country, and that they will not face our men, the dreaded "*Feringhees*," as they call us, unless behind strong positions, and that they are receiving daily some very awkward lessons and have already found that our reign in India is not all over.

These little Ghoorkas are the inhabitants of the Nepaul Hills, and just at present they are worth their weight in gold to us. I should think, from what I have read and heard of them, that there are no better soldiers in the world, if well led; and the

Sikhs that gave us so much trouble in 1845-6 and 1848-9, are not far behind them. We have a regiment of the latter here with us; they are fine-looking men, not at all to be despised. I went, by permission, through the mutineers' camp a few days ago. I was astonished to find that a number of them could speak English—mind, they are all of them disarmed.

We found some of them very talkative, asking all sorts of questions about the Russians, when they found we had been fighting them. I asked one venerable looking officer, with his breast covered with honours, what he thought about the Mutiny. His answer was that it was brought about by bad, wicked men who had eaten the Government salt; that there were good and bad in every regiment, and that the bad men had roused them all. I asked him if he, as an old officer, thought our Government would have given in if we had been beaten at Delhi? "No, never!" was his reply.

He stated that he had served us faithfully for upwards of 40 years, that he had fought many a hard-fought field against the Sikhs, and would never forsake us; they might kill him if they liked, but he would be faithful to the end. This old veteran could say no more, and with the big tears rolling down his furrowed cheeks, he left us with a "*Salam, salam, sahibs.*" We found others looked at us with contempt, but they were silent.

The 16th Grenadiers are one of the disarmed regiments here. I think I never looked upon such a body of men; they may well be called Grenadiers. I am not a waster, and I had to look up into the face of every man I came near. Some rose to salute us, while others sat contemptuously looking at us. I find they have the reputation of being the best fighting regiment in the East India Company.

Some of them cursed the cavalry and said it was all their fault they were disgraced as they were; and that they would go to Lucknow and fight to the death for us, if the Lord Sahib would let them. But I must bring this to a close, or I could keep it up for a week. You ask me if you may publish my letters. Please yourself; I state nothing but facts. I hope this will find you all as it leaves me, in the enjoyment of the best of blessings, good health, and believe me, as ever,

      Your affectionate Son,
       T. Gowing,

Drill-Sergeant Royal Fusiliers.

P.S.—A long letter costs no more to send than a short one, and one feels a pleasure in writing to those we love, but cannot see. Keep up your spirits, mother. T. G.

Meean-Meer, 26th May, 1858.

My Dear Parents,

Well, dear parents, as I have but little to do during the heat of the day, I will try and amuse myself by giving you a little more news. It is extremely hot here at present; in fact, enough to roast one during the day, with a hot wind blowing a perfect hurricane: and, talk about dust and sand, it's enough to blind one. We have been treated of late to several sand-storms, as they are called out here, and I think they have given them their right name.

It's awful to stand and see them coming on: the whole heavens become black, all is still, not a breath of air: all at once we are enveloped in sand, the wind blowing enough to sweep all before it.

All doors and windows must be well secured, and even then it is impossible to see across the room. If one is caught outside, the safest thing to do is to lie down at once: if not, you stand a good chance of being blown clean off your feet and coming to mother earth rather clumsily. Well, this rebellion has received its death-blow at Lucknow, although the enemy will give us a lot of trouble in Oude and Rawalcund; but they will not face our men if there is a back door left open to escape by. As far as I can see, the Fusiliers are doomed to disappointment; we must obey orders.

Our commander got a nasty rap from Sir Colin Campbell for requesting to be allowed to go into Lucknow with us: "Stay where you are; when we require your services we will send for you." But it's as well to keep a good lookout upon the Punjaub, for should the Sikhs break out we shall be in a hornet's nest, as we are right in the midst of a most warlike race of people, and not very far from the Afghan frontier; in fact, the Punjaub extends right up to the mouth of the Khyber Pass. Some of the most distinguished regiments in our army are in the Punjaub at present; fine, stalwart men, that might die, but would never yield!

The Faugh-à-ballagh[1] boys—the 87th Royal Irish Fusiliers—are here with us, backed up by the 27th Inniskillings,[2] both of which noble regiments have taught the French some very awkward lessons. They call the 87th the "*Aigle*" catchers: they captured an eagle from the French on the field of Barrosa, and routed a whole French division with a headlong bayonet charge. They call the 27th the Waterloo lambs, and nice lambs they are at present. Should our turn come, I have not the slightest doubt they will find the Royal Fusiliers still, as at the Alma and Inkermann, true Britons. As it is, we have a good handful in front of us, for they are a cut-throat looking crew; but they stand in awe of us.

I was talking only yesterday (through an interpreter) to a venerable looking, intelligent Sikh, who had fought against us in a number of fields. He informed me that after the fields of Ferozeshah and Sobraon, his men (he was an old general) said they would not face us any more, as we were not men at all, but devils in the form of men, that nothing could resist. As for this war, it would soon be all over, and it would be a good job for the Punjaubees; they would fill up our ranks, and fight to the death by the side of such dare-devils. He farther stated that he had four sons already with Campbell Sahib, and if he had four more, they should all go.

It's all very well to talk like that now. An Asiatic generally carries two faces under his turban, and, mark me, our Government has a long parse, with plenty of that which makes the wheel tarn smoothly. Again, we have been victorious all along the line, and so long as that is the case, we shall have plenty to jump into the mutineers' boats; but with the vast population around as, it would not do to lose a single battle. Nothing mast be left to chance; and our Government, I think, knows well what it is about. Rebellion must be crashed at any cost; then the people may be treated kindly, giving them the right hand of fellowship, with justice: protecting the weak from the oppressor, and shielding the law-abiding subject from the lawless.

Under the old system this was unknown; for a chief *rajah* ruled with despotic monarchy, and might, not right, carried sway in every state. Accordingly, if the *Maharajah* (native king) was in

---

1. "The Faugh-à-ballagh," clear the road.
2. Now the Inniskilling Fusiliers.

any way opposed by one of his subjects, he must die: or if he was left alive, he was horribly mutilated and all his goods confiscated.

Thus, hundreds of thousands are only too happy to be under our flag, although I find the East India Company wink at lots of things they do not want to see or know of. I am sorry to say we are losing a number of men here through fever. They tell as we shall have rain next month, then it will be more pleasant I am happy to say that I have my health remarkably well. I am at it by 3 a.m. daily, drilling first disorderly men; then recruits, then with the regiment, then at the recruits again; so I have a lively time of it, shouting and bawling about six hours every day, except Sunday. I am diving into the *History of India* (Thornton's). The amount of fighting our people have had out here is marvellous. Our men have had to hold on by the skin of their teeth; but the tables have been completely turned, and it would not do for as to lose what our forefathers fought so desperately for. Thus far, our men have proved that they are worthy descendants of the conquerors of Plassey, and that the prestige of our glorious old flag is safe in our keeping.

We still keep on with the executing parades. The rope is used pretty freely. Mr. Calcraft is never complained of for being clumsy. I for one am always glad to get away from such scenes. I sometimes think there ought to be a little more time given; the sentence it passed, and often carried out within less than six hours. But, again, you most remember we are playing for heavy stakes, and they say *all is fair in love and war*. But I most bring this to a close; it has been my fourth attempt. I am writing this without a shirt on, nothing but a pair of thin drawers, but the sweat is rolling off me like rain; so you see we do not require much coal nor yet many blankets to keep us warm. Goodbye, dear Parents.

And believe me as ever.
Your affectionate Son,
T. Gowing,
Drill-Sergeant Royal Fusiliers.

Meean-Meer, October 15th, 1858.

My Dear, Dear Parents,

Well, dear parents, a number of eventful things have taken place since my last. A wing, that is, half the regiment, have gone into the field, with half the 7th Dragoons, so the two sevens are together after the enemy; the one to lather and the other to shave them. A battery of artillery and a regiment of Ghoorkas are with them. Our wing was near 800 strong. We have had a very near squeak with our nice beauties in front of us. They meant mischief, but we have not been caught napping; traitors often have two faces under one hat.

It had been brought to the notice of our commander. General Wyndham, C.B., that these fellows were armed to the teeth, smuggled into their camp, and that as only a slender guard was over them, they would rise and murder all they could lay their hands upon; and, making their way to Lucknow, throw in their lot with their comrades who were fighting the detested *Feringhees*. All was kept quiet. One of their number had divulged the whole plan. One morning, a short time ago, the cavalry, artillery, and the Sikhs marched upon our parade-ground. We did not know what was up; every man had been ordered for parade. Our recruits were served out with arms.

We were ordered to loosen ten rounds of ammunition before we left our bungalows. All sorts of questions were being asked as to who were going to get it. As soon as we fell in, we were ordered to load with ball; but still all was kept quiet. The general rode up to us, and we saluted him. The hero of the Redan called out, "Good morning, Fusiliers; I have a little job for you this morning."

Then turning to Colonel Aldsworth, he said, "I think we shall get over it without much trouble." We then marched off and formed line, with the Sikhs on our left. The cavalry were formed up so that they could act at once if required. The artillery, part with us, loaded with port fires lit, and part with the Sikhs. The mutineers were ordered to fall in. The general and his staff rode up to them, and ordered them to remain there, on pain of instant death. Two troops of the Dragoons—about 120 men—dashed in between them and their camp and faced them.

A number of carts, with about 100 natives with them, with picks and shovels, were close behind us; but still we did not know what was to be the next move, until the general returned to us. He then informed us with a load voice, that in every tent in yonder camp there were arms concealed under the soil. A number of sergeants were ordered to go to the left company, I being one of them. That company were at once ordered to advance.

The whole camp was struck; that is, all the tents were thrown down as quickly as possible by the natives; the picks and shovels brought into play. And true enough, arms of all descriptions were found, wrapped in paper or cloth, just under the soil. We found pistols, swords, guns, spears, and daggers by wholesale. They were thrown into the carts. Some of our men got a good haul in the shape of *rupees* and gold *mohurs* worth about thirty-two *rupees* each, (£3 4s.); but they did not go into the cart. We found daggers in their bed-clothing in many cases.

A nice youth from the Green Isle, a stalwart grenadier belonging to us, found a good *shillagh*, with lead let into the end of it. He had the whole lot of us laughing enough to break our sides, at his expressions and antics. He flourished his stick over his head, and declared that he would "bate" a squadron of yonder traitors with that bit of a "*carbine*,"

The general was with us, and laughed heartily at him, handing him his flask, when he drank to ould England and ould Ireland, as, one handing the flask back to the general, with a salute, he said he hoped that "his 'oner's cow would niver run dry." These weapons had been smuggled in from Wozerabad, the Birmingham of India, about forty miles from here. The disarmed regiment at Mooltan, we found by wire, had bolted, and were coming on to join these gents; but what a surprise it must have been to them when they, many of them, found a strong rope around their necks before the sun set that day, while others were sent flying from the cannon's mouth.

You remember me telling you about a venerable old native officer that had served us for forty years, and was so talkative about his loyalty: that he had fought and would again, as long as he could stand, for the British, and that he would be faithful, to death, and got so excited that he even mustered tears. Well, that very old hypocrite has turned out to be the ringleader. His own letter to his friends at Mooltan, with the whole plan, have condemned the old villain and others to a traitor's death, and he, with nineteen others, were blown to atoms a few days ago. It would have been all up with some of us long ago, but a merciful God has been watching over us.

I have not the slightest doubt that we should have destroyed them to a man, but we must have lost a number of valuable lives. My company's bungalow is the nearest to their camp, about 500 yards distant; so poor No. 7 would have been in as warm a corner as we had on the 18th June, 1855. But, thank God, it has been ordered otherwise. The Mooltan people, (I mean the runaway mutineers), are being brought in daily; one pound, or ten *rupees*, is offered by our people for everyone, dead or alive. The Sikhs are making a harvest.

The mutineers are tried by court-martial, condemned, and executed at once. I think you will say that is sharp work. My dear parents, 400,000 men with arms in their hands are not to be played with; mind, it's death or victory with us. If our Government were to dilly-dally with them we should have the Sikhs against us, as the following, I think, will prove:

It's time for Britons to strike home; our men are, so to speak, fighting with halters around their necks. This is a war of extermination. Some three or four regiments of Sikhs are stationed at Dera Ishmal Khan, about 280 miles from here. These gents have struck for the same pay the British soldier gets, and are determined to fight for it, if required. These are the nice allies that our wing, the Dragoons, artillery, and Ghoorkas are gone against: and news by wire has just come in that they have got a little more than they asked for. They were confronted by our people, and ordered to give up their arms; but would not without a fight: so they got it quick and sharp—grape, shot, shell, and musketry, with the cavalry riding through and through them. It has struck terror into the Sikhs all over the country.

So you see that sharp diseases require sharp remedies. It has reminded their brethren all over the country that we are still the conquering race. The regiment of Sikhs here call them at Dera mad fools; but the tables, you must remember, have been turned. I see by the papers it has had the effect of making our friends, the Sikhs, remarkably civil in all parts of the country. Grape is the best dose that could be administered to traitors; those that escape remember it as long as they live, and will hand it down to their children's children.

Our motto out here must be: *We will surrender India only with* our lives. *Nought shall make us rue, if Britons to themselves will act but true.* Shoulder to shoulder we may die; but so long as India is held in the hands of true Britons, they will never yield. I trust this will find you all quite well. But before I close I have a secret to tell you: before this reaches you I shall most likely have taken a rib to share my joys and sorrows. It will be like all the remainder, *"for better for worse."* I feel confident that her sweet temper will cheer me in prosperity, and soothe me in adversity, and that her tender, loving heart will lighten the burden of life. I always look on the bright side, as I think you know. I never go half way to meet troubles; I have learnt by a little rough experience that the best way to surmount difficulties is to face them manfully. This is a world of ups and downs, and I feel I want a helpmate. . . . I have often thought of your advice to me as a very young man, before I took the Queen's shilling: "Never to think of taking a wife until I could support one comfortably." I can now see my way clear before me, although it's not all gold that glitters. Mine has been love at first sight—our courtship has been short—so we will tie the knot first, and court afterwards. But I must bring this to a close. You may inform Miss H—— that she has played with the mouse until she has lost it. Please tend my kind regards to all old friends.

And believe me,
My Dear Parents,
Your affectionate Son,
T. Gowing.
Drill-Sergeant Royal Fusiliers.

Meean-Meer, (Punjaub),
10th November, 1858.

My Dear, Dear Parents,
Once more a line in health, trusting this will find you the same. This is a changeable world we live in. It will not, I expect, be news to you to inform you that one of the strongest Companies this world has ever seen—that started with but small prospects of success, bat gradually rose to be Rulers of a vast population and a mighty empire, much larger than the whole of Europe in area and population—has passed away. The great East India Company is now a thing of the past, and we are no longer under their control. By proclamation. Her Most Gracious Majesty,

Queen Victoria, is now the supreme Ruler of India.
There has been a lot of pomp and show all through the country. The natives seem to be delighted at the change. They appear to have confidence that they will have justice under the "*Buna Ranee*."[3] One portion of the proclamation must have its effect upon the poor deluded wretches that are still holding out under the Napaul Hills and Central India. The Royal clemency is extended to all offenders, except those who have been guilty of murdering poor defenceless women and children. In accordance with the laws of God and civilized nations, justice demands their lives—"a murderer shall die."
The natives cannot understand how it is possible that we can forgive men that have rebelled against and fought us, time after time. Their wonder is that when we were but few, we destroyed all that came in our way, and now that the whole country is bristling with British bayonets, and the enemy at our feet, we forgive. This is a little beyond their comprehension. The Mohammedans, they say, would not do that. They do not understand mercy to a fallen foe. Hundreds of thousands of them have yet to learn that, as Christians, we are taught to be merciful to our enemies.
I find by the papers that hundreds, yea, thousands of these poor deluded wretches are coming to the various camps and stations and laying their arms at our feet. We may rejoice that this terrible war is now nearly over. As a soldier, I think I have already had enough of war to know the value of peace, and I have no desire to show a bellicose spirit. The man that's fond of war is a lunatic. I know well that at times it is a necessary evil, and duty—stern duty—must be performed. A statesman who hurls his country into war without straining every nerve to avert it, is, to say the least of it, an unwise man, so we hail Her Majesty's proclamation with joy. It will be the means of saying thousands of precious lives. I find that in one province alone (Oude) 350,000 arms of various kinds have been given up already; the mutineers have been pardoned and have gone to their homes.
As far as I can see by the papers from home, they have put a lot of colouring upon the state of things out here, and made them appear to the public much worse than they really are; that's needless, but truth will stand sifting. An honest account will go

---
3. Great Queen.

best when plainly told. I could fill sheet after sheet with what, out here, is called bazaar talk, but only about two per cent, of it is reliable, and sometimes not that; but it often finds its way into the country papers, and home papers copy, and most of it is swallowed as gospel. It's now getting very pleasant mornings and evenings.

I still keep on with my drilling, and am happy to inform you I have got another step up the ladder of promotion—colour-sergeant and pay-sergeant of a company. It gives me a lot of extra work; but I do not mind that at all, so long as I can give satisfaction to my commanders. It gives me near two shillings *per diem* more. I wanted to resign my drill-sergeantship, but the colonel would not listen to me; so I am often at work with my pen when others are enjoying themselves, or asleep. I have much pleasure in forwarding you a small draft to get you a little nourishment. Please to accept it in the same spirit in which it is sent; and if you do not require it, bank it against a rainy day. I must now bring this to a close, and believe me,

   My Dear Parents,
    Your affectionate Son,
     T. Gowing,
   Colour-Sergeant Royal Fusiliers.

         Rawul Pindee,
         28th July, 1859.

My Dear, Dear Parents,

Once more a line in health. This is one of the most lovely, yea, delightful places I have ever clapped eyes upon. The climate is quite refreshing when compared with the burning plains of Meean-Meer. We are just at the foot of what are called the Murry Hills, or Himalaya Mountains. They rise majestically all along our front, and we get a beautiful refreshing breeze morning and evening. I should not mind completing my time here. I am afraid it is too good to last long.

Well, in reference to our march from Meean-Meer. We started on the morning of the 5th April. Nothing particular to note until we came to Wozerabad, the Birmingham of India. As far as I can see, a native will do anything with a pattern. I was astonished, on going through their bazaars, to see the number of arms for sale. I bought a large dagger, and a knife with all sorts of blades in it. I find our Government have bought up the greater portion of the firearms. They are a most war-like race of people about this part of the country, but their teeth have been drawn.

They are on our side, and so long as they can see that we are still the conquering race, they will go with us against all corners. On arriving at the Jelumn, we found it a rushing, mighty torrent, very wide. We crossed it on a bridge of boats on the northern bank. We found a very pretty station, but empty until our arrival. Our other wing rejoined us here. The Headuartera remained at Jelumn, and five companies were ordered on here. I was appointed acting sergeant-major of the wing.

After the first day's march we bade goodbye to all roads and bridges. We struck into a hilly country full of little streams; some about 30, others near 200 yards wide. We had to land on the other side the best way we could—many of them very dangerous places to get over in the dark—with a line of Natives with torches to mark the fords. We had as many as sixteen of these nice places to go through, in as many miles. We found the natives all the way up country remarkably civil; they knew well it would not do to be otherwise.

Although the Mutiny is now nearly all over, the country is still under martial law, and our Government are determined to stamp rebellion out with a strong hand, well rewarding all those that remain faithful. The Sikhs, Afriedies, Ghoorkas, and Beloochees have stood by us well; and they will now reap their reward in the shape of good pensions.

Some of them have had little or nothing to do, but they have completed their portion of the contract with our Government. Sir John Laurence may well be called the saviour of Lidia, for he is the man that saved Lidia. Yes, it was a daring master-stroke on his part. He had spent all his life out here. No man breathing knew the Native character better than Sir John. When the mutiny broke out. Sir John was Governor of the Punjaub. It had only been conquered eight years. Thousands of Sikhs all over the Punjaub, then as now, (*at the time of first publication*), carried the wounds received from the dreaded *Feringhees*.

But Sir John, knowing that we were playing for heavy stakes, at once called upon the chiefs of the Sikhs to rally round the British standard. He requested them to furnish him with 100,000 men; they did so, and arms were at once put into their hands. In the name of our Government, Sir John promised them, if they would serve our Government faithfully for two years, or until the revolt was crushed, a pension for life, according to rank; while for all those who fell in action, or died of wounds or disease, their nearest relatives should reap the reward.

All animosity was thrown on one side, the temptation of the sacking of Delhi and other towns that had revolted being ever before their eyes. Now that it is all over, our Government are faithfully discharging Sir John's promise, and thousands of these stalwart men are returning to their native towns and villages— all loud in their praises of the Big Lord Sahib, as they call our Government. In many cases their sons are off, only too happy to take their fathers' places. I find that all natives are now enlisted to serve us in any part of the world we may require their services.

There are no better men in the world than the Ghoorkas, Sikhs, Afriedees, and Beloochees. If we required 400,000 or 800,000, we could have them in less than one month, and officer them by some of the wildest boys of our much-beloved Isle. They will go anywhere, particularly if they are mixed up with some of our battalions. Should ever the Russians make an attempt on India, they will find a handful. As far as I can find out, the Mutiny was not brought about by anything that has as yet been laid before the public.

There has been a system of bribery all through the service, and the whole scheme of the East India Company was rotten to the core. Such a system of bribery from the highest, one would think, had been handed down from Clive and Hastings. As far as I can see, all the native of India wants is justice; and under their old masters, the much-lauded East India Company, they had a lot of law. But justice was scantily eked out, unless the unfortunate client could stamp up well that which makes the world go smooth, and corers a multitude of sins.

From such cases as the following, now beginning to leak out, you may form some judgment of the laws of the East India Company, there being one law for the native and another for the Lord Sahib, both of whom, remember, being under our much-respected flag of liberty. A European, in chastising one of his servants, killed him. Of course his counsellor (that is, if it was brought to light at all) would represent to the court in most eloquent language that his client had been grossly insulted; or if there was no other loop-hole to escape from—his client, a most peace-loving, fatherly Christian, in the heat of passion, knocked the deceased down with his fist or stick, not thinking for one moment of doing him an injury, but just to teach him better manners. But he died, it must be acknowledged, from the treatment of this peace-loving fatherly Christian. He gets off, or escapes the law by a fine of from 500 to 1000 *rupees*—£50 or £100.

Now just note how justice was doled out to the native, *viz*., if he is a poor man. His *Sahib* hit him, and he returns the compliment, and being a powerful man, he gives his old master a good pounding. Well, the native is duly handed over to the law, and if he gets off with ten years' transportation, with heavy irons, he's a fortunate man. As for the native army rising, I am not at all astonished at it. They have been treated worse than the brute beasts of the field by those they had to look up to, or to whom, according to military law, they were compelled to show respect. The whole system of treatment to which they have been subjected for years was tyrannical; and the Bengal Army, to say the least of it, has been worried into insubordination and, depending upon their strength, broke out into open mutiny.

The upshot of it has been the smashing up of the strongest Company that has ever existed under the old Jack or any other flag. Already we begin to find the country gradually settling down, and I do not think we shall have much more trouble with the mutineers. I find by the papers our Government are determined to root out all evil-doers, and all law-abiding subjects shall be protected from the lawless and have justice; that the same laws that govern the European shall in future guide, govern, and protect the native. And a strong Government has announced that tyranny and bribery shall be stamped out with the strong arm of the law; and that all, from the highest to the lowest in India, shall enjoy liberty of conscience, shall worship God according to the dictates of their hearts, at their own shrines or places of worship, and none shall interfere or make them afraid.

This order or decree has been translated into all the different languages spoken in India. We already see the effect for good upon the natives, and I dare prophecy that it will bind the teeming millions in love to our glorious old flag. We have a regiment of mutineers here, and they are permitted to go where they like about the station. As far as I am concerned, I have a handful—as much as I can get through, with the extra duty of acting sergeant-major, looking after the canteen, "not at all a bad job" I can tell you, and then my Company's work.

But I must say I have some of the sweets, and say nothing about the canteen. A good-tempered, pretty girl to call my own; and, as far as I can see, change of air or new bread is affecting her wonderfully; but all's well that ends well. I must bring this note to a close; I have had two or three goes at it. Trusting this will find yon all enjoying the best of blessings. My wife joins with me in love.

And believe me,
My dear Parents,
Your affectionate Son,
T. Gowing,
C. S., A. S. M. Royal Fusiliers.

P.S.— Do not publish this, but keep it. I have hit out a little too plainly; but facts are stubborn things, and stronger than fiction.

T. G.

Peshawur, 25th November, 1859.

My Dear Parents,

Once more, a line or two in answer to your kind letter, just to hand. As for the small amounts I have sent you from time to time, do not mention it, but rather thank Him who is the great disposer of all. I feel it a pleasure and a duty to contribute a little of what this world mostly prizes towards your comfort: and my fine bouncing rib encourages me. And kindly tell me what a man will not do for a warm-hearted pretty girl, with her arm around his neck, and her sweet lips close to his: "O do send poor mother a little this time; we can spare it."

Please send your photos, with the next letter, in cabinet size. We will send ours by the next mail, as I find there is a good photographer in this station. Our No. 1 is a whopper —a strong healthy child; I hope he will make a man in the world some day. This is a lovely looking station, but it has a cruel name for thieves and murderers, fever and ague. It is much colder here than in any place in which we have been. The Himalayas are on our right, left, and front. We are all served out with an extra warm coat, padded with wadding; and we require them nights and mornings.

Now for a little news about our march up here. We marched out of Rawul Pindee on the 20th October with a regiment of Native cavalry—a portion of Hodson's Horse—that have fought so desperately for us all over the country. I find they are fine-looking men, with a lot of go in them. They have some wild spirits as officers to lead them. We had likewise a regiment of native infantry, and a battery of Horse Artillery with us. We escorted up here more money than I ever saw in my life before. We had some 600 camels and a great number of elephants, carrying bags of *rupees*, 1,000 in each bag.[4]

A camel can carry four bags. The elephants were used to carry tents and other heavy baggage. It was all a job to load up the money; we had thirty *lacs* to load and unload every morning. The string of camels and elephants made a great show; for we had close upon 300 of them with us. Then came all kinds of vehicles, country carts, &c., many of the wheels of which were octagonal, or any shape you like but round; some hundreds of *tattoos* (small ponies), shaggy looking, but strong, most of them belonging to the grass cutters, for the cavalry and artillery.

Then came all the rag-tail of the native bazaars, native women riding on poor pony donkeys; these poor creatures are not much larger than a good-sized Newfoundland dog. Goats by wholesale: and as for monkeys and parrots, these were perched upon the top of the baggage in swarms. The whole of this medley goes swinging along beside the road or track; as for dust, we were not short of that.

We found but few bridges all the way up, and as we came to the streams, which were very numerous—some of them ugly places to get over—we had to land on the other side the best way we could; and a nice lot of beauties we looked, but as all were alike, we could not laugh much at each other, except in a few cases where the men had had a roll in the water, or got into a hole of about seven or eight feet, and had to be pulled out. I managed to pop into one of these nice holes one morning, quite over my head; they pulled me out, and of coarse, had a good laugh at me.

---

4. £300,000.

But laughing is sometimes catching.

At some of the streams there were a number of villagers who offered their services to carry anyone over for about two *annas*—three-pence. Then came the sport. Many of these natives were tripped up, and both native and European would have a roll or flounder for it: all would be taken in good part. As for game of all kinds, they will hardly get out of year way, and one with a fouling-piece can soon have a good bag. There is a very strong force kept at this place. It is close upon the borders of Afghanistan, and our people are not going to be taken short with them; for they are a treacherous lot and know no law, but might is right with them.

We found one of our sentinels this morning lying dead at his post: his rifle and accoutrements were gone, and he, poor fellow, had been stabbed in the heart. I will be bound our fellows will pay them out for that yet—it's only lent. We must keep a sharp lookout. I never attempt to go out here at night without my loaded revolver. I am happy to say we are both of as keeping our health well. I think I told you in my last, a commission was offered me in a native regiment, but I declined it. I shall stop with the old Fusiliers. Trusting this will find you all quite well.

    Believe me, as ever,
      Your affectionate Son,
        T. Gowing,
         C.S.R.F.

P.S.—Wife sends her love to all. Will drop a line next mail.
          T.G.

      Peshawar, April 14th, 1860.

My Dear Dear Parents,

Once more, a line in health from this sickly station. This is, I think, about the worst place we have on all the plains of India— they may well call it the Valley of Death. There is a kind of fever here that brings the stoutest down to the brink of the grave in a very short time. Thank God, I have escaped it thus far. And again, unless we are well on the alert, we do not know when we may get up and find our throats cut, for no other crime than that we are *"Feringhee sowars"*—English pigs. We are surrounded by the scum of the earth—cringing cowards. They will not face our men, but as far as I can see, they take delight in murdering with the dagger, in the dark, any they can pounce upon; but a number of them have already met a traitor's death. I find, by your last, that you are mistaken about Santa Topee. He was not a brother, or in any way related to that fiend of a Nana Sahib, but his right-hand man. He was a black-hearted monster of the deepest dye, but he has met a traitor's death. Hanging was too good for him. To recount his blood-thirsty deeds to poor defenceless women and children, would make your blood run cold. If our laws would have permitted it, he ought to have been tried by a judge and jury of women, and I do not think he would have died in two minutes, for he was a wholesale murderer.

As for that blood-thirsty monster, Nana Sahib, he has thus far escaped the sword of justice. One million of money has been offered for him, dead or alive, by our Government; and as large as India is, if he is alive, he will have to keep very quiet. But the general opinion is that his form no longer disgraces this earth—that he has destroyed himself, or was killed in some of the encounters with our troops on the Nepaul frontier. He knew well that his doom was almost instant death, had he fallen into our hands. The Afghans have become wonderfully civil of late. They have found out that the *"Feringhee ray"*—English reign—is not all over out here, and that civility is much cheaper than shot, shell, cold steel, or a rope.

As for a native army, we *must* keep up one, or send out at least 50,000 more men, to hold this vast country. The old Bengal Native Army has been almost destroyed. There are a few regiments that have remained loyal, and the places of the others are filled up with Punjaubees and Afriedees—inhabitants of the lower range of the Himalaya Mountains. One would almost pity some of the old mutineers that escaped the ravages of war. We have a number of them here. They tell us all sorts of tales as to what brought about the Mutiny. But, so far as I can find out, they were badly treated—buffeted and knocked about by their officers—and it was no use complaining.

The fact is this, with at least thousands of them, it had been prophesied that we should hold the country for one hundred years, starting from Plassey (1757); that none could stand against us; then we should have to bow to them and eat the dust. But they have found the sons of Albion, side by side the heroic boys of Ireland, bad hands at eating humble-pie—that we are still the conquering race, and determined to hold what has been handed down to us. I find the country generally is settling down under the sceptre of Her Most Gracious Majesty.

All those that have been faithful to us are now reaping their reward; and that will have a wonderful effect upon the native mind. All through those dark, troublesome days, with treachery all around, there has been a silver line running. Some have proved faithful until death, although of the same creed and caste with the others; and while in the midst of the ranks of these blood-thirsty villains, have come out boldly, ranged themselves by our side, and fought desperately for us. These men are now reaping their reward.

I have much pleasure in forwarding herewith our photos. You will find a corner for them in the album, I think. Hope you will like them. It's not a good one of my better half, as her attention was upon the child. Most bring this to a close,

And believe me,
My dear Parents,
Your affectionate Son,
T. Gowing.
C. S. R. F

P.S.— I enclose a letter from my rib; and from her long stocking she has desired me to forward you a nice little present of £——. This is the first from her, but if we are spared it will not be the last.

T.G.

Peshawar, October 26th, 1860.

My Dear, Dear Parents,

I think I told you that Rawul Pindee was a perfect paradise upon earth, contrasted with this infernal hole. For if ever there was a hell upon earth, or a hell-doomed place, this is the spot. We are infested with the scum of the earth—thieves and murderers all around us. It's no use trying to tame them or to take them prisoners; they will not be taken alive if they can help it, and the only way to stop their little game is to shoot them. There is nothing too hot or too heavy for them to walk off with. They will creep on hands and knees right into the men's barrack-rooms, and steal their rifles and accoutrements, ammunition, etc.

They are in a state of nudity, greased all over, and armed with a large dagger. Should anyone try to stop or take them, look out for the dagger. We have already had several men killed by them. I think I have encountered the enemies of our country as often as most men of my age. It's far better to have an open enemy to deal with, than such brutes as we are infested with. They come around the barracks during the day, under the pretence of selling all sorts of articles; at the same time they are taking stock of what they will return for at night, under a different garb. I think I told you before, that there are no walls around the barracks out here—at least, we have not met any yet.

An order has been issued to challenge and fire at once, if not answered; but that has been found ineffectual—several men having lost their lives simply by challenging them. So our men have reversed the order,—fire first, then shout out, "Who comes there?" You will say, "that is murder well out." Well, it has been brought in day after day as justifiable homicide; for in every case, that deadly weapon, the dagger, has been found by the side of the would-be murderer.

We have had nearly twelve months' training with these gents, and the Fusiliers, the 93rd Highlanders, the 98th and 19th Hussars or "dumpypice," (as we have called them on account of their diminutive stature), have pretty well thinned them out, one would think. Mind this has been going on since we took possession in 1849. The Afghans then were supposed to be our allies, but in fighting the Sikhs, on the field of Goojerat (21.1.1849), thousands of these nice allies were found in the ranks of our enemies.

The Sikh boundary on their north-west was the River Attock, and as a punishment to the Afghanistan ruler, our people annexed to our dominion the whole slice from the Attook to the mouth of the Khyber Pass, Peshawar becoming our frontier station. Well, since then, hundreds of them have been shot; but still they are as daring as ever. It is not safe to lie down to sleep without a loaded revolver under your head. In the summertime, it is so hot that the doors must be left open to admit air. One of our sergeants caught a fellow very cleverly a short time ago. He had a large hole dug in front of his door, put a slab over it, had it well secured during the daytime, so that it would not tilt, and at night set his trap.

We often laughed at his contrivance. He has a very natty little housewife, and his front room always looked the picture of comfort. He had his rifle and sword so placed, that anyone coming up to the door, during the daytime, could see them. He had not very long to wait before he got his reward, in the shape of a wild-looking savage monster, armed with two murderous-looking daggers. This hole or well was about ten feet deep, with a sort of man-trap at the bottom. The sergeant's quarters were not far from mine. I heard the row, and of course I must go to see the fun. His bâtman or servant is an Irishman. The first salute I heard was: "You murdering villain, an' how the d—l did you git in thir? Arrah! sergeant, dear, the d—l take me if it is not the same identical blackguard that was selling Afghan cats here yesterday!"

We managed to get him out with ropes, but he struck out left and right with his daggers, and before we could disarm him, he got a tap on the head with the butt-end of the rifle, and a taste of the bayonet he was looking after (from the owner). This fellow was transported for life. I have bought one of the daggers for 20 *rupees*. The sergeant got 200 *rupees* from the judge for his ingenious trap, and I think he had the laugh at us. So you see we are in the midst of a nice lot. The noted Khyber Pass is just in front of us, about five miles from the barracks—and this is where most of these gents hail from.

About a month ago, my master-cook came running to me early one morning to report that the whole of the Company's cooking utensils had been stolen during the night; and as they are alls made of copper, they are worth a trifle. It is a pity they did not send a note to inform us where they had taken them; so that we might have sent them, something to cook, if it was only coffee, for it's beginning to get cold on the hills now. By the bye, we can see snow here all the year round, although it's enough to roast one in the valley.

It is the unhealthiest place we have in all India. We have now upward of 200 men down with fever and ague. Last summer, many of our men looked more dead than alive, and were walking about for spite, to save funeral expenses. We have just mustered number two. We shall call him Arthur Henry, after his uncle. Mother and child are doing well. We have had a slice of luck latterly, and I enclose you a little present in the shape of an order for £—. Please to accept it from your wild boy as a mark of love.

Before I close this, I must tell you the latest daring attempt at robbery. An officer of the 98th had been robbed of all he had in his room. He had suspicion that some of his native servants were implicated in the robbery, and was determined, if possible, to find it out. He accordingly furnished fresh; and, next evening, allowed himself to be carried home, apparently drunk. He was laid upon his bed, his native servants attending to undress him. There he lay, to all appearance helplessly drunk. As soon as he was by himself he jumped up, took his revolver (loaded), and lay down again. About twelve o'clock (midnight), a man crawled into the room, and stood over him with a large dagger, ready to plunge it into his heart had he moved, whilst others cleared all out of the room, in the shape of arms, carpets, &c.

As soon as they had got all that they could carry, the signal was given to the would-be murderer to follow. But no sooner was he off his guard, than out came the revolver, and the would-be assassin fell dead. Our cool, resolute officer at once pounced on the others, killing one, and wounding two others—one of them his own servant. But I must bring this to a close. We expect to remove shortly from this "lovely spot" to Nowshira—18 miles from here. They tell us that we shall be jumping out of the frying-pan into the fire—so far as thieves and sandstorms are concerned.

This is the third attempt I have had at this letter. Since writing the above, I am sorry to have to inform you that I have been robbed of every farthing I had in the house—both public and private monies. They have made a clean sweep. But I do not believe that it's a native of India that has robbed me; for in that case all would have gone, including clothing, jewellery, arms, &c.; whereas nothing but cash, and some rum I had bottled for the christening, have been taken.

It was done whilst I was on a visit to my sick wife and child in hospital I was only away from, home about an hour and a-half—from 7 to 8.30 p.m. My servant was found drunk, and, about 10 p.m., we found some rum in bottles, but no cash has turned up. I cannot at present send what I had promised. I have lost in all about £60 (600 *rupees*), including Company's money.

My captain is but a poor man. We were sergeants together at Inkermann, and he shall not suffer by my neglect; for in my absence I ought to have put one of our police at my door, knowing there was so much money in my box.

Whoever has got it, it will not do them much good, and I shall get over it in a few months. But I shall keep my eyes open, and if possible, will bring the thief to justice. We have plenty of "black ones" to look after. I shall discharge my servant at once, and take that good-hearted Irishman who saved my life at the Redan. He is a rough diamond, I know; but as true as steel, and one that I have a right to .respect for his noble conduct to me, when death was all around.

No more at present, must conclude, and believe me, as ever.

     Your affectionate son,
      T. Gowing,
       C. S. R. F.

      Meean-Meer, 26th May, 1862.

My Dear Parents,

In answer to your kind letter of 18th February, just to hand, I am happy to inform you that we are quite well, and doing well. The heat during the day is very trying at present. As for the trifle we sent you last, do not mention it. We both of us are only too happy to be able to contribute a little towards your comfort in your declining days. Send nothing in return but your photos, and as long as it pleases God to give us health and strength, we will keep on repeating the dose as you require it. At your time of life, you want a little nourishment: and it is only a debt of gratitude that I am discharging, and all we ask (for we both pull together in the same boat) is for you to accept it as a mark of love and gratefulness. It will, I hope, help to bind up some of the wounds that the writer, as a thoughtless boy, gave your poor hearts. It's an old saying that a wild colt makes a good horse.

I am thankful to say that I have a partner that is worth her weight in diamonds, and I must tell you we are going on very nicely. We have not yet been married four years, and now we muster five little ones. She has just made me a present of two—a boy and a girl. My captain told me a few days ago he thought I had an eye to business; as I think I told you we get 5s. per month out here, from Government, for every child until they are sixteen years of age. I have the canteen here for my detachment of three companies.

They had to leave us here, as the barracks at Ferozepore would not hold us. We are so strong (near 1,600 bayonets). This detachment is near 500 strong. We are about two miles from the barracks we occupied in 1858. I am heading them every toss. As far as I can see, I prosper in everything I put my hand to. We have some very rich officers, and as drill-sergeant and acting sergeant-major, I have the training of all young officers. I have a lot of trouble with them, and am often hard at work when others are taking it easy. I often get handsome presents from them. I have remarkably good health, and I do not abuse it.

We have been out here nearly five years, and I do not know the taste of any drink stronger than tea or coffee My colonel has very kindly offered me a commission, but I felt almost compelled to decline it, looking at my *little big* family and a strong, healthy wife, not yet twenty-five. I thanked the colonel for his kindness; but on account of my family, requested him to kindly allow me to remain as I was.

Had I been single, I would have jumped at the colonel's kind offer. But I am satisfied: as I have made my bed, so I will lie on it. It is not all pleasure to be an officer, with a smart coat and almost an empty pocket. I am sorry to have to inform you that cholera has made its appearance here. The artillery and the 19th Regiment are losing a number of men daily. Thus far, we have only had one fatal case—a sergeant of my company, cut off in three-and-a-half hours with it. Our commander has left all to me. I have got up all kinds of sports for the men, mornings and evenings—anything but drink, to keep up their spirits. Our general called upon me this morning for a copy of the programme of the sports. He is not a teetotaller, and enquired if I had plenty of rum on hand. He went with me and inspected the canteen, ordering an extra tot of grog for all hands at once, which they had. The men turned out as fast as their legs could carry them when I sounded the grog bugle, and cheered the general heartily.

My wife has gone up to the hills with our little ones, so I am at present a grass widower. I am glad they are off the burning plains. The climate up there is lovely. I hope to start shortly with our eldest boy for the school at Kussoulie; but I shall not leave until all danger is over as regards the cholera. I find a lot of alteration in this place since 1858. The old native huts or barracks have all been thrown down, and beautifully laid out gardens have taken their places. Yes, it is true I was robbed a second time in Peshawur; but I did not like to upset you by telling you.

But since you have got hold of it, I may as well tell you that the second time it was a Khybereen. I lost upwards of 1,400 *rupees*—public and private—my watch (a good English lever), and gold Albert; my wife's gold watch and long chain, and a lot of other trinkets and clothing belonging to myself, wife and children. The fellow was traced to the mouth of the Khyber Pass. The whole of the troops in garrison were on parade at the time; so I think I have cause to remember that lovely spot.

Since then, I have made it a point not to keep much money in the house; but I was not the only victim of our regiment up there. They walked off with our sergeant-major's large box; it took at least two to carry it. There were over 3,000 *rupees* in it, most of it public money. There was a man on sentry close by at the time, but they managed to attract his attention in another direction, and then walked or crept in and slipped out at the back with it. Next morning it was found broken up: the books and papers were left, but the cash had gone.

Now that I am writing upon the tricks of these nice gents, I will give you a few more. The 93rd, whilst on parade, had on one occasion nearly all their medals stolen, and were never heard of more. The artillery had a small guard of three men and a corporal, on their canteen: they walked off with all their carbines, swords, and long boots, including the sentry's (for he was drunk), and then had the cheek to try and take away a six-pounder horse artillery gun; but they had to drop that. It turned out that they were chased, and could not run with it. We had a native policeman to watch our targets. One morning our instructor of musketry found the poor fellow's head stuck upon one of the targets; he had evidently stood in their way. They said we should find them more daring at Nowshera, and true enough, we did.

One of our pay-sergeants, on getting up one morning, found two large stones, larger than his head, by the side of his bed: his three arm-chests, with about twenty stand of arms and accoutrements, gone. The chests were found about a mile from the barracks, but empty. Just as our left wing were leaving Nowshera, the camp being pitched ready for the men to go into, but not occupied—it was almost square—a heavy sandstorm came on during the night, and in the midst of the storm, they walked off with one of the large tents, although there were six sentries with loaded rifles all around the camp.

With reference to the sergeant, he was made a prisoner for neglecting to chain his chests to the wall, according to order. He was a good-hearted, witty fellow. He was brought before our colonel on a charge of neglect; the colonel, who knew well what an honourable, straightforward man he was, said that he was astonished to see the prisoner before him on such a charge. In defence, the old veteran said that he generally slept with one eye at a time, but these fellows had, he must acknowledge, caught him napping. The colonel let him go.

But before I close this I must tell you that our Government do not lose much by them for all that's stolen: a heavy indemnity is laid on all the surrounding villages. As one victim who never got a farthing back, I was only too glad to get out of the Peshawur valley. There were only about fifty men in the whole regiment that escaped the fever and ague, and I am one of them. But I must bring this short note to a close.

And believe me, My dear Parents,
Ever your affectionate Son,
(Our united extra love for Mother),
T. Gowing,
C.S. and A.S.M.,
Royal Fusiliers.

P.S.—The following is too good to be kept back: at Peshawur, one of our staff-officers had a beautiful charger, a very valuable horse. Some of his friends told him he would lose it some night. He laughed at them; he had three men told off specially as a guard for his stables. One morning last winter there were all sorts of rumours going about that the general's horses had been stolen. It turned out that an old man had set himself down to have a smoke with his *hubbybub*;[5] two of the guard joined him, and the third at last thought he would have a pull. Almost as quick as thought, the three men became unconscious. The old man at once gave the signal, when in came the men, stole this

---

5. Native pipe.

beautiful horse, with three others, saddled them, and mounting with all the guards' arms, and ammunition, were away quickly. It was found that the guard had been dosed.

T. G.

Meean-Meer, 20th September, 1862.

My Dear, Dear Parents,

Once more a line, in the best of health, trusting this will find you enjoying the same blessing. I told you in my last that I felt lonely. I have given Corporal Woods a little of my mind. What is the use of upsetting your minds for nothing. It is true I got a touch of the cholera in June last—the doctors only called it a touch—but if that's only a touch, I pray that it may never touch me again. Another wrote to my wife, informing her of it. She, poor thing, was almost distracted: and the only thing that appeased her mind was frequent telegrams informing her that I was alive and had got over the worst of it.

It gave me a good shaking, but not being in the habit of drinking spirits, brandy cured me. The doctors informed me that had I been a rum drinker, the brandy would not have had the effect. I have no objection to Wood writing to his friends; but, as I told him, he might have waited to see the result before sending the news 16,000 miles away, almost amounting to one's death. Well, thank God, I have got over it, but I have had another fight for life since then.

I think it will somewhat amuse you, so I will tell you all. I have put Johnny into the school at Kussoolie, in the Himalaya Mountains: it is about 350 miles from, here. We travelled by bullock cart (Government), changing bullocks every ten miles, travelling night and day. We found it very hot and sultry in July, but still we pushed on. All went well until we came to the banks of the Sutlej, a broad and rapid river which, owing to the melting of the snow on the hills, had overflowed its banks. The point at which we had to cross was over six miles wide, the current running from ten to twelve miles per hour. I obtained a good supply of food, lemonade, and other refreshments from the 81st, stationed in a large fort on the banks of the river. Cart, bullocks, and all, were put into a large Government boat, and off we started.

It was tedious work, crossing each a current. We had four natives to man the boat. As far as I could see, they understood their business. I watched them for some time, and then got into my cart to have a nap. I was informed we should be four hours, at least, crossing. Whilst I was asleep. Master Johnny amused himself by throwing all the food we had overboard, to feed the fishes. On arriving safely on *terra firma* once more, I asked my generous son to hand me a biscuit and a bottle of lemonade. I got the latter, but Johnny said he could not see any biscuits in the box. I told him to look again. The answer I got was; "I cannot see any biscuits, dada."

I was rather annoyed, but I found the child was right. We had then about 140 miles to go, without food, and no sign of habitation—a nice lookout. We travelled all that night, and until about 6 p.m. next day. As I was walking behind the cart, I noticed the child crying; I inquired what was the matter, when he, poor boy, burst out the louder, saying he was hungry. I could not stand that, so, mounting on the top of the cart, I espied a native village about a mile from the road. We drew the cart up under some trees, and telling the driver to take his bullocks out, and stop there to take care of the child until I returned, promising to reward him, I armed myself with a brace of revolvers, loaded, took some empty bottles to hold milk, and with a good strong stick, off I went across the *paddy* fields, up to my ankles, and sometimes knees, in mud and water, until I struck upon a good path.

As I approached the village a number of dogs came at me. I kept them at bay with stones and my stick as long as I could—shooting the most troublesome one, when the remainder were called off. On turning a corner I came upon a number of native women (almost in a state of nudity), milking cows—the very thing I wanted. I walked up to them and saluted them with, "*Salam:*" then mustering my best Hindustanee I told them that I required milk. (Now, mind, don't you laugh). "*Hum-dood, Manta-hi*"—that I would pay them for it. "*Hum piea dada hi.*" They all looked at me with contempt, exclaiming, yea, screaming, "*Jow thome Feringhee sour*"—"Go away, you English pig." I could not stand much of that; I tried once more to make peace with them by telling them I was no thief, that I wanted milk for my hungry child and myself, and that I would pay them what they asked. The following is as near as I can come at it: "*Decco thunb hum loot wallah nay hi Hum-dood Manta-hi, hommoea babba both bokha hi,"* and, to my astonishment, they with one voice screamed out, and sent me to the lower regions—a very hot place for an English pig—*"Jahanham jow tomb Feringhee sour."*

Flesh and blood could not stand that: I was not to be done by a lot of fanatic women. So I at once walked up to one of them, and taking the vessel that she was milking into, drank heartily, throwing down four *annas* (sixpence) for it. Hereupon they all at once jumped up and ran into the village, shouting as though I had killed or kissed some of them.

They had not been gone long when they returned with seven men, armed with *"lathies"*—long sticks with lead let into the end, and brass-headed nails all around from the top, extending about two feet. The women were behind the men, shouting like mad, pitiless creatures, for the men to *"Maro, Maro, Ko Feringhee"*—"Kill, kill the Englishman." It was no use my trying to run, but I must face the lot.

Now for the "tug of war." On they came: the first man rushed at me, delivering a terrible blow at my head; being a fair swordsman, I warded it off, and delivered the six-cut right across his face, when down he went: he had had enough. Another came at me; I warded off his blow, and delivered a point from the hip right into his stomach, which doubled him up and made him pull all sorts of wry faces and down he went. Others rushed at me.

Only one hit me, but I warmed him for that, right and left. In less time than it takes me to tell you, I had them all rolling on the ground: they had each of them received some heavy blows; it was life or death with me. When the women found that the "English pig" was too many for them, they, with one exception, ran back into the village, screaming again. I at once broke all their sticks and threw them into a pond close by, and by way of refreshment, took another good drink of milk, and filled my bottles. I was just about to walk off, when I noticed some men coming after me, with a number of women and dogs, encouraging them to kill me.

I knew well it would be no use me trying to get away, so I made up my mind at once to die hard. My chief thought was about my poor little boy. Hushing to a good-sized tree I stood on the defensive, with my back to the tree, men, women, and dogs pursuing. The first man who came at me was a powerful-looking fellow, a sort of champion or bully. I believe they thought he would be more than a match for me; right manfully did he come at me, but I punished him so severely about the head and legs, that he lay groaning on the ground, rubbing his bead and legs, whilst the blood flowed freely from the side of his head. Others then came on to the attack, but were met with terrible blows, right and left.

At last my stick broke: I dashed the pieces I had in my hand into the face of the fellow nearest me. When the women saw I had no stick, they commenced to shout again: "*Maro, Maro, Ko Feringhee.*" Now for life or death, I thought. Out came the two revolvers. A brute of a dog that had given me a lot of trouble got the first shot right between his eyes, when down he went without a groan. I then fired through one of their huge turbans. It had the desired effect. I did not wish to take life, and told them so, but if they did not let me alone I would kill the whole of them. I then rolled over another dog, one of their pet dogs. This last shot appeared to decide them. The women called their husbands away, begging me, on bended knees, not to kill them. A native has an utter dread of a revolver. They say that it is "*jaddowed*" (bewitched), and that it will fire as often as you like. I still found the dogs very troublesome, and had to shoot another. I made the villagers drop their sticks or send them home, and then made peace with them. I got all the milk I required, and "*chupatties*" (thin cakes of unleavened bread).

Two men went to the road with me, carrying the milk and cakes. I told them I should report them; they begged me not to do it, or they would be heavily punished. I found the child crying bitterly for his dada. The milk and cakes, however, soon put him right, and off we went jogging along again.

I found it exceedingly pleasant at Kussoulie, up about 8,000 feet. We have a large *depôt* up here, and the men look remarkably healthy. I took Master Johnny straight to the school, situated on another hill, and duly handing him over, left him for two days. My wife and little ones were up here, so I spent two days very pleasantly with them, and then went and bade the boy goodbye. The school, so far as I could see, is kept very clean, and the children are well cared for. I found him making himself quite at home with the other children. I think I shall send

Master Arthur there as soon as I can: it will do him the world of good to set off the burning plains.

If ever you see Johnny you will, perhaps, remember the narrow squeak I had while taking him to school. It was the determined front I showed that struck them with awe; they could see I meant mischief. It will not do to stop to count Indians, but go at them determined to conquer or die. I expect to join headquarters at Ferozepore next month. This is my third attempt at this letter. Please excuse all imperfections.

   And believe me,
    My dear Parents, as ever.
     Your affectionate Son,
      T. Gowing,
       C.S., A.S.M.

CHAPTER 19

The Afghan Campaign of 1863

I am now coming to the Umballah campaign. We (the 7th) had been selected by Sir H. Rose, then commander-in-chief, as one of the smartest regiments in India; and, as a feather in our cap, had been directed to escort the Governor-General, Lord Elgin, in his tour through India. Two companies were sent off to escort his Lordship to the plains, and the remaining eight companies (except sick, lame, and lazy, that were left behind at Ferozepore) marched on to Meean-Meer. But the news soon arrived that our two companies had buried his Lordship. We then expected to march back, but to our surprise we were ordered into the field, and to move by forced marches.

When our men, heard the news from the lips of our much-respected Colonel R.Y. Shipley (later Lieutenant-General R.Y. Shipley, C.B.), the shout that they gave startled our native servants. As soon as the cheering had subsided, our colonel's voice could be distinctly heard: "Fusiliers, I want you to use your legs. I will lead you against black or white, I care not who." And during that long march of between 400 and 500 miles, we found we had to use our legs. For the information of my non-military readers, I will just describe camp life in India, and the marching from camp to camp. About retreat, or sun down, all camels that are intended to carry men's kits, tents, &c., are brought and placed against the tents.

The non-commissioned officer satisfies himself that all is right, and that each camel is provided with a good rope. If elephants are to be used, the head *mahout* is told how many to send to each company at the rouse sounding. Tattoo is generally pretty early—say about seven, o'clock p.m. After that, all is quiet throughout the camp—nothing to be heard but the sentinel's measured tread, and the gurgling sound from the queen of the desert (camel). Even the drivers are quiet, and silence reigns until *reveillé* sounds between one and three a.m., according to the length of the march.

All hands at once jump up, strike a light, dress as quick as possible, pack up and clear the tent, down with the sides or *Kornorths*, and set to to load the camels; but not a tent comes down until the bugle sounds, "Strike tents," then one short blast, and down they all come,, as if they were all pulled with one rope; they are at once rolled up, and loaded on the camels or elephants. The quarter-bugle sounds, the men on with their accoutrements in the dark, and at once move to the appointed place to fall in. Coffee is provided for them, if they require it, at the rate of about one half-penny per half pint; the companies are inspected by their respective captains, reports are collected, then away they go, with the band in front playing some lively air, and swinging along at the rate of four miles an hour.

The dust is enough to choke one; often one cannot see the man in front, but all keep jogging along, chaffing and joking. Men who have got "singing faces" are often in requisition. Thus all goes on as merry as a cuckoo until eight miles are covered, when the halt sounds, companies pile arms, and a cup of good coffee is issued to each man with a biscuit, if he requires it, provided by native cooks who are sent on overnight. In half-an-hour the coffee is drank, biscuits are put out of sight, and the pipe is brought to the front; and a nice lot of beauties the men look, covered with dust and sweat.

Fall in again, and off for, perhaps, another eight or nine miles; the baggage and tents keep well up with us, for the camels can swing along at a good pace, although they appear to hang over the ground. The new camp ground is duly reached, all marked out by the quartermaster and his establishment. One would be astonished to see how quickly a canvas city springs into existence; the tents are all up in an incredibly short space of time. The poor *bheasty* (water-carrier; has enough of it. In about an hour the men have had a good wash and brush down, when in come the cooks with breakfast—either beef steaks or mutton chops.

Breakfast over, some of the men who are tired lie down for a little rest. Some get a book, while others play all sorts of games in the tents. Those who do not feel tired get permission to go off shooting. Game of all kinds is very plentiful in most parts of the country, and it does not take long to find a good hare or a brace of pheasants, and there are no game laws in India. When they come back what they have shot is handed over to the cooks. In forced marching not many go out shooting, for the men are pretty well tired out.

From twenty-five to thirty miles *per diem*, with rifle and accoutrements to carry, in a climate like India, is no joke. But it has been proved that our men can beat the natives hollow, and march quite away from them. A camel is soon knocked up if you over-work him; and if you attempt to over-task an elephant, he is liable to turn crusty. Moreover, he wants plenty of room, and he'll quietly shake his load off, and put all hands at defiance.

As acting sergeant-major, I led the Fusiliers through the whole of this march, both to and from the field. On arrival at Nowshera, we soon found that something serious was going on not very far distant, for wounded men from the front were being sent in. We did not stay here long, but left behind all we did not absolutely require, and off we went at a rapid pace. Bidding farewell to all roads and bridges, we had now nothing but a wild tract to traverse, and as we came up to the *nullahs* or water-courses, in we had to go, land on the other side the best way we could, and on again until we came to another. Sometimes we would have six or seven of these nice places to cross, some being about a foot deep, others nearly up to our necks.

As we approached the foot of the mountains, we could distinctly hear the artillery in front at it, and in the stillness of the night the roll of musketry. Other regiments, both European and native, kept arriving, and we had our old friends, the 93rd Sutherland Highlanders, with us. After resting for a day or two, off we went again, with nothing but what we had on our backs. For the first five or six miles we had to push through thick low shrubbery; then we commenced ascending the front of a very high hill, up which we could only go in single file, for it was nothing but a goats' path.

As we topped the first hill, we had a splendid view. The red coats were winding up the steeps like a long red serpent, the head of the column having rested for a time in order to allow the rear to come up. We could now plainly hear the rattle of musketry; and some of our young hands, who had never seen a shot fired, began to ask all sorts of questions. Still on and on, up and up, we kept going. Some now began to fall out to rest a little, for it is very trying with a load such as we had to carry, to be continually climbing.

Each man had to carry 100 rounds of ammunition, his overcoat, a blanket, shirt, socks, boots, towel, brushes, two days' rations, and a number of little nicknacks. I carried a good revolver and plenty of ammunition, for it now began to get a little exciting. About 3 p.m. we could distinctly hear the shrill whistle of the musket balls passing over our heads, which told us that the enemy were not far distant. We had a nice little force with us as a reinforcement—some seven or eight Native regiments, and two batteries of mountain guns. We (the 7th) were about 1,100 strong, and the 93rd about 1,200.

On arrival we were sent straight to the post of honour. We had no tents, so we made the best of it for the night. The enemy appeared on our right, left, and front, and, but for the reinforcements, our small force would soon have been cut off from all communications. Shots were whistling and hissing about us all night. Next morning, we and the 93rd, and two or three regiments of Sikhs, with two of Ghoorkas, let the enemy know that we required a little more breathing room; so in about an hour we cleared them out of their hiding-places on our left flank and front; but we soon found out that they were not to be despised, for they would creep up under the shrubbery, and from rock to rock, and pepper us until they were shot down.

We had a number of strong picquets out, and hardly a night passed but the enemy would attack some of them, coming right up to the muzzles of our men's rifles and fighting with desperation; and, but for the superior weapons that our men had, numbers must have prevailed at times. It was with difficulty that we could get some of our native regiments to face them. One regiment (the 27th Native Infantry) bolted, but we managed to bring them up; they had either to face us or the enemy, and they chose the enemy, and were nearly cut to pieces. Most of the European officers were cut down, for it was close fighting.

We found a number of mutineers mixed up with the Afghans. They knew well that they had no mercy to expect from us, and side by side with the dauntless Afghans they fought with such determination that some of our crack Sikh regiments trembled before them. But, no position that they could occupy did they hold, when once our men and those noble little fellows the Ghoorkas went at them. The Ghoorkas repeatedly proved during that short campaign, as they had often done before, that they were second to none. The honour of Old England had been entrusted to them, and they were never once beaten; but could hold their own by the side of the bravest sons of Britain. And if ever the much-vaunted Imperial Guards of Russia should come across their path, they will remember them, as much as they have had cause to remember us, for in a close fight, with their peculiarly shaped native knives, they are very devils.

As regards the strength of the enemy, they were very numerous; while fresh tribes kept joining them, and it really appeared as if the more we destroyed the stronger they seemed to get. But during the early part of December they were taught some very awkward lessons, and, with all the craft of Asiatics, their chiefs pretended that they wanted to treat for peace. Negotiations were carried on for some days, their chiefs coming daily into our camp, blindfolded, until they entered the commissioners' marquee, when it was found out that they were playing a treacherous game. All they wanted was to gain time, for some thousands of other tribes to join them, in order to exterminate the white-livered *Feringhees* and the dreaded Ghoorkas.

But our people had had more than one hundred years' experience with such crafty gentlemen, and were not to be caught with chaff. So the terms that our Government demanded were laid before them, and twenty-four hours given them to decide. They decided to renew the fighting; and as soon as it suited the time and plans of General Sir T. Garvick and Sir R. Chamberlain, they got quite enough of what they had asked for, but we did not wait for the hordes of reinforcements that were coming from all parts of Afghanistan.

We had three days continuous fighting; and it was of such a nature that it considerably damped their ardour for the fray, and thrashed all the wild fanaticism out of them. They threw up the sponge when they found that they could not make any impression upon us, throwing away their arms and begging for mercy. The "cease fire" sounded all along our line, and they at once found out that we were not half so bad as we had been painted by their chiefs and priests, for they immediately received mercy at our hands, which they could not understand.

We were now right in the Swat Valley, surrounded by the loveliest scenery that the eye could wish to gaze upon; and a number of fine-looking men came into our bivouac with all kinds of presents, which they placed at our feet. The fields for miles around us were covered with their dead or wounded comrades. Poor fellows, they seemed overcome with joy, to think and to see for themselves, that we would not hurt their wounded, but assist them in every way we could. I may here state that the Swattees are a noble set of people, and we now have a great number of them in our Irregular Cavalry regiments; and the Egyptians have lately seen that they are not to be despised.

The campaign ended on the 21st of December, as far as the fighting was concerned, and on the 24th we commenced our march towards the plains of India, right glad to get down from those cold mountains, for snow was all around us. On debouching into the plains, at a place called Pumuailah, at the foot of the mountains, we found our camp already pitched for us, where we could lay our heads down and rest, free from the shrill music of musket balls whizzing past us, or the frantic shrieks of some thousands of native warriors coming upon us in the dark.

Description of Afghan Warfare.

As I have said, the Afghans really seemed to despise death, so long as they could reach us. They have been known to lay hold of the rifle, with the bayonet right through them, and kill their opponent, so that both fell together. On one occasion an entire company of the 101st Fusiliers was cut to pieces, and died to a man; but it was found that a number of these noble fellows had first driven their bayonets through their Afghan opponents and both lay locked in death. On another occasion two companies of the Ghoorkas were sent at(as far as we could see)about 150 fanatic Afghans. These brave little fellows threw in one volley, then dashed at the enemy with their favourite weapon; but instead of 150, some 800 or 900 Afghans rushed out of their hiding-places, and, in less time than it takes me to write it, exterminated the two companies, but not before they had laid low more than double their number of Afghans.

No mercy was shown by these infuriated Hill tribes. The remainder of the Ghoorka regiments obtained permission to go and avenge their comrades; and at them they went, this time backed up by the 101st Fusiliers, who assisted them by throwing in one volley, and that deadly weapon, the knife, did the rest. In marching over the field, about an hour afterwards, the sights that met one's eyes in all directions were sickening. There lay the ghastly fruits of "war to the knife." No wounded; but men of both nations lying clasped in each other's arms, sleeping the sleep of death.

I would suggest that those who are so anxious for war should lead the way at an affair such as I have just described; they would then think well before they set men at each other in deadly conflict; or, in other words, let those that make the quarrels march in the fore front of the battle. But we taught the lawless Afghans how to respect our flag. This had been a short, out a sharp lesson to them, for unprovoked wholesale murder. I must here explain that these neighbours of ours had come down from their hills to the plains, and destroyed whole villages, walking off with the cattle, and all that they could lay their hands upon. Not a man, woman, or child, did they leave alive to tell the tale. The whole country for miles was laid in utter ruin, for no other crime than that the people were British subjects.

So, as the reader will admit, we were almost compelled to draw the sword in this instance; for parleying with such lawless gentlemen would have been looked upon as weakness, and would have had no more effect upon them than water upon a duck's back. But, as usual, the force that was at first sent against the enemy was far too small. It consisted of two regiments of European Infantry (the 71st Highlanders and 101st Fusiliers), seven or eight native infantry regiments, and one of cavalry, with three batteries of artillery.

It was here proved that it is bad policy to despise your enemies, for this little force could barely hold their own. It could hardly be said that they were masters of the ground they slept upon. They had, as it were, to "hold on by the skin of their teeth," in the midst of a host, until reinforcements reached them. Hence our hurried march to their assistance. In this instance again we proved that the bayonet is the queen of weapons, for not all the countless hordes of fanatics could withstand a determined rush of some 10,000 men, backed up by others; for we had ultimately a force of some 25,000 men, with whom we struck terror into at least 150,000 of these sons of the Himalayas.

THE END OF THE WAR.

Well, it was now all over; they had paid the penalty for unprovoked murder, and were submissive at our feet. Although the sword—the victorious British sword—had been uplifted, our people remembered mercy, and that had more effect upon these hardy mountaineers than the mere sight of piles of their dead comrades all around them had produced. We remained for a few days, and then marched on to our frontiers. The natives all around suddenly became wonderfully civil, and all kinds of supplies were brought into our camp; for they had found out that the *Sahib Logs* were indeed lords and masters, and that civility was cheaper than rope.

This short but sharp lesson had such an effect upon them, that one regiment of old women could have kept them in check for years afterwards. We remained for two months on the frontiers, until all was quiet, then broke up camp, and marched to our respective stations. The Fusiliers remained at Ferozepore until the end of 1866, when we marched on to Saugor (central India). It looked a beautiful place, but, alas! many a fine fellow who marched into that lovely vale, in all the pride of manhood, never marched out of it again.

Camp Nowshera, 24th March, 1864.

My ever Dear Parents,

Once more, a line from this troublesome part of Her Majesty's dominions. Yon will have learnt from my wife's pen that I have, thank God, escaped the ravages of war once more without a scratch.

I did not like to write you when things looked so ugly. The war cloud has passed. I have passed through it: and now I will tell you a little. The Afghans, without any warning (*i.e.*, declaration of war—just as the Sikhs did in 1846) invaded our territory, carrying death and destruction into all our frontier villages. All that they could lay their hands upon were destroyed, old and young, male and female, rich and poor, and the cattle walked off with, for no other crime than that they were British subjects. You may be sure our Government would not stand that, so a small army was at once sent against them, to punish them and to teach them better manners.

The Fusiliers were in camp at Meean-Meer, awaiting the Governor-General. We, as a feather in our cap, had been selected by the commander-in-chief, Sir H. Rose, K.C.B., to escort his lordship all through India. Our women and children were left behind, with all delicate men. Our colonel's lady accompanied us, and took Mrs. G. as her lady's maid. We sent two companies from Ferozepore to escort his lordship from Simla here, but his lordship took another route. He died, and was buried in the hills. We expected then to have returned to our station, Ferozepore, but, instead of that, were ordered into the field. The small force our Government (penny-wise and pound foolish) had sent against the Afghans were overwhelmed.

It is bad policy to despise your enemies. Our little force could hardly hold their own: in fact, were hemmed in on all sides by an overwhelming, brave race of men—rather a humiliating position for the conquering race. News in transit out here (bad in particular) will lose nothing. Meean-Meer is near 600 miles from the seat of war, and the news was filing through the native bazaars that our army in Afghanistan had been utterly destroyed.

It was represented to be as bad as the disaster in the Bolan Pass, in 1840—not a man had escaped, and that the conquering Afghans were marching on Rawul Pindee. We were ordered off at once, with a number of other regiments, both horse, foot, artillery. Natives and Europeans, and to force-march, we often covered thirty-two miles in twenty-four hours; so it was no child's play, with a heavy load of ammunition to carry in a climate like this in the month of September. But, dear parents, the honour of our glorious old flag was at stake, and it is then when the true Briton comes out in his true colours. A, brave man can die but once, but a cowardly sneak all his life long: and I do believe that.

Pat has a jealous eye for the honour of that flag he loves so well. We were off to measure our strength with the Afghans. All went swinging along as merry as wedding bells. We had a lively time of it; singing faces were in requisition. I feel I must give a sample of one song we had; but you must not laugh. The man was called upon to sing by our much-respected colonel. He said he would sing if the good lady would ride on out of the way. The colonel gave his lady a hint, and she galloped on ahead. We all thought we were going to hear something nice. We were requested not to laugh, but to come in in chorus. I hardly need say this youth was from the Green Isle. The song:—

I was at the Battle of the Nile,
All the while,
At the battle of the Nile,
I was there all the while.

(Chorus)—*At the battle of the Nile, boys,*
I was there all the while;
All the while I was there,
At the battle of the Nile.

And so this youth kept it up, with about 1,200 men joining in. The natives all along the line of march had heard the bad news: they must have thought we were a jolly lot. This is just a sample of how we got over our long marches. I had the honour, as acting sergeant-major, of leading. We had not a man fall out the whole way. I had promised this youth my go of rum when we got in, if he would sing a good song. As soon as it was all over, our colonel turned in his saddle and called out, "You must not forget your promise, Sergeant-Major."

The man called out in good mellow Irish, "By my soul, then, I shall not forgit it. Colonel dear." Mind, I was in charge of the canteen, so he was likely to have a good tot. Although it was heavy work to be marching night and day, the excitement kept us well on the move, for bad news kept coming in. As we approached Nowshera we began to meet traces of hand-to-hand encounters—wounded officers and men with sword cuts. The wounded informed us that the enemy were very numerous, and as brave as lions, many of them quite fanatics, despising death so long as they could close with you.

We had our old friends the 93rd Highlanders with us. It is a splendid regiment, and I had not the slightest doubt about the result. With the reinforcements that, were going up, one could see our Government meant to make short work of the enemy. We turned off to the right at Nowshera, and bid goodbye to all roads and bridges; but nothing could stop our fellows. We had several regiments of Ghoorkas with us, and we soon found that they had plenty of fight in them. We had a lot of rough marching after we left the plains of India; but still, on and on, up and up, we went. Some of the hills took the singing out of us. In many places we had nothing but a goat's path to get up, and could only go one at a time, but still, on we went. We found our people strongly entrenched, with the enemy nearly all around them. The Swatties are a brave race of people, big, raw-boned, stalwart men, and we found a number of the very worst of the Mutineers mixed up with them. They had nothing to look forward to but death. They knew well that if taken they would be shot, and they fought with desperation. Some of the encounters we had with the foe involved desperate fighting, hand to hand, foot to foot, knee to knee—no quarter asked or given; and but for the superior weapons, with the heavy odds against us, it would have been uphill work with us.

Our artillery (and we had nearly eighty guns with us) simply mowed the huge masses of the enemy down by wholesale. We repeatedly found them as brave as lions; they frequently stood to be mowed down, or came on to certain destruction. Then they would get volley after volley of musketry or be hurled or pitch-forked from the field with the bayonet. But to go into all the fights would be impossible.

We found the little Ghoorkas perfect devils in the fights, but some of our crack Sikh regiments trembled before the foe, while we and the Ghoorkas brought them up and made them face the foe or us. They chose the enemy, and were nearly annihilated. In one of the fights, our Ghoorkas, we found, had killed all they met—both women and children lay all around, dead. Our gallant old General, Sir J. Garveck, K.C.B., would not stand that. As soon as the fight was over and the enemy routed, we formed up and faced the Ghoorkas. A strong force of artillery, with cavalry, were with us, the 71st, 93rd, and 101st. The general at once demanded the men to be given up who had murdered the poor women and children—or instant death. Resistance was out of the question.

Fifteen men were given up by their comrades. They were tried by court-martial, and five of them shot on the spot; the others were transported for life. The general said he would not command murderers: we were fighting a fair stand-up fight against men. This stopped it. At last, after other heavy fights, the enemy threw up the sponge, and begged for mercy they were strangers to—for all who had fallen into their hands, whether Europeans or Asiatics, had had to die. Our chief demanded all the mutineers to be given up. We found they had got into an old mud fort, but in a very strong position.

The arms were given back to a portion of the foe, and they were made to storm the fort and destroy every man. Some five regiments of infantry and about twenty-four guns went with them, with two regiments of native cavalry, to see the order carried out. Remember, these men were all murderers from the Mutiny, so I think we can say that we put the finishing touch upon the mutineers, as the Highlanders did on the Russians at the Alma. Well, thank God, it is all over: we have struck terror into thousands, yea, hundreds of thousands of lawless Afghans. As soon as the last shot was fired and the enemy was at our feet, I wrote the following short note (in blood, for we had no ink) to my poor wife:

The fight all over; enemy beaten at all points. I am, thank God, safe and sound.—T. G.

We marched into the plains of India 24th December last. We had a very long march to finish off with. They said it was thirty-four miles; but we had no mile-posts, and if measured it would have been found a good forty and a wee bit. Now for a bit of a spree before I close this long letter. It is a bit of red tape trampled upon. On marching into Permula, at the foot of the mountains, our colonel sent for me, inquiring as to whether the canteen had come in. I informed him it had not, and from what I had heard, did not expect it for some time to come. Our colonel is a very feeling man—just the sort that the Fusiliers would follow through thick and thin. "Well, Sergeant-Major," said he, "something must be done."

As quick as thought I sat me down on the stones, took a leaf out of my pocket-book, and made out (in pencil) an urgent requisition on the commissariat for fifty gallons proof rum. The colonel read it and signed it at once. I then called out for ten men of my own company to follow me. I had been told to look alive; so oft I started with my men to the commissariat stores close by, armed with the requisition. On inquiring for the conductor, I was informed by a native policeman that the *Sahib* was taking his dinner and could not be disturbed. His tent being pointed out to me, I went at once to it, and inquired through the chick of the tent if the conductor was in. A voice from within answered me in the affirmative. "And what the d—l do you want?" and "Go to h—l out of this."

I said I had just completed one long march, quite enough for one day; and that if he did not know what common civility was, I would teach him. And then, without any more talk, I walked into his tent and handed to him my requisition. After looking at it for about a minute, he said, with all the authority of a lord high admiral: "Sergeant, I shall not issue anything upon that dirty bit of paper." I could hardly keep myself within bounds. My knuckles began to itch, as the Yankees say. I called him some nice name—not a gentleman.

I found he was closely related to that notable firm, Day & Martin. I gave him to understand, in plain English, that if he did not give me the rum, I should take it. He got into a violent temper, rushed out of the tent, called or whistled up a large, ugly-looking dog, and five or six native policemen. I found my gallant friend a perfect swell—patent leather shoes, white ducks, black cloth vest, with red necktie, kid gloves, white linen shirt, *and a black face*. And one would think, by his conduct, that his heart was the same as his face towards us. But I was not to be easily done.

One of my men came up and informed me that they had found the rum. I again asked if I was to have the rum in accordance with the requisition. Throwing the paper at me, he told me to go to the d——l. I could stand no more of that, so I landed my bunch of fives right between his eyes, and followed it up with one, two, three more. His dog and the police came to the rescue; but the dog was the only one that showed fight, the police thinking discretion the better part of valour. I then proceeded to take what I wanted—a barrel of proof rum. I found our colonel had got out of patience, and we met him and the general coming to see what was keeping me.

When I explained all, and how that I had had to fight for it, the colonel and general laughed heartily. The Fusiliers were not to be stopped quite so easily. Ha! Ha! I was reported for striking the conductor, but got over it with flying colours; the general saying I ought to have given him a little more, and that he hoped the lesson the conductor had had in the art of self-defence would teach him to keep a civil tongue with Britons.

So I think you will say the Afghans had not taken all the fight out of me.

But I am getting tired, and must bring this to a close, We shall, all being well, be at, or close to our station, Ferozepore, about the time this reaches you. Please to accept the enclosed £——, as a farther mark of love from as both.

And believe as to remain
    Your affectionate Son and Daughter,
     T. and B. J. Gowing,
      Royal Fusiliers.

P.S.—Mrs. G. is here with me, and we are as happy as the day is long. T. G.

      Ferozepore, 28th September, 1864.
My Dear Parents,
Once more, a line from this dusty station, in the best of health. We are coming close up to the end of a very hot summer. I have had another trip up to the hills with Master Arthur; it will do him the world of good. This is a very pretty station. There are large gardens, beautifully laid out. The River Sutlej is about one mile from barracks. There is a large fort on the banks of it. We keep about 150 men in it. Our men still look very brown from

the last outing we had. The Fusiliers got a lot of soft soap in general orders for their conduct in the late Afghan campaign.

We are to get a medal, and I do not know how many bars, for it someday. I must give in: there is a sand-storm coming up. The doctors say they are very healthy; they may be, but they are very unpleasant—enough to blind one. Well, it's all over; it lasted about an hour: we are almost smothered with sand. About a month ago, we had a flight of locusts; they played "old Harry" with everything green about the place, stripped every bush and tree. There must have been millions of them. The whole heavens were black with them.

Our men turned out to kill or frighten them. The natives caught as many as they could. I have some of them in a bottle. I find the natives make curry of them. Well, we have plenty of fun here. Our colonel has given the men permission to keep horses, tats, ponies, &c. It is very amusing to see our men out by hundreds, practising to ride. They look very smart. Most of them have flannel trousers, in all the colours of the rainbow. I expect they will soon be calling us the 7th Flying Horse, the 7th Dragoons, or the 7th Flannel-bellies. It's enough to make a pig laugh, to see some of them trying to hold on to the saddle, the mane, the tail, or anything they can, belonging to or fastened to their quadrupeds.

It is as good a thing as they could have; it keeps their mind employed and gives them good healthy exercise, and they all look healthy and well. Please to accept the enclosed as a further mark of love, and pass no compliments about it—this is from my rib. Well, dear parents, I hope you will not blame me for the step I have taken. I thought of coming home. I know well you would have liked to have seen me and mine; but you must remember my cap does not cover my head.

We muster six little ones; and I do believe there will be an increase before this reaches you. Whether the number will be brought up to eight, I do not know; and there is something else about it—so long as I have my health and can keep them comfortably, I do not care.

Well, you will say, "What have you done?" I have re-engaged to complete twenty-one years. Had I come home, I should have thrown eleven years away for nothing; and I think I have had ten years of it pretty rough, so I made up my mind to go in for a pension. You see, our house is getting rapidly filled; whether it is the change of air, I must leave you to surmise.

At all events, the bargain was made in '58 for no grumbling, and we pull along pretty well. If I find my old chum wrong-side out, or her temper or monkey up, I just light my pipe and walk over to our mess. In an hour I am back again, and the storm is all over. The old Book is right: *A soft answer turneth away wrath*. I think we could claim the flitch of bacon: we are near six years married, and have not had one cross word.

You ask me about the price of food, clothing, &c. Well, good flour is 3d. per stone. I will give you the prices in English money, you will understand me better. Potatoes almost for nothing, 1d. per stone; eggs (large) sixty for 1s.; fowl (large) fit for the table, 4d.; beef, 1½d. per pound (prime); mutton, 2d. per pound (prime); rabbits, in the season, 2d. each; all kinds of fresh fish for a song; fresh pork, 3d. per pound. Anything from home is very dear, such as Cheshire cheese, 3s. 6d. per pound; hams, from 2s. 6d. to 4s. per pound, and they will not cut them. The cheeses are in tins of from four to twelve pounds. Beer, for the non-commissioned officers and privates, 6d. per quart; but if an officer requires ale, he must drink Bass's or Allsopp's, at 2s. 6d. per bottle. Brandy, from 8s. to 12s. per bottle; gin. whisky, port and sherry, from 6s. to 10s. per bottle.

Clothing for ladies and children is very dear, more than double the price at home, so I hope that you will attend to the order my rib sent you: Snowdon, or Chamberlain's people would only be too happy to comply; get a sample of what they will send. Again, as regards drink. Country drink is very cheap. They call it *Darro*; it is as strong as our brandy, and is sold in the bazaars at 2d. per bottle.

This is the stuff that kills our men. After drinking it for a time, they become quite stupid, and go off like the snuff of a candle, or are sent home invalided, fit for nothing. I have never tasted it yet, and will not, whilst I am in my right mind. I am sorry to have to inform you that cholera, in its worst form, has broken out, and is raging in Cawnpore, Lucknow, Allahabad, Delhi, and Umballa. I hope it will keep from us; we have been very fortunate since '62.

I will send the photos next mail. My kind regards to all old friends,

And believe me. as ever.
Your affectionate Son,
T. Gowing,
C.S. and A.S.M.,
Royal Fusiliers.

P.S.—Wife will drop a line next mail. Keep up your spirits, mother. All is well that ends well. T. G.

P.S. 2.— Before I send this off, I feel that I must give you a little *tit-bit, a relic of the Mutiny,* Just after I had laid my pen down, a respectable looking native came to my door and handed to me a paper to read (he did not speak). I read the document. It stated that he had been a *sepoy*, an unfortunate man; that he had through bad advice, thrown in his lot against as, and fought us at Lucknow: that he was wounded there in a remarkable way by a musket ball: that the shot went in at his mouth, carried away his tongue, and passed out at the back of his head; and that, if you wished, he would take a plug out, open his mouth, and you could see right through his head. I looked at the man, and said *"coolo"* (open). He did so, and, true enough, I could see right through. I gave the fellow a *rupee*. His petition further stated that the man had belonged to a regiment that had not hurt their officers, women, or children; but went over to the enemy and fought for heavy stakes and lost all.   T. G.

REFLECTIONS.

All went on well until the summer of 1869, when we were attacked by cholera, and our poor fellows died like rotten sheep. In fourteen days we lost 149 men, 11 women, and 27 children. I here lost six dear little ones, and my wife was pronounced dead by one of the doctors; but, thank God, even doctors make wonderful mistakes sometimes. It proved so in her case, for she is with me yet, and has made me more than one "nice little present" since. During that trying ordeal we proved the faithfulness of the natives, for, although death was raging amongst us, they stood by us manfully; and a number of them clung so close to our poor fellows, in rubbing them, that they caught the terrible malady, and died rather than forsake their masters.

I say now, after nineteen years in the midst of the burning plains of India, treat the native with kindness, be firm with him, but let him see that you are determined to give him justice, and I'll be bound that you will find him a good, kind, loving, obedient creature, and a loyal subject. Thousands, yea tens of thousands, of the natives can speak our language as well as we can, and see plainly that they have justice, that the rich cannot oppress the poor, and that under our flag they are safe from all oppression. The highest positions are attainable by all, if they will only qualify themselves for them.

Our equal laws have bound them to us in love, and if our Government required 500,000 more men we could have them in less than a month. They will tell you plainly if you will lead they will follow. There are no better troops in the world than the Ghoorkas, Sikhs, and Beloochees; all they require is leaders. But give me old England, with a crust, in preference to India, with all its luxuries, although I had my health remarkably well all the time I was there.

I had, however, a very strong objection to the hot winds, the sandstorms, the flying bugs (and those that could not fly), the mosquitoes, and to a slow bake, for in summer the thermometer would often show 125°' Fah., and the air would be so sultry that one could hardly breathe without being fanned. But I must be honest. A number of our men wreck their constitutions with heavy drinking and then complain of the climate, which certainly is very trying. After all, give me "home, sweet home."

Saugor (Central India),
25th September, 1869.

My Dear Father and Mother,—

This is a world of troubles and sorrows; my heart is almost too full to say much. Since my last from this place, it has pleased an All-wise God and Father again to lay the hand of death upon our once happy circle. I told you in my last that cholera, in its worst type, had broken out among us and the artillery, and that we were burying the poor fellows without coffins—sewed up in blankets, twenty and twenty-five a-day.

As you know, this is not my first experience of that fearful scourge. But, dear parents, the heavy blow that I have received is enough to give one a stroke of apoplexy. My poor heart is near bursting with grief. The stroke has been so sudden that I can hardly realise it. But it is the stroke of One who is *Too wise to err; too good to be unkind*. So we, poor short-sighted mortals, must bow to His all-wise decree.

Six of my dear children have been called away to the bright realms above, all in a few hours. On the morning of the 16th inst. they were all well. Eight dear little ones, wife, and self sat down to breakfast, all hearty and well. Before the breakfast was over, little Freddy complained of a pain in his body. I took him on my knee, but that did not cure him. One of our doctors was passing; at the time; I called him in. He ordered the child off to the cholera hospital at once.

Mother went with him. But, dear parents, I cannot dwell upon it. Before four o'clock, six of my fine boys and girls had passed away into the arms of Him who does all things well. We shall never hear their sweet prattling tongues any more: all is silent in the tomb. Before six o'clock p.m. on the 15th, they were all laid in one common grave, wrapped in sheets, without coffins. Three of them the same morning, about five o'clock, were singing the following hymn in bed:—

I'll praise my Maker with my breath;
And when my voice is lost in death,
Praise shall employ my nobler powers:
My days of praise shall ne'er be past
While life and thought and being last,
Or immortality endures.

Their mother and myself stood at their bedroom door, listening to their sweet voices. We little thought that they would so soon be numbered with the clods of the valley. But further, I am sorry to have to inform you that my poor dear wife was pronounced dead by one of our doctors, and carried to the deadhouse, or mortuary, about 2.30 p.m. on that fatal 15th. Thank God, however, life was found in her: she was carried back to hospital, and is still alive. She, poor thing, does not yet know how she has been bereaved; the doctors having given strict orders that she must not know it for some time to come.

I am thankful to say that she is rapidly improving. But I sometimes feel that I cannot live: all, all are gone that we loved so well. Out of our heavy family we have lost eight dear little ones, snatched from us in this, to all appearance, *paradise* (?) on earth. A dear old friend said to me this morning, when I told him the blows were more than I could bear: "My boy, your partner is left to you; it might have been worse." Then, grasping my hand, he said, "Look to your father's God for strength, look to the strong for strength." My dear parents, I feel it is there I must look. My officers, from the colonel downwards, are very kind to me. The colonel and his lady called this morning to sympathise with me in my sore trials.

I cannot say more at present. Will write again in a short time if I am spared. Goodbye, and may God bless you all. And believe me as ever.

In health or in wealth.

Your affectionate Son,

T. Gowing, Sergeant-Major,

Royal Fusiliers.

P.S.—Please to accept the enclosed; use it if you require it, or put it in the bank.   T. G.

Saugor (Central India),
20th October, 1869.

My Dear Parents,

Once more, a line in health, in accordance with promise. Thanks for your kind letters and Christian advice. I know well that you are ripe for the Master, and that in a few short years at most, we shall all be where time shall be no more. But I am truly happy to learn that your health and that of poor mother is still good. You must remember, dear father, that you have passed the allotted time of man by ten years, and mother by seven years. I know that you must be drawing on for your diamond wedding, as you married much younger than I did. I hope the Lord will spare you to celebrate it, and me and mine with you to cheer you up.

I am exceedingly happy to inform you that my dear partner has been spared to me; she, poor thing, has been terribly shaken, and does not look the same woman. Our colonel's lady kindly undertook, with other ladies, to break the sad news of the loss of our dear children to her. She bore it with a Christian fortitude beyond what I had expected; and thanked God fervently that I had been spared to comfort her, and that we had yet four left to us. I am bringing my boys from the school. They will help to fill up the void, or empty chairs, and cheer us up a little.

But bad as our case was, there was one in the regiment worse. A whole family, of father, mother, and eight fine boys and girls, all in a few days. The mother and children died on the 16th September, and after they had been interred three days, the poor distracted father bribed the native in charge of the cemetery, obtained a pick and a shovel, and digged down to his poor wife to have a kiss. But it was a fatal kiss for him, and in less than two short hours he was laid beside those he loved so well.

Our men have subscribed and put a nice stone over him, with a suitable epitaph. I have put up a monument over my dear little ones. I am happy to inform you that cholera has now entirely left us. Some of our poor fellows who got over it are nothing but wrecks of humanity, and will all have to be invalided home.

Now that it is all over, I will tell you a little. My poor wife hardly ever left the side of the poor women and children that were dying of it, but stuck to them like a true Briton until she, poor thing, caught the terrible malady from our little Freddy.

And, further, I never left the men, but did all that lay in my power for them. I pitched the sergeant-major's coat on one side, tucked up my shirt sleeves, and rubbed the poor fellows as long as there was a chance of life. Poor Corporal Woods died in my arms. I promised him that I would write to his widowed mother in Norwich. I have his watch; he wished me to send it to his mother. I will do so by this post. Go and console the poor widow. Mind, this is the same man who wrote home about me in 1862.

The cholera lasted only fourteen days with us, and in that short time we lost 149 men, 11 women, and 27 children, out of a total strength of about 340. We have strong detachments out at Nowgong, Putchmuny, and Jhansie. We had no parades nor drills. What was to be done? Our doctor asked the colonel to leave me to him. I found it all through as I have frequently found it before—in Turkey, the Crimea, in Meean-Meer (in 1862), and here— that it is almost impossible to keep the men's spirits up. They get it into their heads that they are going to die, and die they will.

Others fought against it manfully. Some said they would sooner face the foe, twenty to one; they might have a chance to sell their lives dearly or to die hard. But here there was an unseen enemy, with no chance to combat it.

Well, thank God, it is all over, and I am still in the land of the living, whole and hearty.

My wife joins with me in love; she will drop you a line as soon as she gets a little stronger. Please to accept the enclosed from the old girl's long stocking, that has never seen daylight for years, so far as I know.

     And believe me as ever,
      Your affectionate Son,
       T. Gowing,
        S.M., R.F.

TAKING THE CENSUS.

During the taking of the census in India, in 1871, I was garrison sergeant-major of Allahabad, and had some eight or ten native male servants, all of whom were married, but I had never troubled myself about the number of wives or children they had, so long as they performed their duties in my service. Schedules were issued to all officers and non-commissioned officers detached (employed on the staff). I gave direction to my head *sirdar*-bearer to parade the whole of my native establishment, male or female, old or young, at a certain time in the verandah, opposite my door.

The time arrived. All the men and children were duly paraded, but not a woman put in her appearance. I enquired where the wives were, and was told that they were in the house. I informed them that I must see them. They all looked at each other in blank despair. I gave them to understand that it was a Government order and that it must be obeyed. One man stated that I might kill him if I liked, but I should not see his wives. I had to be very firm with them, assuring them that I would not lay a finger on them, but that there was the order and it must and should be obeyed, even if I had to force my way into their *harems*.

My wife came to my assistance, and, with a little coaxing from her, we succeeded in unearthing some forty "dear creatures" encased in *chudders* (or sheets) perforated about the face. They all sat down in families. I then commenced to take from the husbands their names and ages. On inquiring of the men the names and ages of their respective wives, I found they knew neither the one nor the other in many cases, and had to enquire of their spouses. Some of the dark ladies seemed to enjoy the joke, which they expressed in titters of laughter, but were only too glad when they were told they might go to their homes.

SERVANTS AND CASTE.

A gentleman in India is compelled to keep at least eight or ten servants, their salaries ranging from four *rupees* (8/-) to ten *rupees* (£1) per month; for the man who cooks your food will not put it on the table for you, or look after the table in any way; the man who brings you clean water won't take away the dirty; the one who sweeps your house will not clean your dog; the one that grooms your horse will not drive you; and the one that looks after your clothing and cash will do nothing else.

The gardener will look after the garden, but should he come across anything dead, he will not touch it. The female servants will attend to the mistress and children in dressing them or walking out with them, but will not wash them or do any manual work. The *dhoby* (washerman) will wash and get up your clothing, but will do nothing else. Such is caste.

Fort Allahabad, 15th July, 1872.

My Dear Mother,

In answer to your kind letter, just to hand, with the sad news of the death of poor dear father. Truly, as you say, he was beloved by all who knew him. I do believe his enemies could be put into a very small room, whilst his friends were numbered by tens of thousands. I know, mother dear, that you will feel his loss more than tongue can tell; but do try and console yourself with this fact that he is not lost, but gone before; that he is now in the midst of that blood-bought throng that no man can number; that he is now with Him whose name he tried to extol for fifty-six years; that he is now with untold millions singing, "Unto Him that loved us, and washed us from our sins in His own blood, and hath made us kings and priests unto God," thus helping to swell the anthem of the skies,

While heaven's resounding mansions ring
With shouts of sovereign grace.

We can mourn the loss of a good, loving earthly father. You, dear another, will miss his sweet counsel, his noble, loving, manly heart. But we cannot mourn him as one whose work was not done. He has gone to his grave full of years (nearly 83[1]). And you have another consolation, that he died at his post, like a good soldier— faithful unto death. He tried to live as he would wish to die, that he might be able to sing in death—"Looking unto Jesus." What an end! He can now shout, "Victory, victory

---

1. Born May 11, 1789; died April 8, 1872.—*Extract from Family Bible.*—T. G.

through the blood of the Lamb." There will be no sorrow there, no more pain, no more tears, but one continual song of praise unto Him who has done All things well.

Again, remember, dear mother, in your bereavement, what a family of us have gone before, leaving behind them the record that they were on the Lord's side: Grandfathers on both sides, grandmothers on both sides, uncles on both sides, aunts on both sides, my eight little ones; and now our beloved father has gone to tune his harp, and to sing forever of redeeming love. Do not fret, dear mother; we shall meet again, and be able to sing when time «hall be no more. Keep up your spirits. Again, do not be uneasy.

About money; we are not short of a few pounds, and as long as I live you shall never want for anything that will help to make the remainder of your days comfortable, so please rest contented on that score. I enclose a draft on Gurney's Bank, that will, I think, put all straight, set the doctors smiling, and leave a good shot in the locker to make all things comfortable. I should like to have some of poor father's books; do not sell one. I should advise you to go and live with Sarah; she could look after your comfort until I return. If I am spared we will then take you, and do all we can for your comfort.

As for the furniture, sell it, but do not let the broker rob you. Give it to the poor rather than be imposed upon; and take the best of the things, including the books, to S—h. My wife will write you next mail. I want her to go home, take the children with her, and look after you. But, no; she likes mother very much, but the loadstone is at this end. Now, my dear mother, try and keep your spirits up; looking to the Strong for strength and guidance through this dark hour of trouble. Give my kind regards to all kind friends.

And believe me, my dear Mother,
Your affectionate Son,
T. Gowing, Sergeant-Major,
Allahabad Garrison.

Fort Allahabad, 5th April, 1876.
My Dear, Dear Mother,
In answer to yours, just to hand, I drop a line. This, I hope, will be the last letter from the land of pestilence, blacks, and bugs.

I have had quite enough of it, and so has my partner. I have found the last three or four summers very oppressive. Remember, I have had eighteen summers on these burning plains; quite enough, one would think, to get used to the excessive heat, or to get acclimatized, as people call it. But I begin to find that the climate is playing old hack with me, and the sooner I have a change the better. Although I have kept to my post throughout, I have continued for many summers to send my best half up to the hills with ladies, or at my own expense.

Remember, dear mother, I have served the State for upwards of twenty-two years. I have more than completed my portion of the contract, and have tried to do my duty on many a hard-fought field, both in the Crimea and out here; and if spared a few months more, we will see what the Government will give me. They must give me the pension of my rank, *viz.*, the large sum of 2s. 6d. *per diem*. I see by the papers there is some talk of increasing the rate of pensions for. all ranks. I hope to be home sometime next month, all being well. The doctor's words have come true about my poor wife—that she would never be the same woman again after, the attack of cholera. I almost long to come home.

It will be nearly nineteen years since I left England; and what an eventful time of it I have had—death all around me, from water, famine, pestilence, shot, shell, grape, sword, musketry, and the assassin's dagger; yet I have passed through it all. Truly I have much to be thankful for. My life of forty-two years (today) has been, I must acknowledge, watched over by an all-wise God, who can see from the beginning to the end. Mother dear, that is nothing more than I expected.

Some of my letters out here have been little newspapers. It is no new thing: there is a class of people in this world that like to pry into other people's business. I am sorry that you have lost some of my letters, but do not let that trouble you. I thought they might come in handy for some of my children, just to let them see a little what their father had gone through. There are many things that I have omitted in my diary; and again, I have neglected it of late years.

And, dear mother, in order to have something nice when we arrive, please to accept the enclosed cheque for £—. Will drop a line from Bombay, if possible, and another as soon as we land.

And, as I have escaped thus far, I hope the same powerful hand and watchful eye that has attended me and mine, will guide us safe to the land of liberty; and then, dear mother, we will sing—

Home, sweet home!
I love thee still.

I am only bringing home two of my children—Arthur and Amy. Keep up your spirits, dear mother. We will meet again, all being well. Till then. Believe us as ever,
    Your affectionate Son and Daughter,
     T. & B. J. Gowing, S.M.,
       Allahabad.

CHAPTER 20

The Royal Fusiliers

We will claim for this noble regiment the honour of being second to none—either in the field for its dashing intrepidity, or in quarters for its steady, soldier-like qualities. It is one of the most famous regiments in the British army. It has fought and conquered in all quarters of the globe, and has proved that neither the storms of autumn, the snows of winter, nor the heat of an Indian summer—that neither the sword nor the bayonet, nor musketry fire, can subdue them. Napier might well call them "the astonishing infantry." It has traditions of glory which inspire and maintain that *esprit de corps* so valuable in the hour of peril—so animating in the crisis of battle.

The Royal Fusiliers was raised in June, 1685, as an ordnance regiment, not from any particular county, but from every part of the United Kingdom. Some of the noblest sons of Albion and Erin's Isle have served in its ranks, and the haughtiest sons of Adam's race have had to bow before them, and give up the palm to the matchless Fusiliers.

We find that Lord George Dartmouth was appointed its first colonel; its second was no other than the brave and talented nobleman, the Duke of Marlborough, who made the French to quail before him on field after field. Its third colonel was Lord George Hamilton. And on the 9th of April, 1789, His Royal Highness Prince Edward, Duke of Kent (Her Most Gracious Majesty's father) was appointed its commander. The following pages will show that his Royal Highness was a soldier of no mean sort, and his courage knew no bounds.

In their maiden fight with the French (25th August, 1689) the regiment evinced firmness and intrepidity, for they rolled the enemy up in a masterly style, killing some 2000 of the frog-eaters. King William was well satisfied with the conduct of his Fusiliers. This was the first field, but not the last, on which they well stamped their initials upon the French. On the field of Steenkirk (24th July, 1692) they again confronted the foe, and taught the French to respect our flag.

On the field of Landen (19th July, 1693) they again displayed the stem valour of British soldiers. Their loss was heavy, but they proved that they were worth their title, and taught the French such a lesson that they did not forget it for some time to come. In the battles following they proved by their contempt of danger, when the honour of the nation was at stake, that they were determined to overcome all difficulties or perish in the attempt. And, reader, when a fine body of men have so made up their minds, it is better to build a bridge of gold for them to pass over than to try and stop them.

At the siege of Nemur, in 1695, the old corps fought with desperation. The French here got a taste, and a good taste too, of what they were destined to have plenty from this dashing corps, *viz.*, the bayonet. We next find them at Vigo, in 1702, dressing the Spaniards down, and they did it well. In 1703 we find the old regiment afloat, acting with the fleet; but the enemy kept out of their way. Again, we find the Fusiliers defending the deadly breach at Lerida, in 1707, with admirable courage.

Once more we find the gallant old regiment afloat, acting as marines. They were in the action with the French fleet on the 20th May, 1756, and proved that they could fight for the honour of old England on the raging billows as well as on land. We next find them, in 1775, defending Quebec, and repulsing the Americans with a terrible slaughter. We also find them on a number of battle fields against the Americans, ever prompt in performing their duty, throughout the unfortunate War of Independence.

The Fusiliers again were in collision with their old hereditary enemy, the French, in March, 1794, at Martinique, commanded by His Royal Highness the Duke of Kent. The old regiment went at the enemy in masterly style. His Royal Highness addressed the storming column as follows: "Grenadiers, this is St. Patrick's Day. The English will do their duty in compliment to the Irish, and the Irish in compliment to the Saint. Forward, Grenadiers!" And away went the Fusiliers. And a number of poor Gauls paid the penalty for opposing such a dashing body of men. During the five years that His Royal Highness was in command of the Fusiliers, no fewer than eight non-commissioned officers were rewarded with commissions, as suitable acknowledgments for meritorious service. His Highness endeared his name to the grateful remembrances of both officers and men.

The Fusiliers were next employed at Copenhagen, in 1807. Napoleon's plans had been frustrated by the destruction of his fleets at the Nile and Trafalgar, by the immortal Nelson, and the Corsican tyrant was determined, if possible, to obtain possession of the Danish fleet to help to carry out his plans. But our Government were not to be caught napping; a strong fleet and a nice little land force was despatched, and demanded the whole of the Danish fleet, by treaty or by force. The brave Danes fought for it, and lost all—"except their honour;" and the Fusiliers returned to England with the victorious fleet.

We will now trace the gallant old Fusiliers through one of the brightest pages in the history of our dear old isle—the Peninsular War. No heavier effort had been made by our army since the days of Marlborough. Our noble Jack Tars had carried all before them, and their gallant deeds resounded throughout the world. All were compelled to admire. But the time was now approaching when the matchless "thin red line" taught Europe to beware; for all the brave sons of Albion and Erin's Isle were not yet afloat. The proud and haughty Imperial Guards had stood as conquerors on field after field, and had polluted every capital in Europe except ours.

But the usurper met his match for the first time on a grand scale on the 27th and 28th July, 1809, on the bloody field of Talavera; and the so-called "invincible pets of a tiger" were, so to speak, lifted or pitchforked from the field by this dashing old corps. The old "second-to-none" boys took the conceit out of the haughty legions of Napoleon, and captured seven guns from them; and all the attempts of the enemy to retake them were in vain. The bayonet was used with terrible effect, and the guns remained in the hands of the Fusiliers. Wellington, with the eye of an eagle, watched the desperate fighting, and thanked the Fusiliers on the field for their conduct.

The next field on which the Fusiliers made the acquaintance of the French was that of Busaco (27th September, 1810)—"Grim Busaco's iron ridge," as Napier, the military historian, terms it. Here the enemy were driven from crag to crag and rock to rock, and the "thin red line" followed them up. All the regiments engaged seemed to take delight in thrashing the invincibility out of the boasting enemy. The grim-faced old veterans had been victorious on the fields of Austerlitz, Jena, Wagram, and Eylan, and had never once been defeated; but they had now met their match, and more than their match, in the "contemptible" sons of Albion.

The columns of attack came rushing forward with such impetuosity that it appeared impossible to stop them; but they were all driven back with fearful slaughter, and the Fusiliers had a good hand in the pie. Thus ended the vain boasting of the French that they would drive all the English leopards into the sea. So they would if weight of numbers could have done it; but that nasty piece of cold steel was in the way, and in the hands of men who might die, but who had a strong objection to a watery grave; and at the close of the desperate fight the Fusiliers were one of the regiments that stood triumphant on that grim rocky ridge. About this time the 23rd Royal Welsh Fusiliers joined the army from America, and the famous Fusilier Brigade was formed, which was destined to shake the bullies of the continent out of their boots, and play "Rule Britannia" on the field.

The Fusiliers were engaged in a number of minor affairs about this time. Our conquering commander was determined, after the fall of Ciudad Rodrigo, to wrench Badajoz from the hands of the enemy, and the Fusiliers assembled under its walls. But Marshal Soult was not asleep, and a strong army under that crafty commander flew to the rescue of the brave General Phillipon, and Marshal Beresford was compelled to raise the siege, and retire to the heights of Albuera—a name that shortly afterwards resounded from one end of Europe to the other. Again we would repeat, the fame of the mere handful of Fusiliers echoed throughout the civilized world, and Europe stood amazed at their doings. Lo! the Fusiliers had in a desperate struggle routed a host—an entire army—of the proudest and haughtiest sons of Adam's race from the bloodstained heights of Albuera.

They rushed upon the enemy with vehement courage; bayonet crossed bayonet; sword clashed against sword. Backwards and forwards rolled the eddying fight. The din was terrible, the carnage awful. But in the end, although the Marshal of France did all he could to encourage and animate his countrymen, they had to yield to the Fusiliers. The conduct of the Fusilier Brigade on this field was the admiration of both friend and foe. "Gallantry," says one of the bravest of the brave (Lord Hardinge) "is hardly a name for it. In this terrible charge, which swept the veterans of France from the field, the Fusiliers lost 638 men, 34 sergeants, and 32 officers. It was here Sir William Myers fell, and no man died that day with more glory, yet many died; and there was much glory."

Happy the nation which can find such true-hearted men to meet the foe. But the remainder stood triumphant on that fatal hill. The list of killed and wounded proclaim with dreadful eloquence the sanguinary character of the contest the Fusiliers had just decided. Decided what? A doubtful field? No; but won back a lost field, and once more fastened victory to our glorious old standard. The word "Fusilier" after this was almost enough for a Frenchman's breakfast. We again find the old regiment advancing with rapid steps to assist their hard-pressed comrades, the 5th Fusiliers, on the field of El-Bodon. And on this occasion the determined appearance of the Fusilier Brigade was enough. They stopped the pursuit of the boasting steel-clad squadrons of France.

Again, at Alder-de-Pont, the dear old corps charged the enemy with such vehemence as to drive them from the field. And now we retrace our steps to Badajoz. After no end of hardships in the trenches, the hour of assault draws near. Everything that could be thought of was done to repel an assault. It was known that the enterprise was a desperate one; powder-barrels and live shells, hundreds were embedded in the earth just at the foot of the deadly breach, all ready for an explosion. A large *chevaux-de-frise* was placed across the breach, and at the bottom of the ditch long planks with spikes, bayonets, and sword-blades fastened into them, and pointing upwards, ready for our poor fellows to jump upon.

The Fusiliers led the way at the deadly breach of Trinidad with heroic valour. The fires of hell seemed to have broken upon them to destroy the old regiment. With a tremendous cheer, however, they mounted the deadly breach, only to fall back into the ditch below. Others then rushed up, nothing daunted, to be hurled back upon their comrades. The enemy fought with desperation. More men pressed forward while the dying and wounded were struggling in the ditch. At other places the ladders were too short, while, to add to the horror of the scene, a mine was sprung. But the Fusiliers never quailed. At length an entrance was forced, and in a short time Badajoz was at the conqueror's feet. But, alas! five thousand poor fellows lay in front of those deadly breaches. The loss to the Fusiliers was heavy—18 officers, 14 sergeants, and 200 men.

After a number of minor combats, in all of which they came off victorious, we trace the old corps to the field of Salamanca. The enemy were taught a short but sharp lesson on this field. The Fusiliers were in the thick of it, but they were determined to maintain the honour of the corps, and, with cheer after cheer, they rushed at the enemy with levelled steel. Here again their loss was heavy—12 officers, 8 sergeants, and 199 men; but the remainder stood as conquerors.

Then, after a lot of marching and counter-marching, we again find the old regiment on the field of Vittoria. On this field they had the post of honour, and were the admiration of all except the foe. It was here that the French lost all, including their honour. It was a most decisive victory for the English.

We now trace the Fusiliers to the sanguinary battles of the Pyrenees, where, with rapid and headlong charges, and with shouts of victory, they stormed position after position which appeared almost impregnable, hurling the enemy down the mountain sides. The old regiment, side by side with the 20th, 23rd Welsh Fusiliers, and the 40th, fought valiantly. As the ranks of conquering bayonets rushed at them, the shock of cold steel was too much for Napoleon's spoilt invincibles. Each column was met in mid-onset, and forced back with great slaughter. Four times the Fusiliers precipitated themselves on a host of fresh opponents, and in each case proved victorious. Here our Commander again thanked the men on the spot, and in his despatch to the Government expressed his admiration of the deeds of the gallant old Fusiliers; for his Grace openly affirmed that the Royal Fusiliers had surpassed all former good conduct, and that the valour of the Fusiliers had won his approbation.

His Grace might well say, "With British soldiers I will go anywhere and do anything." The loss of the old regiment was heavy, being 11 officers, 14 sergeants, and 188 men; but they inflicted a terrible loss upon the enemy. They had been forced from ten strong mountain positions, and all had been carried with the queen of weapons—the bayonet. The passage of the Bidassra followed. Then the enemy's army was driven from a strong position on the Neville. The gallant regiment now stood triumphant, firmly established on the "sacred soil" of France. Retribution had overtaken guilty, haughty, insulting France.

The tyrant Napoleon had hurled the thunderbolts of war against the nations of Europe. The whole of the sovereigns of the continent had been on their knees before this tyrannical usurper, but he now saw them attack him with fury. The enemy took up a formidable position at Orthes, but no advantage of position could stop our victorious army. Marshal Soult (Napoleon's pet General) here got a sound drubbing.

The old Fusiliers are again side by side with the Royal Welsh, well to the front, for our victorious General opened the ball with them. The enemy were beaten at all points, and routed from the field. After a number of minor engagements, in all of which they were victorious, we come to the closing scene—the field of Toulouse. But Dame Fortune would not smile upon the French eagle, for the enemy got another sound beating, and had to retire from the field, leaving it in the hands of the conquering sons of Albion. Thus the Fusiliers had carried our triumphant standard from victory to victory. We pass from one brilliant deed to another with almost breathless rapidity.

The succession of victories had dazzled the whole of Europe, who stood amazed at the gallant deeds of the "astonishing infantry." Peace was now declared, and the Fusiliers returned home, after an absence of nearly seven long years of toil and triumph. We need hardly say that they got a worthy reception, being greeted with hearty cheers from crowds of their fellow countrymen. They had frequently been acknowledged to be a most brilliant, heroic, and dashing body of men by those who were competent judges. Their conduct had often been the admiration of all, for where all were brave, they were acknowledged to be "the bravest of the brave."

The Fusiliers' stay at home was of short duration. Our big cousins across the Atlantic, thinking our hands were full, must "kick up a row" with us; so the Fusiliers were despatched to teach them better behaviour. After a number of engagements with our kinsmen, with but little honour on their part (and it is not at all pleasant to thrash one's own flesh and blood), peace was patched up, and the Fusiliers returned home; for the disturber of the world was again in the field, and on the red field of Waterloo. The conqueror of nations, backed by an army of old and grim veterans, threw down the gauntlet at the feet of our conquering chief, Wellington, and the bright dream of the "hundred days" was rudely dissipated.

But the old Fusiliers this time were not in it; they landed at Ostend on the day of the battle, and pushed on rapidly, but all was over with Napoleon before they reached the field. They marched on into France with the victorious army, and remained with the Army of Occupation until 1818. A long period of peace and tranquillity followed. Europe had had enough of war. And the old Fusiliers, as the sequel of this book will show, nobly maintained, on the heights of Alma, and Inkermann, and throughout the siege of Sebastopol, the reputation acquired by their forefathers. Lord Raglan knew well what he was about when he selected the Royal Fusiliers, together with the Royal Welsh Fusiliers, to lead the way at the Alma. The two old regiments had often been shoulder to shoulder; and his lordship on this field was not disappointed, for they urged each other on to desperate deeds of valour, up they went, forcing back a huge column of the enemy, until they gained the bloodstained heights, and then stood triumphant.

And repeatedly during that trying campaign the Royal Fusiliers led the way. Since then the mutineers could not say that the Fusiliers were napping when wanted; and I am confident that their countrymen are well satisfied with their conduct in the Afghan campaigns of 1863 and the late go-in at Candahar; and that the honour of our dear old flag may still with safety be left in the hands of the Royal Fusiliers.

Their mettle has been well proved on the following fields:—Walcourt, Steenkirk, Landen, Namur, Cadiz, Rota, Vigo, Lindau, Minorca, Quebec, Satur, Montgomery, Clinton, Philadelphia, Newhaven, Charleston, Cowpens, Copenhagen, Martingal, Oporto, Talavera, Busaco, Olivenze, Albuera, Aldea-de-Pont, Ciudad Rodrigo, Badajoz, Salamanca, Montevite, Vittoria, Pampeluna, Pyrenees, Bidassoa, Orthes, Toulouse, New Orleans, Fort Bowyer, Alma, Inkermann, throughout the siege of Sebastopol, India (1857-8-9), Lalo, Umbeyla Pass, and Candahar (1880). Their valour was displayed on the heights of Alma and Inkermann in a manner most heroic. Multiplied and almost unheard-of proofs were given, I do not say merely of courage, but of devotion to their country, quite extraordinary and sublime.

The following are a few of the "Second to None" boys who have been presented by Her Most Gracious Majesty with that priceless decoration.

THE VICTORIA CROSS.

Lieut. H. M. Jones, 1st.
Lieut. W. Hope, 2nd.
Ass.-Surgeon T. E. Hale, 3rd.
Private W. Norman, 4th.
Private M. Hughes, 5th.

And during the Afghan campaign, at a sortie from Candahar, Private James Ashford won the cross by carrying wounded comrades from the field under a most tremendous fire, after all the troops had re-entered the fortress.

The Fusiliers have, as the records prove, been largely recruited from Norfolk, Nottinghamshire, Derbyshire, Yorkshire, and Lancashire, with a good sprinkling of the boys of the Green Isle.

HEROES OF THE SEVENTH ROYAL FUSILIERS.

Lieutenant Henry Mitchell Jones (afterwards Captain in the regiment; retired 28th August, 1857).—Date of act of bravery, 7th June, 1855.—

For having distinguished himself while serving with the party which stormed and took the Quarries before Sebastopol, by repeatedly leading on his men to repel the continual assaults of the enemy during the night. Although wounded early in the evening, Captain Jones remained unflinchingly at his post until after daylight the following morning.

Lieutenant William Hope (retired 3rd March, 1857).—Date of act of bravery, 18th June, 1855.—After the troops had retreated on the morning of the 18th of June, 1855, Lieutenant W. Hope, being informed by the late Sergeant-Major William Bacon, who was himself wounded, that Lieutenant and Adjutant Hobson was lying outside the trenches, badly wounded, went out to look for him, and found him lying in an old agricultural ditch running towards the left flank of the Redan. He then returned and got four men to bring him in. Finding, however, that Lieutenant Hobson could not be removed without a stretcher, he then ran back across the open to Egerton's Pit, where he procured one, and carried it to where Lieutenant Hobson was lying. All this was done under a very heavy fire from the Russian batteries.

Assistant-Surgeon Thomas E. Hale, M.D.—Date of act of bravery, 8th September, 1855.—1st. For remaining with an officer who was dangerously wounded, Captain H. M. Jones, 7th Fusiliers, in the fifth parallel, on the 8th September, 1855, when all the men in the immediate neighbourhood retreated, excepting Lieutenant W. Hope and Dr. Hale; and for endeavouring to rally the men in conjunction with lieutenant W. Hope, 7th Royal Fusiliers.—2nd. For having, on the 8th September, 1855, after the regiments had retired into the trenches, cleared the most advanced sap of the wounded, and carried into the sap, under a heavy fire, several wounded men from the open ground, being assisted by Sergeant Charles Fisher, 7th Royal Fusiliers.

Private (No. 3443) William Norman.—On the night of the 19th December, 1854, he was placed on single sentry some distance in front of the advanced sentries of an outlying picquet in the White Horse Ravine, a post of much danger, and requiring great vigilance; the Russian picquet was posted about 300 yards in his front; three Russian soldiers advanced, under cover of the brushwood, for the purpose of reconnoitring. Private William Norman, single-handed, took two of them prisoners, without alarming the Russian picquet.

Private (No. 1879) Matthew Hughes,—Private Matthew Hughes, 7th Royal Fusiliers, was noticed by Colonel Campbell, 90th Light Infantry, on the 7th June, 1865, at the storming of the Quarries, for twice going for ammunition, under a heavy fire, across the open ground; he also went to the front and brought in Private John Hampton, who was lying severely wounded; and on the 18th June, 1855, he volunteered to bring in Lieutenant Hobson, 7th Royal Fusiliers, who was lying severely wounded, and in the act of doing so was severely wounded himself.

CHAPTER 21

Military Commanders in the Army

THE LEADER OF THE CRIMEAN ARMY.

In the hour of need Britons will ever do their duty. Our gallant Commander, Lord Raglan, K.C.B., or, as he was known for many years. Lord Fitzroy Somerset, was of noble blood, being the eighth son of the late Duke of Beaufort, and was born in 1788. He entered the army in 1804, being then a mere boy. Having wealth and plenty of influence at his back, and a brilliant spirit, he soon brought himself into notice. He was a captain in one of we finest disciplined regiments in our army (the 43rd Light Infantry), which has proved itself on many a hard-fought field second to none. At Vimiera (August 21st, 1808) this regiment contributed largely towards routing the proud legions of France from the field.

That great General, Wellington, with the eye of an eagle, soon detected our young hero's worth, and placed him on his staff, and we find him by the side of his chief through field after field. It was on grim Busaco's iron ridge (September 27th, 1810) that his Lordship received his first wound, and it was there that the tide of French glory was rolled back with terrible slaughter, upwards of 2000 being killed by the British conquering bayonet alone. Again we find our hero on the field of Fuentes d'Onor, May 3rd and 5th, 1811, distinguishing himself most brilliantly—again wounded but not subdued. We next find him, on the 6th April, 1812, foremost among the storming party at the bloody parapets of Badajoz, fighting with determination, and encouraging the 43rd to desperate deeds of valour.

How he escaped that terrible night's slaughter was almost a miracle, for near 5000 of our poor fellows lay in front of those deadly breaches. Then we find him beside his chief on the field of Salamanca, July

Field-Marshal Lord Raglan. K.C.B. &c.

22nd, 1812, taking a distinguished part on that memorable occasion. A French officer stated that 40,000 of his unfortunate countrymen had been rolled up and routed from the field in forty minutes. Wellington was one too many for Marshall Mormant, who was completely outgeneralled, and his army defeated in detail by the conquering sons of Albion, side by side with the heroic boys of the Emerald Isle.

It was on this field that the 88th, or Connaught Rangers, immortalized themselves. Lord Fitzroy Somerset was to be seen in all parts of the field, delivering orders from his commander. Next we hear of him on the plains of Vittoria, June 21st, 1813, by the side of his chief wherever the fight was hottest, doing all that he could to encourage and animate the men. Here it was that the legions of France were completely routed, leaving all their guns in the hands of the victors. This was the most disastrous defeat the French had as yet received; they lost all, including their honour, for they ran like a flock of frightened sheep, throwing away their arms in order to escape the devouring swords of our Cavalry, who chased them for miles from the field.

We next trace his lordship through all the battles of the Pyrenees—ten in number. At times Wellington moved so quickly that Lord Fitzroy was the only one of all his brilliant staff who could keep up with him. Napoleon's pet General, Soult, had to bow before the all-conquering British bayonets. Our young hero still kept by the side of his chief, and we find him on the fields of Nevelle, Orthes, and Toulouse, adding to his renown through all those memorable struggles, ever prompt in performing his duties, and amongst the foremost and the bravest of the brave; not second, even to the fiery Picton, Crawford, Evans, Brown, Campbell, or Napier. He was a true type of a Briton. If there was a "hot corner" he was sure to find it. He had now fought his last fight in the Peninsula. Buonaparte had been crushed by combined Europe, whose armies had been kept in the field by English gold through two campaigns, *viz.*, 1813-14.

Napoleon's wings being clipped, he was sent to the Isle of Elba, as a state prisoner, with an annual revenue of 6,000,000 *francs* to be paid by France. Peace was signed on the 30th May, 1814, between the allied Powers—England, Austria, Russia, and Prussia on the one hand, and France on the other; and our young hero returned home with his commander. But the peace was of short duration. Napoleon burst from his narrow prison, and once more landing in France, set the whole of Europe in a blaze. An army was consequently sent into Belgium, under command of the Iron Duke. Lord Somerset again accompanied him, and was present at the memorable battles of Quatre-Bras and Waterloo, where the conqueror of nations, backed by an army of grim Veterans, again essayed to bid defiance to the British hosts. I must not, however, attempt to go into the details of those fights now. Some of the best blood of Britain: was spilt there, and Lord Somerset was desperately wounded; but he helped to strike the tyrant down to rise no more.

After the lapse of only a few months, our hero, though he left his right arm on the field of Waterloo, again joined his chief in France, and remained at his post till the conclusion of peace. Subsequently he was employed in various capacities at the Horse Guards, until the breaking out of the Crimean War, when he was selected to command the army sent out to Turkey, and from thence to the Crimea. I have not the slightest hesitation in saying that his lordship was looked up to by the whole army with veneration. Under fire he was as "cool as a cucumber"—did not seem to put himself out in the least; he was very kind in his manner, but yet as brave as lion. At the Alma his lordship was in the thick of the fight, giving his orders as calmly as if no bullets or shells were flying around him.

At Inkermann he sat his horse as collectedly as on parade, although death was raging around. But, I must not here attempt to enumerate his deeds through that trying campaign. On the return of the victorious troops, after taking the Quarries and the Circular Trench, his lordship thanked us for the manner in which we had done our duty, and promised to report all for the information of Her Most Gracious Majesty. Such words when uttered by a commander-in-chief are always grateful to soldiers' ears, and go far to reward them for any arduous labour they may have undergone; but praise coming from Lord Raglan was felt to be more than ordinarily inspiring, for his lordship was no stranger to the trying ordeal we had just passed through.

The fighting had been terrible, and he could appreciate the manner in which his orders had been carried out; all had been left to the bayonet. It was then, as it had often been in his lordship's younger days, England and Ireland side by side. But our noble commander's end was now fast approaching. His lordship was not at all well, although his indomitable spirit would not yield; but the weighty responsibility of the disastrous mishap, or repulse, of the 18th June, 1855, was too much for him: it broke his heart, and he sank rapidly.

But, reader, "his end was peace." He could say with Job, "I know that my Redeemer liveth;" and he quietly sank into the arms of that

Lord and Master, whom he had not been ashamed to acknowledge before men.

The Generals of Division.

The following is a brief statement of the vast amount of service of the gallant veterans who commanded the three divisions (Light, 1st, and 2nd) that were destined to bear the brunt of the fighting from the Alma to the fall of Sebastopol; and under this head we will include the hero of Inkermann, Sir G. Cathcart, the commander of the 4th division.

Lieut.-General Sir George Brown.

The commander of the Light Division was Lieut.-General Sir George Brown, K.O.B. Sir George was a Scotchman. He joined the army in 1806, and his first service was in Sicily. He went all through the Peninsular war, under our great captain, Wellington, and frequently distinguished himself; but as he was a poor man, and had none to help him on, he was "left out in the cold." Others who had plenty of cash and influence jumped over his head, although they had never smelt powder.

Sir George was present at the following battles in Portugal:—Roliça, 17th August, 1808; Vimiera, 21st August, 1808; Almeida, September, 1808. At these places he showed the metal he was made of. The Duke acknowledged that he had "done his duty," and there it ended. At Busaco (September 27th, 1810), he was engaged in a severe hand-to-hand conflict with one of the staff of Marshal Massena, and proved the victor.

At Badajoz he greatly distinguished himself, proving to the whole army that he was one of the bravest of the brave. Here he was wounded, and the Duke again acknowledged that he had done his duty. From Roliça (1808) to Toulouse (10th April, 1814), in storming parties and battles in Spain, Portugal, America, and the Netherlands, he had proved himself a cool, determined man, but was still only a captain; his crime was that he was poor; talent and bravery were not in those days taken into consideration. But still he held on and served his country faithfully wherever he was sent, and the sequel will show that the fire was not all out of him; his conduct at the Alma was grand, and at Inkermann he gave his orders as coolly as if he had been talking to his gardener, and firmly faced the foe until he fell wounded and reluctantly left, the field.

Lieut.-General Sir George Brown. K.C.B

LIEUT.-GENERAL SIR DE LACY EVANS.

This general had proved himself second to none on many a hard-fought field in India, Spain, Portugal, America, the Netherlands, and Spain again—where all were brave he would lead the way. He was an Irishman; and his drawback, under the old dispensation, was his obscure position. Mr. Evans entered the army as a volunteer, and by his dauntless bravery obtained a commission on the 1st February, 1807. He was present at the taking of Mauritius, and for his valour was promoted to a Lieutenancy, in December, 1808. But here he was destined to stop for years, although his conduct had been brought to the notice of the then commander-in-chief and the public at large, but a "piece of red tape" had got in front of him.

He could lead the way through the deadly breach repeatedly, but that bit of red tape he could not get over. The facts may seem incredible, but they are true, and history will attest it. His next service was in India, in the Deccan. He remained in India until 1810; was engaged against Ameer Khan, and was once more brought to notice for his talents and bravery, but still he remained a plain Lieutenant. In 1812 he joined the army in Spain, and greatly distinguished himself at the retreat from Burgas; he was wounded, but kept his post throughout the battle.

At Vittoria, June 21st, 1813, his conduct was such that he was the admiration of his whole regiment—the 3rd Dragoons. At Salamanca he attracted the notice of Wellington, who, unfortunately, never troubled himself much about daring obscure men. All he got was, "Evans has done his duty;" but he remained a lieutenant still. Shortly afterwards his horse was killed under him, and he received a contusion in the fall. At Badajoz, he led the forlorn hope, and was wounded. At San Sebastian, he volunteered to lead the assault and was wounded. At Toulouse (April 10th, 1814) he had two horses killed under him, and was twice wounded.

Will it be believed that this gallant veteran, so often wounded, after all his brilliant services, remained at the end of the Peninsular war still a lieutenant? Peace having been made with France, our hero sailed for America with General Ross, his fellow-countryman. At the battle of Bladensburg Mr. Evans had two horses killed under him, and was again wounded. He received the thanks of his commander for his conduct. The same day, Lieut. Evans led the stormers at Washington, and took it, with an enormous booty; the upshot was the complete rout of the enemy and the American Government: and although Gen-

Lieut.-General Sir De Lacy Evans
K.C.B., &c.

eral Ross did his best to obtain promotion for Mr. Evans, the hero of Washington remained a lieutenant still.

At Baltimore the Americans were again defeated, and Mr. Evans was once more thanked by his commander for the dashing manner in which he had led a portion of the 3rd Dragoons, but no promotion followed, although strongly recommended by the General commanding. The next exploit of our hero was to lead a boarding expedition at a part of the American fleet. Mr. Evans was the only military man employed; he was thanked for his conduct, but there it ended. At New Orleans our arms suffered a reverse, but Mr. Evans was said to have nobly done his duty. He shortly afterwards returned to England, and was made a captain in (what do you think, reader?) a West Indian regiment—thus adding insult to injury.

Well, well, those days are past, but if this is a sample of the "good old times," it is a happy thing that they are long gone by. War soon again broke out with Napoleon, and Captain Evans's services were requisitioned. On the field of Waterloo, he was again wounded; and it was acknowledged by those in high position that Captain Evans fought with conspicuous gallantry, leading our heavy cavalry on against Napoleon's *Cuirassiers*; but no further promotion followed. He next entered the Spanish service, commanding a British Legion, and there he carried all before him. He reached the rank of Lieutenant-Colonel in 1835, after twenty-eight years' service (it took Wellington only twenty-six years to reach the rank of Field Marshal).

This was the "grand old man," who commanded us at Little Inkermann, October 26th, 1854. His conduct at the Alma and the two Inkermanns, was that of a tried veteran, cool and determined to conquer or die; the music of shot, shell, grape, canister, and musketry, had not much effect upon his nerves; but he would not throw his men's lives away unnecessarily.

On the morning of the 5th November, he was on board ship at Balaclava sick, but when he heard the booming of the guns, his practised ear knew well that something serious was going on; the honour of the flag he loved so well was in danger, and, as a true and loyal son of Emerald's Isle, he at once landed, and rode on to the memorable field of Inkermann. Although his arm was feeble he could assist with his counsel, for nothing could disturb his iron will but death. He passed through that fiery ordeal without a scratch. He was in all parts of the field, but as tranquil as if he was out for a country ride. Such was the hero of a hundred fights.

Major-General Sir Colin Campbell.

This hero joined the army in 1808, and few lived to see more hard fighting—he was a regular fire-eater. He started from humble life, and, by dint of rough soldiering and an unconquerable spirit, fought his way to the top of the tree; and I may say honestly that few officers in our army, or any other, have been in half the number of battles. From 1808 to 1858 his was one continual blaze of triumph in all parts of the globe. We trace him from the field of Corunna, on which his noble countryman, Sir John Moore, met a soldier's death, to the final relief and capture of Lucknow. Neither Sir De Lacy Evans, Sir George Brown, Sir Charles Napier, nor the great Dukes of Marlborough and Wellington, ever fought more battles than Lord Clyde; and I might almost challenge the admirers of the great Napoleon I. to show such a catalogue of victories as this gallant son of Scotland.

In his maiden fight he proved he was of the right sort of stuff to make a soldier. He was cool and collected, and evidently determined to achieve victory or perish in the attempt. He joined the Walcheren expedition, participating in the cruel sufferings that destroyed nearly the whole army. It was an ill-fated enterprise, and badly commanded—so much for favouritism; but the less we say about it the better. However, even here Sir Colin Campbell contrived to reap some "glory"—as our neighbours delight to call it. From 1809 to 1814 he served under Wellington, in the Peninsula, upon field after field, from Vimiera through such fights as would make the much-lauded heroes of Tel-el-Kebir blush. We trace him through all the great conflicts that won for his commander a dukedom, and compelled the nations of Europe to respect our glorious old flag.

The so-called "invincible" sons of France had to yield the palm to the sons of Albion, and in struggle after struggle their much-vaunted battalions had to give way before our irresistible wall of steel. Shoulder to shoulder with Napier, Evans, and Brown, Sir Colin Campbell was among the foremost in the forlorn hope at Ciudad Rodrigo and Badajoz, and at the deadly breach of San Sebastian,—leading on to almost certain death; and, although repeatedly wounded, nothing could daunt, nothing dismay, this valiant Highland Laddie. He was ever prominent, and helped very materially to achieve some of the grandest victories ever won by British soldiers.

But he was poor, and little notice was taken of him; it was recorded of him that he had done his duty, and there it ceased. Nevertheless, he carved out for himself a name that will not readily be forgotten.

Lord Clyde, K.C.B. &c.,
Better known as Sir Colin Campbell.

The hero of San Sebastian, Chillianwallah, Alma, Balaclava, and Lucknow will be remembered, I fearlessly assert, not only in Scotland, but throughout the British Empire, with pride for ages to come; for he was ever prominent wherever hard knocks were to be served out, and he was acknowledged by those who were competent to judge to be a most brilliant, heroic, and dashing soldier. He led no end of storming parties, and some of the most desperate forlorn hopes that ever man undertook, in all parts of the world. Repeatedly wounded, as I have said, his spirit was not subdued. This gallant soldier appeared to have a charmed life, for he always turned up at the right time and place, to have the lion's share of the fighting. He had a good share of fights in India, as Colonel Campbell, under Lord Gough.

It was he who decided the doubtful field of Chillianwallah by leading the 61st regiment on to a rapid, though prolonged and headlong, bayonet charge. He was wounded, but kept his post, as he had often done before. Again, on the field of Goojerat he fought with the same dauntless courage, which elicited the highest applause from the hero of Borrosa, Lord Gough. We next find him beside the conqueror of Scinde, Sir C. Napier. We shortly after trace him up to Peshawur, fighting the lawless hill tribes, subduing them, and returning to England just in time to take part in the Crimean expedition. At the Alma, he gave the finishing stroke to the Russians, exclaiming, with all the fire of youth, and waving his sword high in the air—"We'll have none but Highland bonnets here."

After the enemy had been routed. Lord Raglan, in thanking him for his conduct, asked him if there was anything he could do for him, and his only request was *to be allowed to wear a Highland bonnet,* which was granted. And ever after that. Sir Colin might be seen wearing his Highland bonnet (to the great delight of the Highland regiments) instead of the usual head-dress of a general. He fought throughout that campaign, and returned home—one would have thought, to end his days in peace, having spent nearly half a century in the service of his country; but no, in 1857 the Indian Mutiny broke out. The brightest gem in Her Most Gracious Majesty's diadem was threatening to break loose. It was held only by a few desperate men, who might die, but would never surrender. Men of Sir Colin's stamp were wanting. He was sent for; and when asked how long it would take him to prepare to proceed to India to assume the command, his answer was—"In twenty-four hours;" history will tell how he rolled back the Mutineers on field after field—all had to yield to his conquering sword.

He left the Empire safe, and won for himself a Field-Marshal's baton and a Peerage. But his end was now fast approaching: he had fought his last fight and made his way to the top of the tree in his old days. The only thing that had kept this grand old hero back, had been, as they say in India, "*pice, pice,*" or money, money. Red-tape is never friendly to the poor man, no matter how brave, or what his talents are. Sir Colin Campbell had displayed a dauntless contempt of danger, wherever his country's honour was at stake; and he lived to receive from his countrymen addresses of the highest thanks and some of the most eloquent eulogies that were ever penned or spoken about a British soldier. But at last he had to ground his arms to King Death; and we may be sure he was ready for the change.

LIEUT.-GENERAL SIR GEO. CATHCART.

It can be truly said of him that he was another of Britain's bravest sons. He was born in the year 1794; at the age of sixteen he joined the army, and was appointed to the 2nd Life Guards, remaining with them a little over one year, when he exchanged into the 6th Dragoons, or Carabineers. His whole soul was alive to the honour of the flag of Old England, and he seemed to long to measure his sword with the enemies of that flag. Napoleon Buonaparte was then at the summit of his power; and, as he was backed up by upwards of 1,000,000 bayonets, it took brave hearts with strong arms to subdue him. We first find young Cathcart in Russia, by the side of his father, who had been appointed British Ambassador to the Court of St. Petersburg. He went out as *aide-de-camp* to his sire, and as such had various duties to perform.

During the invasion of Russia by Napoleon in 1812, young Cathcart attended upon the Emperor, and engaged in some exciting and important scenes. He was continually employed carrying despatches at the peril of his life, and during that momentous period was never known to shirk his duties, but ever courageously pressed forward, having frequently to swim his horses across deep and rapid rivers, and to ride them until they dropped dead beneath him. The Emperor of Russia often expressed both his astonishment and his approbation at the fortitude of our young hero. At the battles of Lutzen and Beautzen he showed prodigious strength, activity, and courage. At the battle of Dresden he fought desperately, and was by the side of one of the greatest generals of the day (Moreau), when he met a soldier's death.

Lieut. Cathcart had now shared in eight pitched battles, and any number of combats. Napoleon had at last been baffled by Russia's snow and England's gold, had to bow to the dictates of combined Europe, and retire to the Isle of Elba, with the empty title of Emperor. Lieut. Cathcart, although of a noble stock, had no friend in the red-tape office, and the excuse for not promoting him was that lie had not served with the British army—although the Russian, Prussian, and Austrian armies had been kept in the field by means of British gold. But when the disturber of the world broke from his prison-house, on the Isle of Elba, young George was again called upon to face his old enemy, and we next find him on the fields of Quatre-Bras and Waterloo.

For his valour he was promoted, as was the hero of Washington, into a West India or black regiment. But he was as true as steel; he was skilful in times of peace, and as brave as a lion in the presence of the foe. He well-merited the highest eulogy that could be bestowed upon a Briton. He had only just returned from the Cape of Good Hope, after subjugating the lawless *Kaffir* tribes, when the Crimean war broke out. He had served his country for forty-four years, had passed through many a hard-fought field, and had lived to trample beneath his feet and silence some of the red-tape gentlemen. Sir George was now well-known, and those at the head of affairs appointed him to command a division in the East. He had been made a Knight Companion of the Bath, and had only just time to pay his homage to Her Most Gracious Majesty and depart.

His division was not engaged at the Alma, but at Inkermann it fought courageously, and it was on this field that our hero met a glorious death. He fell while engaged in repulsing one of the bloodiest attacks made by the enemy on that memorable field. Thus fell, in the hour of victory, one of Britain's bravest sons; and if a chariot of fire had been sent to carry him to the skies, he could not have departed in a brighter blaze of glory.

Sir George had sprung from a family of warriors, who had often cheered their men on to victory; and in him Britain lost a true hero, while posterity will point to the field on which, for England's home and glory. General Sir George Cathcart victoriously fell. Inkermann will never be forgotten.

Before I close this branch of my subject, I must say a few words about another of the commanders, and then my non-military readers will be able to see more clearly the advantages which money and position in life could secure in our army.

The Earl of Cardigan did not enter the army until he was about twenty-seven years of age. He joined the 8th Hussars, in May, 1824, and had scarcely learnt his drill when he was promoted lieutenant; in eighteen months more was advanced to a captaincy. He smoothly passed through the different grades, and in six years from the date of joining, found himself a lieutenant-colonel and commander of a regiment. He had never smelt powder, and, in fact, had never seen the enemies of his country; influence and money had done the whole. I think the reader will agree with me that it was not a bit too soon that the purchase system was discontinued.

When the army was formed for Turkey, in the early part of 1854, this distinguished veteran of the ballroom was selected to command our light cavalry brigade; and right gallantly did he lead that brigade at Balaclava, October 25th, 1854. It was a dashing piece of work, and he did it well; but that was the sum and substance of his lordship's services in the field, and of which we shall never hear the end. Poor old Sir George Brown, Sir De Lacy Evans, Sir Colin Campbell, Sir George Cathcart, and a host of others too numerous to mention, had gone through and seen ten times as much service long before they had reached the ripe age of twenty-one. So much for money and position.

Punch, in 1855, might well put it that the Crimean army was an army of lions led by donkeys. More than half the officers did not know how to manoeuvre a company; all, or nearly so, had to be left to non-commissioned officers; but yet it would be impossible to dispute their bravery, for they were brave unto madness. The writer has seen them lead at the deadly bayonet charges, and at the walls and blood-stained parapets of Sebastopol, as freely as they would have led off in a ballroom; and our officers at Inkermann let the enemy see that they knew how to fight as well as to dance, for there was no manoeuvring, nothing but plain hard-hitting, and fair English fighting (not cooking).

There are none more loyal than the sons of Albion, and none more fond of seeing royalty at the head of their fleets and armies. As far back as Cressy, fought on the 26th August, 1346, when we gained a glorious victory over the French, Edward III. commanded, and there his son, the Black Prince (as he was named from the colour of his armour) had to, and did, win his spurs. The last action when royalty was in command, was Dettingen, fought 27th June, 1743. There George II. commanded. His son, the Duke of Cumberland, was with him and was wounded. The King and his son were in the thick of the fight, setting a bright example; and the same language as he used was adopted by the

Duke of Cambridge at Inkermann, to animate the men, namely, "Stick to them, my boys; now for the honour of old England."

The gallant bearing of the Black Prince, particularly his behaviour to his prisoners after the battle, was well imitated by the Duke of Cumberland and the present Duke of Cambridge, for they showed on each occasion the greatest attention to the poor wounded prisoners. The Duke of Cumberland refused to have his wounds dressed or attended to in any way until the French officers who had been wounded and taken prisoner, were first looked after. "Begin," said His Royal Highness, "with that poor man, for he is more dangerously hurt than I am." The Duke of Cambridge, at Inkermann, was in the midst of the battle and it was almost a miracle how His Royal Highness escaped.

His Royal Highness has for many years proved himself a good soldier's friend, both in the field and out of it; and, when those of royal blood will lead, the enemy, whether black or white, may look out, for they are going to get it hot. At Inkermann things looked desperate. Our weak battalions were being fairly mobbed off the field. At times the day appeared to us to be lost; but our troops quickly recovered themselves, at last closed upon the enemy with the queen of weapons, and then was seen with what determination Britons can fight.

At a critical moment, when almost surrounded by the overwhelming numbers of the foe. His Royal Highness the Duke of Cambridge and a few other officers again rallied the men, and on they went with a desperate headlong charge. The bayonet was then used with effect; the vast columns of the enemy came on and on again, to be repeatedly hurled back by those who would die rather than yield an inch. Such was Inkermann, with the soldier's friend in the thick of it. The Guards had a warm corner of it: if there was one place hotter than another on that field they got into it.

ALSO FROM LEONAUR
AVAILABLE IN SOFTCOVER OR HARDCOVER WITH DUST JACKET

IRON TIMES WITH THE GUARDS *by An O. E. (G. P. A. Fildes)*—The Experiences of an Officer of the Coldstream Guards on the Western Front During the First World War.

THE GREAT WAR IN THE MIDDLE EAST: 1 *by W. T. Massey*—The Desert Campaigns & How Jerusalem Was Won---two classic accounts in one volume.

THE GREAT WAR IN THE MIDDLE EAST: 2 *by W. T. Massey*—Allenby's Final Triumph.

SMITH-DORRIEN *by Horace Smith-Dorrien*—Isandlwhana to the Great War.

1914 *by Sir John French*—The Early Campaigns of the Great War by the British Commander.

GRENADIER *by E. R. M. Fryer*—The Recollections of an Officer of the Grenadier Guards throughout the Great War on the Western Front.

BATTLE, CAPTURE & ESCAPE *by George Pearson*—The Experiences of a Canadian Light Infantryman During the Great War.

DIGGERS AT WAR *by R. Hugh Knyvett & G. P. Cuttriss*—"Over There" With the Australians by R. Hugh Knyvett and Over the Top With the Third Australian Division by G. P. Cuttriss. Accounts of Australians During the Great War in the Middle East, at Gallipoli and on the Western Front.

HEAVY FIGHTING BEFORE US *by George Brenton Laurie*—The Letters of an Officer of the Royal Irish Rifles on the Western Front During the Great War.

THE CAMELIERS *by Oliver Hogue*—A Classic Account of the Australians of the Imperial Camel Corps During the First World War in the Middle East.

RED DUST *by Donald Black*—A Classic Account of Australian Light Horsemen in Palestine During the First World War.

THE LEAN, BROWN MEN *by Angus Buchanan*—Experiences in East Africa During the Great War with the 25th Royal Fusiliers—the Legion of Frontiersmen.

THE NIGERIAN REGIMENT IN EAST AFRICA *by W. D. Downes*—On Campaign During the Great War 1916-1918.

THE 'DIE-HARDS' IN SIBERIA *by John Ward*—With the Middlesex Regiment Against the Bolsheviks 1918-19.

AVAILABLE ONLINE AT **www.leonaur.com**
AND FROM ALL GOOD BOOK STORES

ALSO FROM LEONAUR
AVAILABLE IN SOFTCOVER OR HARDCOVER WITH DUST JACKET

FARAWAY CAMPAIGN *by F. James*—Experiences of an Indian Army Cavalry Officer in Persia & Russia During the Great War.

REVOLT IN THE DESERT *by T. E. Lawrence*—An account of the experiences of one remarkable British officer's war from his own perspective.

MACHINE-GUN SQUADRON *by A. M. G.*—The 20th Machine Gunners from British Yeomanry Regiments in the Middle East Campaign of the First World War.

A GUNNER'S CRUSADE *by Antony Bluett*—The Campaign in the Desert, Palestine & Syria as Experienced by the Honourable Artillery Company During the Great War.

DESPATCH RIDER *by W. H. L. Watson*—The Experiences of a British Army Motorcycle Despatch Rider During the Opening Battles of the Great War in Europe.

TIGERS ALONG THE TIGRIS *by E. J. Thompson*—The Leicestershire Regiment in Mesopotamia During the First World War.

HEARTS & DRAGONS *by Charles R. M. F. Crutwell*—The 4th Royal Berkshire Regiment in France and Italy During the Great War, 1914-1918.

INFANTRY BRIGADE: 1914 *by John Ward*—The Diary of a Commander of the 15th Infantry Brigade, 5th Division, British Army, During the Retreat from Mons.

DOING OUR 'BIT' *by Ian Hay*—Two Classic Accounts of the Men of Kitchener's 'New Army' During the Great War including *The First 100,000* & *All In It*.

AN EYE IN THE STORM *by Arthur Ruhl*—An American War Correspondent's Experiences of the First World War from the Western Front to Gallipoli-and Beyond.

STAND & FALL *by Joe Cassells*—With the Middlesex Regiment Against the Bolsheviks 1918-19.

RIFLEMAN MACGILL'S WAR *by Patrick MacGill*—A Soldier of the London Irish During the Great War in Europe including *The Amateur Army, The Red Horizon & The Great Push*.

WITH THE GUNS *by C. A. Rose & Hugh Dalton*—Two First Hand Accounts of British Gunners at War in Europe During World War 1- Three Years in France with the Guns and With the British Guns in Italy.

THE BUSH WAR DOCTOR *by Robert V. Dolbey*—The Experiences of a British Army Doctor During the East African Campaign of the First World War.

AVAILABLE ONLINE AT **www.leonaur.com**
AND FROM ALL GOOD BOOK STORES

ALSO FROM LEONAUR
AVAILABLE IN SOFTCOVER OR HARDCOVER WITH DUST JACKET

THE 9TH—THE KING'S (LIVERPOOL REGIMENT) IN THE GREAT WAR 1914 - 1918 *by Enos H. G. Roberts*—Mersey to mud—war and Liverpool men.

THE GAMBARDIER *by Mark Severn*—The experiences of a battery of Heavy artillery on the Western Front during the First World War.

FROM MESSINES TO THIRD YPRES *by Thomas Floyd*—A personal account of the First World War on the Western front by a 2/5th Lancashire Fusilier.

THE IRISH GUARDS IN THE GREAT WAR - VOLUME 1 *by Rudyard Kipling*—Edited and Compiled from Their Diaries and Papers—The First Battalion.

THE IRISH GUARDS IN THE GREAT WAR - VOLUME 1 *by Rudyard Kipling*—Edited and Compiled from Their Diaries and Papers—The Second Battalion.

ARMOURED CARS IN EDEN *by K. Roosevelt*—An American President's son serving in Rolls Royce armoured cars with the British in Mesopatamia & with the American Artillery in France during the First World War.

CHASSEUR OF 1914 *by Marcel Dupont*—Experiences of the twilight of the French Light Cavalry by a young officer during the early battles of the great war in Europe.

TROOP HORSE & TRENCH *by R.A. Lloyd*—The experiences of a British Lifeguardsman of the household cavalry fighting on the western front during the First World War 1914-18.

THE EAST AFRICAN MOUNTED RIFLES *by C.J. Wilson*—Experiences of the campaign in the East African bush during the First World War.

THE LONG PATROL *by George Berrie*—A Novel of Light Horsemen from Gallipoli to the Palestine campaign of the First World War.

THE FIGHTING CAMELIERS *by Frank Reid*—The exploits of the Imperial Camel Corps in the desert and Palestine campaigns of the First World War.

STEEL CHARIOTS IN THE DESERT *by S. C. Rolls*—The first world war experiences of a Rolls Royce armoured car driver with the Duke of Westminster in Libya and in Arabia with T.E. Lawrence.

WITH THE IMPERIAL CAMEL CORPS IN THE GREAT WAR *by Geoffrey Inchbald*—The story of a serving officer with the British 2nd battalion against the Senussi and during the Palestine campaign.

AVAILABLE ONLINE AT **www.leonaur.com**
AND FROM ALL GOOD BOOK STORES

www.ingramcontent.com/pod-product-compliance
Lightning Source LLC
Chambersburg PA
CBHW031618160426
43196CB00006B/189